OXFORD MONOGRAPHS ON MUSIC

MUSIC IN LATE MEDIEVAL BRUGES

The Lucca Choirbook (fol. 17v): Beginning of the *Missa Caput*. Flemish illumination of *c.*1470.

Music in
Late Medieval Bruges

———◆———

REINHARD STROHM

CLARENDON PRESS · OXFORD
1985

Oxford University Press, Walton Street, Oxford OX2 6DP
Oxford New York Toronto
Delhi Bombay Calcutta Madras Karachi
Kuala Lumpur Singapore Hong Kong Tokyo
Nairobi Dar es Salaam Cape Town
Melbourne Auckland

and associated companies in
Beirut Berlin Ibadan Mexico City Nicosia

Oxford is a trade mark of Oxford University Press

Published in the United States
by Oxford University Press, New York

British Library Cataloguing in Publication Data

Strohm, Reinhard
Music in late medieval Bruges.
1. Music − Belgium − Bruges − History and criticism −
Medieval, 400−1500
I. Title
780'.9493'1   ML265

ISBN 0-19-316327-6

Library of Congress Cataloging in Publication Data

Strohm, Reinhard.
Music in late medieval Bruges.
"Catalogue of the Lucca choirbook": p. 192
Bibliography: p. 257
Includes index.
1. Music − Belgium − Bruges − 15th century − History and
criticism.   I. Title.
ML265.2.S77   1984   780'.9493'1   83-23966

ISBN 0-19-316327-6

Printed in Great Britain by
Biddles Ltd, Guildford and King's Lynn

PREFACE

————◆◆◆◆◆————

THIS book has been written out of admiration for the Belgian people and their history. It is not a fortunate history: the Belgians have always wanted to live in peace with their neighbours, but always became the victims of aggression from outside and of painful internal conflicts. Their contribution to European civilisation has never been politically rewarded.

The readers of these pages will be aware of the significance of early Netherlandish painting; the musicians among them may know about the musical 'Art of the Netherlanders' of the fifteenth and sixteenth centuries, which is a cornerstone of our Western musical heritage. Our respect for the works of composers such as Dufay, Binchois, Ockeghem, Obrecht and Josquin is, in a sense, only a token recognition. Whilst it is so convenient to speak of a 'Netherlandish' or 'Franco-Flemish' school of composition, little effort has been made to look beyond the achievements of individuals, and to identify the contents of a 'Netherlandish' or 'Flemish' tradition, let alone the actual 'schools' which generated it.

What I hope to offer in the following pages are some results of a conscious attempt to meet the Flemish musicians 'at home', and to reassess the cultural significance of their native environment. Bruges was not only the artistic and commercial centre of Flanders at the end of the Middle Ages, but also one of those urban communities in the Low Countries whose coherent and pervasive organisation obviously demanded the contribution of musicians. The city of Jan van Eyck and Hans Memling, in particular, cannot have been a musical backwater. Sooner or later, the music of Bruges will have to be studied in much more detail than can be done here, and similar studies of other great cities in the Low Countries will have to follow, if we want to take the concept of the 'Franco-Flemish' tradition seriously.

I have not found it necessary to express my respect for Flemish music of the fifteenth century by using the keyword 'Renaissance'. It is open to discussion to what extent the term can be stretched without becoming purely decorative – perhaps that is already the case when it is applied to music at all. Even if one does not want to be so restrictive, the onus of explaining what is 'Renaissance' in music and what not is on those who decide to adopt the term. With regard to the musical life of Bruges, I cannot see a major transformation before the end of the fifteenth century, i.e. of the 'Middle Ages' in the accepted chronological sense of the term. The culture of the town developed coherently from the Carolingian era until the period after the fall of Charles the Bold (1477), when the previous balance of civic, ecclesiastical and territorial government was broken by the Habsburg rulers. Only at this time, the individualist and humanist traditions in art and learning, which had long been cultivated, faced the increased challenge of clerical oppression, on the one hand, and religious radicalism, on the other. Flanders, like other Germanic areas of Europe, experienced Renaissance and Reformation together and, indeed, as a conflict.[1]

This book is much more the product of collaboration than it might appear. Even the main idea is not entirely my own. I had originally intended to write a monograph on a musical source from Bruges which I had discovered, the Lucca choirbook, and on its background. It was the wish of the editors, Anthony Mulgan and Bruce Phillips, to make this background the main theme. As this meant studying people rather than manuscripts, I have never regretted the decision.

In this way, I was led to undertake archival studies, mainly in Belgium, which have proved a delightful and unforgettable experience. This is mainly due to the unfailingly charming support which I received from the archivists and librarians, with their staff, of the following institutions: the Stadsbibliotheek, Algemeen Rijksarchief, Bisschoppelijk Archief, Archief van het Klooster van de Ongeschoeide Karmelieten, Stadsarchief, Archive and Museums of the O.C.M.W., Provinciaalbibliotheek van West-Vlaanderen, Groeningemuseum and Archief van het Grootseminarie (all in Bruges); the Manuscript Department, Bibliothèque Royale Albert Ier, Brussels; the University Libraries of Ghent, Utrecht and Leiden; the Archivio di Stato, Lucca; the Archivio Arcivescovile, Pisa; the British Library, Reference Division, London; the Stadtbibliothek, Nuremberg; and the Bayerische Staatsbibliothek, Munich.

The archivists and other scholars of various fields who gave advice, and generously shared their knowledge with me, include Canons B. Janssens de Bisthoven, Jozef Decleer and Paul Declerck (†), P. Lawrence van Assche O.C.D., Drs J. Mertens, L. Danhieux, N. Geirnaert (all of Bruges), Profs. Albert Derolez (Ghent), Gerard I. Lieftinck (Leiden), Albert Schouteet (Bruges), Otto Pächt (Vienna), Julian T. Brown (King's College, London), Dr T. M. Guest (Bedford College, London), Martin Staehelin (Bonn), Chris Maas (Amsterdam), Jaap van Benthem (Utrecht), Barton Hudson (University of West Virginia), Leeman L. Perkins (Columbia University), Craig Wright (Yale University), Lewis Lockwood (Harvard University), Keith Polk (University of New Hampshire), Alejandro Planchart (Brandeis University), Margaret Bent (Princeton University), Brian Trowell

(King's College, London), Pierluigi Petrobelli (Bologna); Thomas Walker (Ferrara), David Fallows (Manchester), John Caldwell (Oxford), Andrew Wathey (Oxford), Rudolf Bockholdt (Munich), P. Hermann Watzl (Heiligenkreuz), Ludwig Finscher (Heidelberg), Jeremy Noble (Buffalo), Tom Ward (Urbana), Wulf Arlt (Basel), Wolfgang Osthoff (Würzburg), Walter Salmen (Innsbruck), Ronald Woodley (Liverpool) and F. Alberto Gallo (Bologna).

The bibliography may show to what extent my work has depended on the research of Alfons Dewitte of Bruges, whose personal help and advice I also enjoyed. His publications are obligatory reading for further researchers interested in the musical history of Bruges.

The book could not have been completed without the support of my wife, Janet M. Smith, who shared all the pressure but too little of the pleasure of the undertaking. The task of publishing a book in a foreign language would have been impossible for me, had Mary Whittall (London) not helped me along by translating chapter II and providing much linguistic advice, and had Ian Rumbold (Cambridge) not corrected and improved the style of chapters III to VI. To both of them, I also owe my apologies for the departures from their texts which became necessary for reasons other than language. I very much hope that the reader will condone my pretentiousness of presenting an English text which has had to be cobbled together in this peculiar way.

One of the problems concerns **terminology**. I may not always have succeeded in finding the right historical equivalents in English for the many Latin and Flemish terms encountered in the sources. Original Latin and Flemish texts have mostly been translated or paraphrased; geographical names and technical terms are spelled according to modern Flemish usage. **Proper names**, which may appear in the sources in concurrent Flemish, French or Latin forms, have not been modernised; I have chosen the French, Latin or Flemish form of the name in accordance with the status and main occupation of the person, as the native language of a person can rarely be established. In family names which include prefixes such as 'van', 'de', 'le' etc., only the noun has regularly been capitalised, and the nouns also determine the alphabetical order of the names. Only the names of modern writers are ordered alphabetically according to the modern spelling and capitalisation. The name of 'Flanders' is used in this book as denoting the political unit, the county of Flanders, which from 1384 was ruled by the dukes of Burgundy. The adjective 'Flemish', however, is used for the whole ethnic and linguistic area of the Southern Low Countries; 'French Flanders' is the French-speaking (Southern) part of the county of Flanders.

All **chronological references** have been adjusted to modern usage (nearly all original documents use the style of Easter). Account books and similar registers often begin the year with 24 June or another feast-day; in these cases, quotations such as '1375/6' indicate the year of account, whereas '1375–76' indicates a period covering both years according to the modern style.

Currency is invariably quoted in Parisian pounds (£), sous = shillings (s) and deniers = pennies(d). The Parisian £, at 20 s. of 12 d. each, was valued from 1390 as approximately 1/12 of the Flemish £, and 1/6 of the *livre de Tournai*; the *franc* and the Rhenish guilder were valued at 33 (Parisian) sous. In Bruges, a regular income of one shilling per day (i.e. £18 5s. per year) would have represented an acceptable living standard – although it should be noted that regular income as such reflected a privileged social position.

The **music examples** of this book are not critical editions, but mere transcriptions from one reliable source in each case; only obvious errors have been tacitly corrected. I would have preferred to present the music in facsimile as well, which was, of course, not possible; as the music examples span a hundred years and are transmitted in very hetero-geneous original notations, I have been forced to use modern score notation as a common denominator. The responsible performer will wish to consult the original sources in any case. It is my greatest hope that this book may contribute to the revival of the music of Bruges as a living reality.

R. S.

CONTENTS

LIST OF PLATES

Frontispiece. The Lucca Choirbook (fol. 17v). Beginning of the anonymous *Missa Caput* with Superius 'Deus creator omnium' and Tenor 'Caput drachonis' (Lucca, Archivio di Stato, Biblioteca Manoscritti 238).

1. Religious procession (Corpus Christi?) in a Flemish town, possibly in the Blinde-Ezelstraat, Bruges. School of Rogier van der Weyden, mid-15th century. (Courtesy of the British Museum, Department of Prints and Drawings, Inv. no. 1895. 9. 15. 1001.)

2. 18th-century drawing of the Collegiate Church of St Donatian, and a plan of the church with cloister and 'burg' square. Recueil généalogique Pierre de Molo, MS 595, Stads-bibliotheek Brugge, vol. 2, Annex p. 22 and 25. (Courtesy of the Librarian.)

3. Calendar page for May from a Book of Hours, Bruges *c*.1500 (ex coll. Dyson Perrin, Malvern). Courtauld Institute of Art, University of London, neg. no. 236/66(22). (Courtesy of the Courtauld Institute.)

4. Choirbook fragment from St Stephen's, Vienna, *c*.1400 (Stadtbibliothek Nürnberg, Fragm. lat. 9, fol. 2r). Motetus 'Rector creatorum' of the ceremonial motet 'Comes Flandrie' for Count Louis de Male, 1381 or 1382 (Courtesy of the Manuscript Department, StB Nürnberg). See music ex. 1.

5. Chansonnier with works by Thomas Fabri, early 15th century (Heiligenkreuz, Archiv des Zisterzienserstifts, frg. without shelfmark). Rondeau 'Die mey so lieflic' (fol. 1v) and ballade 'Ach Vlaendere' (fol. 2v), see music ex. 2 and 3. (Courtesy of the Archivist.)

6. The Lucca Choirbook (fol. 25v). Beginning of Gloria of the anonymous *Missa Te gloriosus* (No. 6), quoted by John Hothby in his *Dialogus de arte musica*, *c*.1470–80. (Lucca, Archivio di Stato, Biblioteca Manoscritti 238.)

7. Works of Seneca. Universiteitsbibliotheek Leiden, MS BPL 43A, fol. 196r. Apparently copied in the same *scriptorium* as the Lucca choirbook: Bruges, *c*.1470. (Courtesy of the Librarian.)

8. The Lucca Choirbook (fol. 38v). From the Gloria of the anonymous *Missa Hec dies* (No. 10); John Hothby or one of his students at Lucca cathedral added a fifth voice at the end of the Superius. (Lucca, Archivio di Stato, Biblioteca Manoscritti 238.) See also music ex. 8.

LIST OF MUSIC EXAMPLES

CHAPTER ONE

Townscape – Soundscape

LATE medieval Bruges is known to us through the stillness of pictures. Motion and sound are contained in them, but in a frozen form: reduced to an infinitely small fraction of time. Given time, the pictures would start to move, and the music would be heard.

In the Ghent panels by Hubert and Jan van Eyck, an angel is seen playing the organ: she is about to press the keys F, c and a. The time lapse between her action and the perception of the chord is extended to eternity. Next to the organ-player another angel, holding a harp, counts the time with her fingers on the shoulder of the partner in front of her, who holds a viol and is ready to play, but is resting. In the opposite wing of the picture, eight angels are singing mensural polyphony. Musical measure determines the precise moment in time in which the whole picture is set.[1]

The moment in which Giovanni Arnolfini raised his right hand to confirm the oath which he was to pronounce – that he was to marry Giovanna Cenami who stood beside him – this moment was witnessed by the painter Jan van Eyck, who recorded 'Johannes de Eyck fuit hic' ('was here'), using the past tense which was customary with dated signatures on legal documents or letters. In his signature, written on the back wall, van Eyck used the calligraphy which normally began and ended the text of a charter or roll. Arnolfini's commitment is not for eternity but for a human lifetime, which will consume itself like the candle that is burning in the chandelier. The small space of Arnolfini's Bruges townhouse is reflected in the mirror on the back wall. In the reflection, two people can be seen standing in the open door: the painter and witness, and a procurator of Giovanna's father – the banker Guglielmo Cenami of Paris. The mirror-frame is ornamented with ten small pictures showing the Passion of Our Lord, a symbol of human life and of the liturgical cycles of the week and the year. This picture is a document of a ceremony which took place in Bruges in the year 1434, and is therefore placed in time by reference to human life and its history of salvation.

The betrothal of St Catherine to the infant Jesus was painted by Hans Memling as that delicate moment when the child was about to touch the finger of the young princess. Mystic suspense and happy leisure are juxtaposed, as St Barbara keeps reading her Book of Hours, and a smiling child-angel enjoys the sound of the portative organ which he is playing.

These pictures also encapsulate motion and space. We are aware that the townscape of Bruges is just beyond – or rather, on our side of the picture, facing them. Here, where we now stand and look at the pictures, there were the people, the houses and the activities of a city whose hectic business, disorders and violence cry out from page after page in the archives. It is strange that the works of the painters have come to resemble more the Bruges of today – a peaceful and orderly town whose medieval architecture spells nostalgia – than that of the fifteenth century: the liveliest, wealthiest and most complex urban community of North-Western Europe. It was the home of more than 30,000 people – princes, priests, friars, soldiers, housewives, prostitutes, artists and artisans, bankers and beggars. The noises of the market-place, the inns, the workshops, the stock-exchange, the public baths – they have all died, and so have the music and the song of the nightingale in the orchard. And yet, these sounds have shaped the townscape, contributing to its order and to its disorder. The sound of music is still frozen in the shapes of Bruges.

Bruges is not on the map of the leading musical historiographers. They have ignored the cultural achievements of the European medieval towns, and distorted those of medieval Flanders. The country is interpreted by them as one of those areas which humbly supplied the great Renaissance courts with musical talents, but not as a home of music in its own right. Bruges, like all other cities of this size, had its own musical life, whose patterns were more complex, indeed, than those of the great cathedrals, abbeys and royal courts.

The medieval city is a circumscribed space of human life which defends itself within walls against the poverty and desperation of the countryside, and against the silence and the cold of woodland, marshes and the sea. Against the extreme unpredictability of life and death, the townspeople build patterns which transcend individual lives: social patterns like families, guilds, corporations, confraternities; time-patterns for working, praying, feasting and sleeping, of which they remind themselves by the peal of the church-bells.

The cycles of the calendar – day, week and year – are filled and ordered by the liturgy of the church, which uses music as a means of representing time. Music also represents the sacred space: the two halves of the choir who sing in alternation are also seated on opposite sides of the choir. At one end, space is reserved for the priest with the ministers, and for the cantor with his assistant; at the other, for the cluster of clerks and choirboys who sing under the succentor's direction;

the organ on the choir-screen accompanies, or alternates with, the full choir. Beyond, there are the nave where the parishioners can hear mass and vespers, and the many chapels around the choir and along the aisles, where private individuals and confraternities attend their private services behind closed doors or curtains. They also have their special liturgy and music, which is performed by clerks and boys, gathered around a small organ in front of the altar. They almost form one picture with the image of Our Lady or the saint in the altar panel.

The spatial arrangement of the church is reflected in the timetable of its services, which overlap or happen simultaneously in different places. Also the various cycles of the liturgical year form layers – the patterns of movable and immovable feasts, the weekly and daily repetitions of 'ordinary' services and the fixed yearly pattern of the saints' feast-days. In the sacristy, there is a kind of painted calendar which identifies all these cycles throughout the year, and which distributes the clergy's tasks accordingly. This is the *arbor paschalis*, so named because everything depends on the date of Easter. It is normally the work of the succentor – a learned musician who masters arithmetics and mensural rhythm.

The rhythm of urban life conforms to the church's calendar. The three 'greater hours' (matins with lauds, vespers and compline) mark the beginning and the end of the day, and the four 'lesser hours' (prime, terce, sext and none) divide the working day into four equal segments. Everyone is aware of these seven hours, as they are announced by the church-bells. The townspeople are reminded to pray the 'Seven Hours' of the Dead on Monday, of the Holy Ghost on Tuesday, of the Trinity on Wednesday, of the Holy Sacrament on Thursday, of the Holy Cross on Friday, of Our Lady on Saturday and of Our Lord on Sunday. There is one moment, at least, on each day when everyone in the town thinks the same: the *Angelus*. When night breaks and the colours and noises of the working day recede, the bell recalls the visit of the Archangel Gabriel to Mary in her chamber: 'Angelus ad virginem subintrans in conclave'. The people say to themselves the salutation of the angel: 'Ave Maria, gratia plena . . .'. The major bell of the church of St Donatian, pitched *ut*, sounds nine strokes, three times three, and after each stroke there is an interval for the saying of one *Ave Maria*. This happens every day at the same time, throughout the year. Other forms of urban music just elaborate this basic pattern.

The bells and clockworks of the various towers form a magnificent hierarchy of sound-signals.[2] Each bell has its name and its special significance (as its individual tone can be recognised): as an indicator of the hour; as a reminder to close the inns; as a signal for the beginning of masses in the churches, of the sessions of the magistrate, of school-hours and tribunals; as a warning against thunderstorms, fires and approaching armies; as a messenger of death. The bells can also be sounded together in many combinations, for example for solemn or happy events. In Bruges, one used to peal three bells together throughout mass (which was called *triplicare*; Flemish *beyaerdene*) for celebrations – while the musicians were singing inside the church. Many a group of bell-ringers had developed individual ways of pealing, which the people could distinguish. A chaplain of St Donatian's, Bertinus Moens, was known for his particular style of bell-ringing during the 'O-Antiphons' in Advent. When he died in 1480, part of his bequest was allocated for the support of the continued pealing 'in his manner'. This must have been an unwritten 'composition' – a mode of performance fixed in rhythm, pitch and measure. We know that Moens was familiar with polyphonic music as well. Some composers of the time have given the bell a place in their scores, which is not only a symbolism, but also a realistic reflection of the acoustic environment of church music.[3]

The soundscape of the town comprised much other music which had its specific function. Among the bells, there was also the clockwork in the city's belfry above the market square, the *beyaerd* or *carillon*, one of the most cherished traditions of Bruges.[4] It existed before 1400 and became a musical instrument in the sixteenth century. Even today, its tunes (which now include Schubert and Gounod) can be heard over most of the town.

The horns and trumpets of the city waits and minstrels were the next strongest instruments; the musicians played on the belfry, on the city gates or from other dominating positions. Their signals and fanfares related to events of common civic interest, such as the arrival of prominent guests or, indeed, hostile armies; the beginning and end of public proclamations, processions, jousting tournaments in the market square, public meetings and executions. Announcements made by the magistrate were communicated throughout the town by public criers (*clinkers*) who called for attention with strokes on a kind of cymbals. The soundscape of the town was, of course, characterised by the human voice: the cries of the coachmen, shopkeepers and traders, buskers, heralds and servants of noble passengers, and of the beggars and lepers – and most of these also had bells or other noise-making instruments. Women and children were amply represented in this concert. The focal point of all the noises as well as of all outdoors music was the market square.

A marvellous way in which music helped order time and space within urban life were the great processions. The sacred chants, sung by the numerous participants, and the festive sounds of the accompanying city trumpeters, were carried through the streets, thus linking music with movement and evoking the spiritual significance of the townscape. The idea of the procession itself must have been born in a city; western civilisation inherited it from the ancient urban cultures of the Near East. The monastic processions of the earlier Middle Ages were only an interlude; it was the medieval towns which developed and multiplied the practice. Bruges had countless processions, whose functions were hierarchically distinguished. The great majority were held by individual churches and convents within the space of the church itself; on some occasions one went round the churchyard or the parish. The great general processions, supervised by the city magistrate and the chapter of St Donatian's, united the personnel of secular bodies and guilds, and the clergy of all major churches and convents; mendicant friars and sisters often conducted them. In some years, there were more than twenty general processions, many of them on occasions of civic interest such as a victory of the ducal army or a threat of the plague. The main procession of Bruges, which still exists, was dedicated to the venerated relic of the Holy Blood, which is kept in the chapel of St Basil. It was carried in procession on many days of the year, but above all on the feast of the Invention of the Cross (3 May). It is typical for the pervasiveness of the urban culture that this day coincided with the secular festivities of the May Fair, which attracted merchants and prominent visitors from many other towns and countries.

Of the musical ingredients of the Holy Blood procession, only a series of plainsongs survives in written form. It is contained in two almost identical processional books of around 1510, which once belonged to members of the sister–house of the Beguines,[5] an order to which the direction of the procession was often entrusted. The rubrics in these manuscripts indicate exactly at which point which chant was performed. Two processions are recorded for the main feast-day. The first started and ended at the sister–house of the Beguines and went round the inner city. On the way out of the convent, the sisters sang the responsory *Summe Trinitati*; during a 'station' in the chapel of St Julian, the antiphon *Ave virgo gloriosa*; on the way back to the city centre, the hymn *Veni creator spiritus* and the antiphon (*sic*) *Veni sancte spiritus*; when passing the church of St Saviour, the antiphon *Salvator mundi*; in the *Steenstraat*, the busiest street of the town, the very popular responsory *Stirps Jesse* and the antiphon *Ave regina celorum*; in the market square, the antiphon *Regina celi letare*; near the chapel of St Basil, the antiphon *Miles Christi gloriose, Basili sanctissime*, followed by the antiphon *Dulcis sanguis* for the Holy Blood; when leaving the square in front of the church of St Donatian and entering the passage called the 'blind donkey', the sisters sang *Confessor domini pater Donatiane, astantem plebem corrobora* ('Confessor of God, father Donatianus, strengthen the bystanding crowd'). Later on, the church of Our Lady was greeted with the responsory *Felix namque* (with the versicle *Ora pro populo*) and the *prosa Inviolata, integra et casta* – a tune which probably everyone in Bruges knew, so often does it occur in the liturgies of the various churches. The last group of chants referred to St Boniface, another patron saint of Our Lady's, and to St Elizabeth.

The second, larger procession went round the city gates and also had its appropriate chants for the respective places. The chants were performed on the approach to, and during stations at, the gates themselves and the chapels and convents nearby. The emphasis was again on plainsongs which the people knew and loved, such as *Argentum et aurum, O crux gloriosa, Regnum mundi, Letare Germania, Inter natos mulierum*, and so on; there was also a litany and the Te Deum.

It is as if Bruges had a tune for each of its squares, gates and street-corners. The people who participated in the procession could explore their own material and spiritual environment while walking and singing. There is no doubt that the watching crowd also sang. The sound of the sacred chants was coloured by the many voices of women and children, and the rhythmic pace of the procession must have influenced the musical rhythm; at least the syllabic chants such as hymns and sequences were most probably sung in fixed metre. Together with the sound of the city trumpeters and of the pipers of the guilds who walked in the train, the overall acoustic impression must have been one of brightness and brilliance, quite unlike the dark, amorphous sound which the Romantics used to associate with medieval plainsong. One may add to this the many visual stimuli provided by the blue costumes of the city minstrels, the red and black of the representatives of the guilds, the silver trumpets which were decorated with the city's coat of arms (a red lion in a blue and white field) and the many other banners which were carried or which decorated the houses; by the white, grey, black and red habits of the regulars and the secular clergy; by the gold and silver of religious vases and shrines – altogether a feast for the eye which contemporary painters and miniaturists such as Jan van Eyck or the Limburg brothers could not possibly exaggerate.[6]

Not only the processions, but also the civic festivities which took place in the streets, united music and other arts. Two observations can be made about the street pageants, in particular, which Bruges used to offer to visiting princes: firstly, the imagery of these secular ceremonies was predominantly sacred until about the mid-fifteenth century; and secondly, the visual display was normally part of actual performances, dramatic as well as static. The former, the mystery plays which were acted amidst processions and pageants, used instrumental music in the form of fanfares and interludes, but also sacred songs for the dialogue and the narrative. The latter were the so-called 'living pictures' (*tableaux vivants*) in which living people, dressed up as sacred or mythological figures, displayed a picture of well-known arrangement and significance: the Resurrection, Mary and the Angel, the 'Tree of

Jesse', King David playing the harp, the City of Jerusalem, the Mount of Olives, the Nativity with musician angels, and so on. The actors, seen on a podium against a painted and plastic background, had to stand or sit motionless 'as if they were a picture' – as is explicitly stated in contemporary descriptions. They were, however, accompanied by live performances of vocal and instrumental music, or they sang and played themselves. For greater clarity, the texts which they sang or which explained the meaning of the picture, were displayed on banderoles – *Ave regina celorum* or *Hec est dies quam fecit dominus* or *Ecce ancilla domini*, and so on. The performers of the music were often children, dressed up as angels, or men and women musicians, posing as prophets and sybils. Curtains could be drawn at specific moments to cover or reveal the picture. The similarity between the practice of the 'living pictures' and the imagery of contemporary painting is astounding. Mutual influences must be assumed.[7] As regards music, however, there is an important difference.

A 'living' representation of a Nativity with musician angels can give us the sound, which the painting cannot give. Nearly all music historians and even some art historians who have commented upon the representation of music in paintings, have undervalued or ignored the 'living pictures' as a bridge between art and reality. The people of Bruges, for example, could actually *hear* the angels' concerts in the streets, and the boys and girls from church and conventual schools were experienced in performing as angels, vocally and instrumentally. Artists of the period painted music as a reality, albeit as an artistic, theatrical reality. They may have gone beyond everyday life in adding symbols and theological significance to the arrangement of their pictures – but then, symbolism and allegory were the very essence of the 'living pictures' as well! If a group of nine angels, playing various kinds of instruments, is required as the background of an altarpiece, it can equally well be required for the display on a podium in the streets, where the instruments can be heard.

We do not know precisely what this music was like – but it is clear that performance practices did not have to match those that were admitted inside the church. The limits that had to be respected here were those of the education and skills of the musicians themselves.[8] They would normally distinguish between performing groups on *haut* and *bas* instruments; they would perhaps have some difficulty in combining the plainsong or the polyphony sung by the clerks and boys with the practice of the instrumental group – but such combinations could be rehearsed for the occasion. The city minstrels were used to perform sacred tunes in the open air – what else would they have played in the general processions in which an almost uninterrupted series of sacred chants was sung? We know that the civic wind band of Bruges played mensural polyphony from the 1480s at the latest, both in church and in serenades from the town's belfry.

The practice of polyphonic music was shared between various classes of Bruges, despite the strict social distinctions. Polyphony was, of course, usually performed indoors, and often enough behind closed doors. But it was also heard at high mass in the churches, when all parishioners could attend. The daily polyphonic *Missa de Salve*, performed in the Lady-chapel of St Donatian's from 1421, was probably open to everybody, although space was limited there; the daily singing of the *Salve regina* in polyphony from 1480 took place in the nave of the church, and had been instituted expressly for the population at large. Besides, there was an enormous amount of polyphonic performance which was endowed by guilds and confraternities in private chapels. Although one used to reserve the access to members of the confraternity and even made sure that the doors of the chapel were closed or the curtains drawn, almost every working individual in the town belonged to one or more confraternities who all had their musical 'programme'. Their musical and theatrical gatherings in churches, convents and guild-houses were really 'subscription concerts'. Taken together, the performances of mensural polyphony in the churches of late fifteenth-century Bruges must have averaged three to four per day – and this is disregarding the non-written or non-mensural polyphony which was accessible outdoors, or during public balls and other festivities in the town hall.

Although Bruges was a home of secular song and theatre, most of the art-music which the ordinary citizen could listen to was sacred. Just as the church ruled society – often with unjust means – and as the spires and the sound of the bells dominated the townscape, so the fantasy of the individual was imbued with sacred images, texts and sounds. The churches, chapels and churchyards were the spiritual homes of the townspeople, and they encountered their saints and angels whenever their thoughts wandered away from daily work. The altar-paintings in the chapels, and the miniatures in the prayer-books, were perfectly realistic insofar as they externalised what was really in the mind. Some people actually entered the pictures, being portrayed as donors on the wings, or as praying shepherds. All the others who did not have this opportunity, and could not afford a tomb-stone or funeral brass which transmitted their image to posterity in a sacred context, have at least left us their murmured prayers which appear in the pictures: *Ave regina celorum, O mater Dei, memento mei, Salve sancta facies*. All this was really once heard: it was part of the environment in which the pictures existed. And music was very much part of this environment as well.

The very precision of the great Flemish paintings has made us forget that they are longing for completion in life, motion and sound. They are silent mirrors of music. The 'Queen of Heaven' in the painting did not only watch the people in front of the altar; she also heard what they sung to her: *Ave regina celorum*. Her angels continue to reflect the music which was made by the humans in front of the picture – on our side of the picture.

CHAPTER TWO

The Collegiate Church of St Donatian

A sketch of the early history

Flanders is not a land of great cathedrals. The county of Flanders was politically a single unit throughout the Middle Ages; but its ecclesiastical government[1] was divided between bishoprics whose cathedrals were all situated outside its borders. Some parts to the east, beyond the river Escaut, belonged to the diocese of Cambrai, which also covered large regions of Brabant and Hainaut; the south-western coastal area (with Dunkirk and Ypres) was subject to the bishops of Thérouanne, a town in the French province of Artois. The centre and the north, with the major cities of Bruges, Ghent, Courtrai and Lille, all belonged to the diocese of Tournai; but Tournai itself was politically independent and not part of the county of Flanders. Even the Dutch diocese of Utrecht had some possessions along the northern border with Zeeland. The situation still reflected the original role of Flanders as a frontier–land, colonized and christianized in the early Middle Ages by the Frankish kings advancing from the east and south. It was only in the sixteenth century that Flanders got its own bishoprics (Bruges and Ghent), whose present cathedral churches (St Saviour's in Bruges, and St Bavo's formerly St John's in Ghent) were only parish churches during the middle Ages.

The absence of a central and all-embracing spiritual power in Flanders did no harm, however, to the ecclesiastical life or the culture in the country. On the contrary, an advantageous interplay was able to develop between secular and ecclesiastical institutions under the counts of Flanders and their successors (from 1384), the dukes of Burgundy. Just as these princes spread their residences between the wealthy commercial centres of Lille, Ghent and Bruges, so too these cities and several others had rich collegiate churches, whose clergy were so bountifully provided with privileges and land that centres of ecclesiastical culture were able to flourish independently of the bishops. A smaller, though still significant role was played by great monasteries and abbeys, especially in eastern Flanders. But the focal points of church life, to a steadily increasing extent, were the cities. Here, the collegiate churches such as St Peter's in Lille, St Donatian's in Bruges, Our Lady's in Courtrai, St Martin's in Ypres and St Pharailde's in Ghent, also had their share in secular administration and jurisdiction, being invested with rights of coinage and with their own seals, and the provosts of St Peter's and St Donatian's were *ex officio* chancellors of Flanders. They were also 'court' churches in a certain sense, in that the counts of Flanders maintained their private chapels in them, and the clergy served the counts in the functions of a civil service. The right of collation (of making appointments) to the majority of the rich prebends belonged to the counts, though some prebendaries were appointed by the Curia in Rome, and a smaller number by the bishops of Tournai, Cambrai and Thérouanne, by the archbishop of Rheims, the king of France and the University of Paris. Clerical appointments were made without regard to regional origins, and of course the clergy were bilingual; the fact that Flanders was a meeting point of French and Germanic influences was a cultural stimulus. A maritime and trading community from its earliest times, and fully converted to Christianity during the seventh century, Flanders established its own identity in the age of the invasions by the Northmen in the ninth century; the flood-plains of the coastal region proved a military defence that northern France lacked. Trading boats with a shallow draught were able to ply peacefully in this region, and at an early date the Flemings, like the Dutch, learned the skills of constructing dykes and strongholds to which the surrounding channels acted as defences.

The foundation of the collegiate church of St Donatian itself[2] was connected with the building of a castle by the counts of Flanders on the bank of the little river Reye, on a site that had already been fortified as part of the defensive measures taken against the Northmen. The church of St Mary belonging to the *castrum* was re–dedicated to St Donatianus, archbishop of Rheims, in 842, when his relics were translated there, and he has remained the patron saint of Bruges to the present day.

A charter of privileges of 1089 raised the provost of St Donatian's to the rank of a chancellor of Flanders with the same rights as the provost of St Peter's in Lille; he exercised secular lordship over all the inhabitants of the 'burg', who were also parishioners of the collegiate church: in the fifteenth century that included all members of the Burgundian court.

The rectangular complex of buildings in the city centre, still called the *burg* today (see plate 2), consisted of the original castle built by the counts of Flanders on the east side (this site is now occupied by the baroque Palais de Justice), the church and the provost's palace on the north side, the prison (the 'steen') on the west side, the castle chapel of St Basil, later the church of the Holy Blood, in the south-west corner, and the City Hall (the present building dates from the late fourteenth century) and the Palais du Franc de Bruges, the assembly hall of the Flemish nobility, on the south side. The mingling, in close proximity, of the seats of secular and spiritual authority is characteristic of the age – and at the same time the *burg* was an enclave of princely power within the city of Bruges, which was invested with its own rights and privileges, and whose belfry on the adjacent Great Market overtopped the crossing-tower of St Donatian's. The capitular church shared in the city's cultural flowering in the Middle Ages, and in its later decline. Raised to cathedral status in 1560, the old Romanesque building (see plate 2) was pulled down in 1797, during the revolutionary wars.[3] Since the nineteenth century the church of St Saviour has been the cathedral of the diocese of Bruges.

Internal organisation

The pastoral duties of the clergy of St Donatian's were light – the parish consisted of the *burg* alone – but they had a lot of administrative work in addition to the daily celebration of mass and the divine office. As was customary with collegiate chapters of the time, they imitated the practices of monastic communities. As well as a daily high mass (*summa missa*), prime, terce, sext and none (the 'lesser hours'), and vespers, compline and matins (ending with lauds, *matutinae laudes*) were all celebrated. The chapter's income from its land and other endowments provided for the sustenance of the thirty-one canons and numerous chaplains and clerks. In the later fifteenth century, there were twenty-two chaplaincies *de gremio chori*, and forty or so, with fewer privileges, *extra chorum*, ten vicariates (mostly held by clerks who deputised for the canons by taking the masses assigned to them), and eighteen clerkships (posts of *clerici installati*). The power of decision on all internal matters rested with the canons, assembled in the chapter, over which the dean presided; second to him came the *cantor*, who directed the plainsong in the daily services, normally assisted by a *coadjutor* on the other side of the choir, unless either place was taken by a deputy. During the course of the Middle Ages the business of the chapter, indeed, increasingly turned away from worship and towards secular administrative functions; the counts of Flanders played a large part in this process, using their rights of collation so that the prebends went to pay their own senior officials and courtiers. These gentlemen could be exempted from their duty to stay in residence, and this led to the accumulation of benefices and the appointment of numerous vicars and other deputies. This is not to say that some of the canons were not also learned musicians (and even composers), but they took a less active part in the music of the church, especially as many of them were often absent. In the late Middle Ages, a canon of St Donatian's *in absentia* might be active, for example, at court, at a cathedral or the Curia of the bishops of Tournai or Cambrai, at the papal Curia, or at a University such as Paris, Louvain, Orléans, Angers. The canons had normally to be in holy orders: the right to vote in the chapter rested upon this condition. Many of the canons were of noble birth, and a number of prebends were actually reserved for the nobility.[4]

The administration of finance and justice, secretarial duties and the supervision of the church school (*magna officia*) were divided between the canons; the chaplains and *clerici installati* undertook such functions as those of the *magister scholarum*, succentor, organist, verger, sexton, bell-ringers (*parva officia*). The duty of singing in the mass and in the divine office devolved principally upon the chaplains, vicars and *clerici installati* who often owed their positions in the choir solely to their musical abilities. The *clerici installati* were normally supposed to be in minor orders only, although many of them got dispensation to proceed to the priesthood, thus becoming eligible for a chaplaincy.

The division of labour between higher and lower offices undoubtedly benefited the cultivation of music.[5] As early as 1251/2 an account roll of the church (preserved in isolation) mentions the offices of organist, *rector scholarum* and succentor, the latter two with an annual salary of £5 each. In 1306/7 the name of an organist appears for the first time – Johannes Rogerii – and he earned 50s a year. From the middle of the fourteenth century, the account books are continuously preserved, giving us a long series of names of musical specialists employed by the church (see Appendix A). The first succentor known by name was Willelmus Tasset alias Barbier, appointed in 1365, but present at St Donatian's already before 1360 as a *clericus installatus*.[6] The succentor's part in church music had now become crucial: in addition to supervising the singers-clerks in the choir he was responsible for the musical training of the boys. In 1312, the chapter had made an endowment providing for eight schoolboys with vocal gifts, who were to receive special training by the succentor. The primary duty of the eight *chorales*, as they were now called to distinguish them from the *pueri scholares* or *refectionales* (boys receiving other forms of bursary), was to sing under the succentor's direction at mass, matins and vespers, especially in the psalms and the lessons, while the antiphons and hymns were normally led by the cantor and sung by the church choir as a whole.[7]

Choirbooks and the rise of polyphony

The quickening of musical activity at St Donatian's can be deduced from the records which mention large numbers of new choirbooks in the later fourteenth century.[8] These were written, notated, illuminated and sometimes even bound by specialists among the clergy. Apart from the chapter library itself, which by 1274 already contained no fewer than 136 codices, the church accounts (from 1354 onwards) furnish a record of the liturgical books, including missals, psalters, sequentiaries and ordinals. Some of them were specially prepared for the use of the *pueri chorales*. Between 1354 and 1402, these special books included the following items:

1354   2 new antiphonals and 1 new *graduale puerorum*

1365   1 new *libellus de ludo dominice resurrectionis ad opus puerorum chori*, i.e. an Easter play

1376   1 new *legenda sanctorum innocentium ad usum puerorum*, i.e. a special office for the Feast of the Holy Innocents, 28 December

       1 new *legenda lamentationum jeremie scribenda cum notulis ad usum . . . puerorum*, for Easter week

       A *graduale puerorum* was rebound

1377   2 *libelli sequentiarum ad usum scholarium* – which implies that the other boys in the school also sang the sequences – were rebound

1387   An *antiphonarium puerorum* was rebound

1397   1 new *breviarium ad usum sancti donatiani . . . ad finem quod chorales et alii horas suas canonicas legere valeant*, i.e. the breviary was used by the choirboys and the clerks seated next to them in the choir

1400   1 new *graduale puerorum*, and the old one was repaired and rebound

1402   2 new *libri puerorum*, with a total of 280 leaves, were made.

The frequency with which these codices – and the other liturgical books in the choir – were repaired and rebound indicates very heavy use and the continual enlargement of the repertory. It also emerges that the *pueri* had special duties on certain festivals, such as singing the Lamentations during Easter week, and performing mystery plays, surely under the direction of the succentor and *magister scholarum*. Unfortunately, none of these interesting codices containing special liturgies have survived.

This is also the case with the books containing polyphonic music. As early as 1377 the accounts refer to a *liber motetorum*, to which on that occasion twelve new leaves were added. In 1402 the succentor purchased an additional *liber motetorum*. As well as motets in the proper sense of the term, the 'motet' books will have contained sections of the Ordinary of the mass, and perhaps even secular music for use in the school. As the motet books are not specially designated as *libri puerorum*, the polyphonic music was probably sung mainly by expert clerks, but the choirboys will have started to take part as well before long: an endowment of 1415 for the feast of the Exaltation of the Cross (14 September) stipulated the performance of motets at the end of first and second vespers, by the succentor and the choirboys.[9] According to another endowment of 1417, the *kindercanter* (i.e. the 'children's cantor', the succentor) had to assemble the singers to perform a motet during the procession on the octave of the feast of Corpus Christi.[10] By that time, a mixture of men's and boy's voices for the singing of polyphony was probably the rule: the choirboys (not necessarily more than two at a time) sang the *triplum*, the succentor and two or three other clerks the *motetus*, the *tenor*, and, in case of four-part polyphony, the *contratenor*. The services of the organist were usually required too, to support the polyphonic singing on a positive or portative organ. The text of an endowment made in 1417 by Dino Rapondi, a rich and famous merchant from Lucca, describes the practice.[11] Every year on the day of St John *ante portam latinam* (6 May) the chapter was to:

'. . . faire déchanter ladite jour une messe en ladicte chapelle saint jehan avec les petites orgles avant heure de prime par six compagnons portans habit en nostre dicte église, et par ung de nos dis vicaires se dira la dicte messe, come on a acoustumé de déchanter les messes de hors du cuer cest assavoir de saint machut et de saint liénart'.

Déchanter is not a variant of *chanter* but a French translation of the Latin *discantare*. The specification of six musicians for polyphony, a number which may or may not include the organist, occurs frequently in Bruges documents from this date onwards. In the case of a three–part mass each part would be taken by only two singers (with or without boys for the triplum), and the organ would double one or perhaps even more than one part. We do have specific proof for polyphonic playing on the organ of St Donatian's from as early as 1384 (see p. 18). The terms of Rapondi's endowment reveal that other polyphonic masses were already sung in the church also, namely on the feasts of St Machut (Maclou or Malo, 15 November) and St Leonard (6 November); both were celebrated 'hors du cuer'. In fact, the church accounts for the year 1385/6 already mention the payment of £3 to organist and singers in the chapel of St Machutius for mass and first and second vespers on the saint's feast-day.[12] This sixth-century Breton bishop had special significance for St Donatian's, which possessed some of his relics, including his crozier, which survives to the present day. This used to be carried in solemn procession on 15 November, and was permanently exhibited in the chapel. In the collecting box beside it the faithful placed their alms – to the tune of £150 in 1377, for example.[13] This money was certainly used to meet the relatively high cost of the feast, which included two motets at vespers and a discant mass as well as plainsong and many other ceremonies. More discant singers took part than in the case of the Rapondi mass, nine in 1400, for example, and as many as eleven in 1401.[14]

St Leonard's day was another very popular festival, with processions and the collection of alms from the public; the mass is not mentioned in the *fabrica* accounts, so must have been paid for from a different fund whose accounts have not survived. The most important festival at St Donatian's, the patronal feast-day on 14 October, was also celebrated with a lot of music. The annual total spent on music for this feast is not clear from the accounts of the *fabrica*, but those of 1380/1 record even specially composed works.[15] Here, the succentor Petrus Vinderhout was paid a total of 12s for writing out and notating four *O Christi pietas*. The same ledger records that he was paid at the rate of 3s for every page he wrote in an antiphonal; thus each of the four *O Christi pietas* averaged a page in length. This popular antiphon for St Nicholas, which in Bruges was also sung on the feast of St Donatian, has about 60 notes, and therefore fills at most three or four lines in an antiphonal; moreover there would be no reason for making four copies at once of such a well-known melody. It follows that what Vinderhout wrote out was four different polyphonic compositions, possibly by himself, based on the antiphon. They will have been sung by the church's discant group in connection with the great processions on 14 October, and on the Sunday in the octave, at first and second vespers. A fifteenth-century composition from Bruges on the cantus firmus *O Christi pietas* survives – the motet *O Sanctissime presul Donatiane*, probably of the 1430s (see music example 6). In 1478, two Magnificats 'in discantu de O Christi pietas' were written down in a discant book of the church.[16]

The feast of St Donatian included instrumental performances. In the procession of the saint's relics through the city five or six *tubicinantes* walked in front of the shrine, and usually a *turpisonans* as well – presumably a trumpeter (*trumpisonans?*), as he is sometimes counted as one of the group of six wind-players. These must have been the city minstrels, playing on trumpets and shawms; the occurrence of the term *bucinatores* for them points to the use of the slide-trumpet (*bucina*, sackbut). This musical contribution to the procession of 14 October was a regular occurrence, referred to in documents throughout the fourteenth and fifteenth centuries.[17]

It is characteristic of Bruges that the instrumental music and the polyphonic singing at church festivals were rooted in popular faith, and also supported by the munificence of rich citizens and merchants. Endowments did not always consist of money; the citizen Petrus van Oostkerke, for example, gave the church a small organ on 14 February 1385.[18] Alms and endowments were needed, for the singers-clerks had to earn their living by piece-work, taking part in as many services as they could (with only some of them including polyphonic music), and the annual stipends of the succentor and organist were relatively small: from *c*.1387 until 1427 the succentor was paid £18 and the organist

£12, whilst the canons got £40 at the very least. It was the voluntary gifts that nurtured ecclesiastical life in general and the cultivation of music in particular. Sometimes they came from the chapter itself (as with the endowment for eight choirboys of 1312) or from individual members of the clergy, but increasingly from the citizens and merchants of Bruges, and from the counts of Flanders and members of the court. The cultivation of music at St Donatian's – as in the other churches of Bruges – was the achievement not of the clergy alone but also of the city and of all Flanders. One of the great festivals celebrated by the clergy of St Donatian's was, indeed, sponsored directly by the city magistrate of Bruges: the feast of the Invention of the Cross (3 May). This was the day on which the Holy Blood procession took place, the highest religious solemnity of Bruges until the present day. This day also marked the beginning of the urban May Fair, and was as much a civic as an ecclesiastical feast (see also p. 85 f.). On 23 April 1419, the city magistrate decided that the rank of the feast was to be raised to that of a *festum triplex*, and in order for the appropriate liturgical ceremonies to be carried out, the city fathers endowed the church of St Donatian with an annual income of £24 (later more).[19] Some of this money must have been spent on polyphonic music.

Nevertheless, providing opportunities for the performance of polyphonic music was not, at that date, the prime purpose of the many and various endowments which wrapped round the great, and before long the small, feast-days like filigree. All the members of the clergy were rewarded for their various activities, and apart from the costs of the ceremonial a lot of the money was diverted to charitable purposes. With private endowments, the focus was most often a requiem mass for the donor and his family, or an anniversary service during his lifetime. The terms of the endowment made by the canon Johannes de Hagha in 1415 are typical of many.[20] The donor's particular interest was in the feast of the Exaltation of the Cross (14 September), which he had the chapter raise to a *festum solemne*. Some of the payments of bread or money, to be distributed in tokens (*pitancie*), covered the presence of the clergy at the four 'lesser hours'. The emoluments for the high mass were as follows: 6s for the celebrant, 3s each for the cantor and his *coadjutor*, 4s for the curate or *major custos* who had to put out the vestments for the choir and the altar cloths, 2s each for the sacristan and the two *virgiferi chori* (who carried the cross and torches), 6d each for the four schoolboys who sang the psalms at matins, 2s each for the servers (deacon and sub-deacon), 10s altogether for the organist and organ-blower, but 18s for the bellringers. The *hostiarius* (keeper of the sacrament) received 1s, whilst the *fabrica* (the office of works of the church) was paid no less than £5 for candles. The succentor got only 2s, which he had to share with the choirboys, for the singing of two vespers motets. The clergy were paid 8s for each attendance at the antiphon *Alma redemptoris mater* for the *Benedictus* at lauds, and another 6s for attending the whole of matins. There was 16s each for everyone who took part in the procession inside the church before the high mass, and 10s for those present at the antiphon *O crux gloriosa* at second vespers. It can be seen that these sums were intended to attract even the well-paid canons to attend matins, the procession and second vespers.

A mass with suffrages and collects for the dead was to be read daily during the octave of the feast in the Chapel of the Holy Cross for Johannes da Hagha and his relatives. On 14 September the *receptor obedientie* (the chapter chamberlain) was to distribute 60 white shilling loaves and 48 sixpenny jugs of mead to the inmates of the city prison (the *donckercamere*). He himself was paid 4s for performing the task.

At the same time Hagha also left money for celebrations on the feasts of St Barnabas and the Transfiguration and on all the feasts of the apostles, as well as for two masses for the souls of his kinsman Hugo de Hagha and himself, with vigils on the eve, and accompanied by further distributions of bread and mead to the 'pauperi incarcerati'. All this was paid for by the income, expected to be £40 a year, from houses and land, the titles to which were legally transferred to the *receptor obedientie* Jean Ondanch as the representative of the chapter.

This example may perhaps help to place the music at St Donatian's in its proper context in the life of the church. At the time it was made, Johannes de Hagha's endowment was one of the richest, but it was followed during the course of the fifteenth century by dozens of similar ones, some even more comprehensive.

Musicians among the clergy, and connections with other chapels

Already in the late fourteenth century, the cultivation of music at St Donatian's is closely associated with the Burgundian court and chapel; but there were connections with other centres as well. When Duke Philip of Burgundy (Philip the Bold) became count of Flanders after the death of his father-in-law Louis de Male in 1384, and made his ceremonial entry into Bruges on 26 April of that year, this was not the first occasion when the musical forces of the court and of the collegiate church were combined. Among other celebrations, Bruges saw the new duke take the traditional oath to uphold the privileges of Flanders at the high altar of St Donatian's. According to an old custom, the clergy sang the responsory *Honor virtus* during the duke's procession to the altar, and 'after the responsory the organist played a motet on the organ'.[21] According to the accounts, the organist was paid 10s;[22] he was in all probability Jean Visée, then newly employed by Philip the Bold, who had already been in the service of Louis de Male. His fame reached as far as Aragon, and he must have stayed mostly in Bruges, where he received free board ('tenetur de mensa') at St Donatian's between 1380 and 1388 during at least four of those years.[23] On 25 April 1384, the day before his entry into Bruges, Philip the Bold took into his employment two singers who probably lived in Bruges at the time: Henri Potage, from the chapel of Louis de Male, and Symon le Corier. Both had previously sung in the papal chapel in Avignon.[24] Jean Visée's effective successor as court organist, from 1384, was Jean Ondanch.[25] He seems to have been a chaplain of St Donatian's as early as 1370;[26] in 1387 he acquired a house in Ghistel, not far from Bruges; in 1390 he became a chaplain of St Basil's, and from 1394 to his death in 1425[27] he was a canon of St Donatian's. There he was more or less regularly in attendance from 1406, despite his many musical activities at court. He never performed the duty of organist at the collegiate church itself, but in his position of canon, he must have influenced church music there, too. He may have supervised the repair of the great organ carried out in 1411–12 by the Delft organ-builder Rogerus (Roegaert) de Noorthende; the large endowment made by the chapter for a daily polyphonic mass in 1421 may have been due in part to his initiative – at all events he presented his own son (or pupil?) to the chapter as a choirboy on 21 April 1421 under the terms of the new endowment (see p. 22).

One of the earliest canons of St Donatian's known in the history of music was the *scholasticus* Jean Champion, who held this position from 1361 to his death in 1383. He was a poet as well as a musician, and conducted a literary correspondence with Jean de le Mote and Philippe de Vitry in the period around 1350.[28] Champion was a follower of the school of the *seconde rhétorique* and its curious, mythological, early humanism, which is reflected in the texts of many motets and ballades of the late *ars nova*. Literary sources for such texts can have been some of the books which Champion borrowed from the chapter library before 26 April 1372: Boethius, Quintus Curtius, Jordanus, Thomas de Capua, various books *de dictamine* (prosody), the comedies of Terence and the epigrams of Martial.[29]

In 1378 a prebend of St Donatian's was given to a Johannes de Bosco, whom Ursula Günther equates with a known composer of the papal chapel in Avignon.[30] The contact with the Curia was important, and the ripples of the conflict between the 'Urbanists' and the 'Clementists', the adherents of the pope in Rome, Urban VI, and those of the pope in Avignon, Clement VII, from 1378 onwards spread through Flanders and even through the chapter of St Donatian's. Thus the canon Jean Guinoti (from 1374, resident from 1383) was *scriptor* at the Roman Curia, while the chaplain and *magister fabrice* Johannes Scavere was excommunicated by Rome in 1378. That a new altar of

Our Lady in the nave was consecrated in 1387 by the bishop of London was in keeping with attempts of Bruges to free itself from the Avignon allegiance imposed by the bishop of Tournai. But because of the ties with the court of the Valois, and in contrast with the rest of Bruges, the majority of the chapter pursued a pro-Avignon policy. Prebends were given to a whole group of canons who had previously been singers at the papal court in Avignon, and several of whom were now at the Burgundian court: Eligius de Bray (c.1386–96), Nicole Fessard (1396–1400), Eynard le Fevre (Fabri: 1398–1400) and notably Jean de Watignies (1394–1402), of whom Craig Wright says that he 'typifies the extensive interchange of personnel between the papal and Burgundian chapels that took place at the end of the fourteenth century'.[31] This famous musician must have visited Bruges quite often between the journeys he also made to Paris and Avignon, all on Duke Philip's business.

This is not the place to pursue the contacts that the chapter also had with various universities, and which extended certainly as far as Prague. But it should be remembered that in 1394 the chapter elected the most famous theologian of the age, Jean Carlier de Gerson, as dean. An indication of his great interest in music is contained in the chapter minutes. Only three days after his assumption of the office, on 15 October 1396, he summoned the chapter to a meeting 'super reformationem divini officii'. The outcome was a reform of the liturgy that is breathtaking in its clarity. More regulations on similar lines followed, which must have done music at St Donatian's a world of good. Unfortunately this did not prevent the chapter, after the great mystic and music-lover had returned permanently to the University of Paris in 1404, from stopping his stipend for dereliction of duty in 1408, and finally deposing him in 1411.[32]

Around that time, we find already several canons of St Donatian's who are known to have been composers. Jean Charité (Caritatis) was a canon from 1406 to 1411 but was then 'auctoritate apostolica privatus',[33] having perhaps been caught up in the wheels of the Great Schism; he was chaplain and secretary to Duke Jean de Berry and also presided at Philip the Bold's Court of Love in Paris. Jacques Vide, a composer of several widely distributed chansons, was a canon in 1410–1411; he owed his benefice to Pope John XXIII, who was recognized by Burgundy.[34] Jean Carbonnier held a canonry from 1417 and was *valet de chambre* to Duke John the Fearless at the same time (see also p. 88). These musicians may not have resided in Bruges for any amount of time; but the following case is different.

On 14 January 1411 Henricus Sandewin, a canon, armed with a letter of appointment from Pope Alexander V (Pisa 1409–10), had his brother Robertus nominated to a clerkship in the choir. Robert

Sandewin was a canon himself by 1414, and in the following decade also accumulated benefices in the Bruges churches of Our Lady and of St Saviour. This musician sang at the Council of Constance in the papal chapel,[35] of which he was probably a member already in Pisa and Bologna, at the courts of Alexander V and John XXIII. After that, he spent most of his life in Bruges, becoming cantor of St Donatian's in 1447; he died in 1453.

Long before that, the church of St Donatian's had developed frequent interchanges with the great musical establishments of the age. The succentor from 1412 to 1415, Thomas Fabri, was known as a composer and a pupil of Jean Tapissier in Paris. He left some extremely interesting chansons in French and in Flemish (see p. 109 ff. and music examples 2–4), and a canonic motet whose text connects him with Bruges and with the composer Egardus (see p. 111), who may have served Pope John XXIII (1410–15). The succentor of 1422–25, Simon Ranarii, had been a singer in the chapel of King Sigismond during the Council of Constance (1414–18).[36] We do not know where Jacobus Coutreman had received his training, who, as a 'musicis notabilis', became a *clericus installatus* in 1417. In spite of several occasions when indignation was expressed at his immoral life – he was alleged to be a 'bigamist' – he was succentor from 1419 to 1422, and again from 1428 to 1429, on account of his 'particular musical industriousness'; from 1427 to his death in 1432 he was also organist. He did a great deal for the instruction and the polyphonic repertory of the choirboys. He bought a motet book for them in 1421 and copied several motets in the *Libri puerorum choralium* in 1427 and 1429; in the former year, these consisted of 'quibusdam motetis, scilicet Patrem, Et in terra, ac Sanctus'. In 1431, he wrote out four Passions in a paper codex of the church, which were perhaps polyphonic.[37] He had already been awarded an increase in salary in 1420 for instructing the boys in motet singing, and it was probably for him that the succentor's salary was raised, in 1428, from £18 to £24.[38]

Coutreman's only surviving work is a chanson, however: *Vaylle que vaylle, il faut s'asseürer*[39] – this seems to quote, in an oblique manner, the name of a Burgundian singer, Pierre Vaille, and Duke Philip himself, who carried, after his accession in 1419, the sobriquet 'l'Asseüré'. The piece belongs to a specific genre of chansons, those connected with the 'moys de May' (see p. 100 f.).

A few sacred works are known by Jacobus de Clibano, who was succentor from 1430 to 1433, and remained closely connected with St Donatian's until his departure for Soignies after 3 June, 1449.[40]

The choral foundation of 1421

Very early in the reign of Philip the Good, the chapter of St Donatian's showed the way to renewing and increasing the practice of sacred polyphony. Its main concern was the sustenance of the choirboys. As the funds provided by the 1312 endowment had dwindled in value, the chapter decided on 7 May 1421 to provide a large new endowment, worth £84 a year, for four choirboys and nine more schoolboys (*refectionales*), whose duties were exactly specified.[41] The *chorales* and the succentor (and probably some of the clerks, though that is not actually mentioned) were to sing a polyphonic mass in honour of the Virgin every day in the Lady Chapel behind the choir. This mass was known as the *Missa de Salve*, since it began with the introit *Salve sancta parens*. According to the text of the endowment its celebration was already an established practice, but hitherto it had often been performed in a slovenly, 'syncopated' manner.[42] From now on it was to be sung 'with counterpoint', in correct measure without hesitation, in the manner of the chaplains ('cum contrapuncto seu discantu et mensura cursim depromere more capellanorum'). In other words, the more expert singing of the chaplains and clerks was to serve as a model. Another model named in the text was the practice of the *Missa de Salve* observed in the cathedrals of Tournai and Cambrai and other churches in the neighbourhood (possibly Our Lady's church in Courtrai) – although no documentary evidence is known for this practice, the earliest extant polyphonic mass cycle is, in fact, the 'Mass of Tournai' of the fourteenth century.

The 1421 Bruges document also stipulates that the four *chorales* had to attend the daily high mass and vespers in the choir, and 'sing counterpoint' at these services, i.e. whenever the rank of feast required it. For polyphony at high mass, the evidence is otherwise scanty, but in 1442 the chaplain Symon Coene was reproached for not having participated as much as he could have done, in the polyphonic singing of the Gloria and Credo on all higher feasts. In 1421, the chapter also stipulated that the *refectionales* should be instructed by the succentor in the correct recitation, at least, of the psalm verses for matins. The more gifted of them were also to be trained in discant and counterpoint, so that there were always a reserve of boys capable of augmenting the four *chorales*. The musical skills of the latter must have been high; one was accepted in 1420 who already knew 'his counterpoint'.[43]

Philip the Good, who visited Bruges in 1419 for the first time, seems to have taken the endowment of St Donatian's as a model for his own choral foundations of 1425, in the Sainte-Chapelle of Dijon, and in St Peter's in Lille (see p. 94).

The performance practice and the musical repertory of the Bruges *Missa de Salve* are not directly documented. The succentor and one or two of the clerks must have sung the tenor and contratenor; there is no mention of the organ, but there was a small one in the Lady-Chapel at least from the middle of the century. New choirbooks were certainly needed: in 1418, a special missal 'de Salve' and a (new?) *liber motetorum* were bound; in 1421, Coutreman bought a motet book from the clerk and bookbinder Willem van den Driessche.[44] It is likely that the music for the *Missa de Salve* was still assembled from individual mass movements spread through the *libri motetorum*; the 'motets' notated by Coutreman in 1427 were, indeed, movements of the Ordinary of the mass (see above). Many such movements from the early fifteenth century are known, some of which are identifiable as Marian music through cantus firmi or the Marian trope *Spiritus et alme* for the Gloria; Binchois and Dufay contributed to the genre. Only England seems to have produced a unified mass cycle, on the tenor *Salve sancta parens*, by the 1420s;[45] it cannot be ruled out that this or a similar work was known in Bruges.

Some minor private endowments[46] at St Donatian's still tend to emphasize the use of individual movements in this period: there was, for example, a 'Sanctus solemniter decantandum' (i.e. 'discantandum'?) on the feast of SS. Peter and Paul (29 June) from *c.*1430; an *Et in terra* and *Patrem* and a motet on the feast of SS. Simon and Jude (28 October) from 1439; those same movements on the feast of the 11,000 Virgins (21 October) from 1445, and several others. The *Missa de Salve* itself was further supported by three additional endowments until the 1460s. In 1434, the citizen Johannes Scateraers also endowed the singing of a *Salve regina* in discant every Saturday;[47] this was a genre not hitherto sung in polyphony.

Famous musicians

In the reigns of Philip the Good (1419–67) and Charles the Bold (1467–77), many well-known musicians such as Grenon, Binchois, Dufay and Joye were canons at St Donatian's. The musical life of the collegiate church must have benefited from the exchanges with the ducal chapel and other establishments. Music produced at court was probably heard during the increasingly frequent visits of the dukes and their entourage: Philip the Good was in Bruges as often as in Lille or Brussels, and certainly more often than in Dijon.[48] Because many singers of the ducal chapel held their prebends *in absentia*, the collegiate church actually subsidised the music of the court. (It should not be forgotten that the church's own income came from its estates all over Flanders, and was thus ultimately the product of the labour of Flemish peasants.) On the other hand, the liturgical music which the court wanted to hear when visiting St Donatian's was performed by the musical experts of the resident clergy, with or without assistance from the ducal musicians. The clerks lived to a large extent on the donations and endowments of citizens and merchants of Bruges (thus, this social class too made its contribution to the musical glories of the court).

The non-resident singers and composers who held canonicates or chaplaincies could at least be relied upon to send compositions, recommend new singers, or give general advice. The canonicate of Nicholas Grenon (1424–25), who was at the time *magister choralium* of Pope Martin V, seems too short even for that. Another papal singer, Johannes Redoys, applied for a prebend in 1425 and again in 1430 – unsuccessfully, but he seems to have remained in touch with the chapter which elected him to be one of the procurators at the court in 1454. Egidius de Binch alias Binchois became a canon on 7 January 1430 (he was in Bruges at that time) as a result of a ducal nomination, and held the prebend *de privilegio* without interruption until his death in September 1460. On 29 August 1430 the chapter approved the nomination of Georgius Martini, at that time a singer in the chapel of the new pope, Eugene IV. He took up residence in 1432 and remained in Bruges until his death in 1438 (see also Appendix A and p. 117). On 3 September 1431 a representative of Guillaume Dufay applied for a prebend for the papal 'cantor et capellanus'. The application was approved as late as 28 April 1438, and then evidently under pressure from the new provost Jean de Bourgogne, a step-brother of duke Philip, in whose election in 1438 Binchois had taken part.[49] Dufay received not only the twenty-fourth canonry, reserved for law graduates, but also the chaplaincy of St Lawrence. As Dufay's appointment had been initiated not by the duke, but by Pope Eugene IV, to whose patronage he also owed his canonry in Cambrai where he resided from 1439, further ducal support was needed to make the chapter of St Donatian's actually pay his prebend. For the period from the summer of 1439 to 2 February 1440, the duke actually attested Dufay's presence in his *familiaritas*[50] (it was the time when Dufay had taken residence in Cambrai!); after that, Dufay had to apply every year in Bruges for his prebend, sometimes personally, and the chapter, which was under no legal obligation to pay him, granted only the minimun annual emolument of £40 nearly every year[51] as a gratuity, 'out of respect' for the ducal protection. But its objections led to the duke himself promising in 1446 that he would make no further requests for such payments to be made. When another patron of Dufay, Philip's cousin Jean de Bourgogne, Count of Estampes, did exactly that on 23 June 1446 the chapter refused once and for all, and Dufay's procurator the Seigneur d'Archy threatened revenge. It came to nothing; Dufay resigned his canonicate on

4 October 1446, a proceeding for which he appointed not the customary one procurator to represent him in Bruges but five: the duke's squire Charles de Rochefort et Bossu, himself a benefactor of St Donatian's; three chaplains of Philip the Good, Gilles Binchois, Pierre Maillart and Nicaise Dupuis; and Pierre's brother(?) Clemens Maillart, cantor to Jean de Bourgogne.[52] With this blatant parade of his exalted patrons and famous friends Dufay soothed his wounded pride; the annual £40 from Bruges had been tossed at him like alms, and in spite of his absence, whereas the chapter of Cambrai at once made an appropriate deduction from his stipend when he set off on his travels in 1452.[53]

Musicians like Binchois, who were court singers with special privileges, had an easier time of it in Bruges than Dufay. Among the canons intermittently resident in Bruges, there were the court singers Pierre Godefroy (can. 1435–45), evidently a friend of Binchois, Estienne Petault (1438–†1442) and Mathieu de Bracle (1439–†1460), whose prebend at St Waudru's in Mons passed to Dufay in 1446. He was a councillor of the duke and an active diplomat; in 1459–60 he was provost of Our Lady's in Bruges. The careers of the court chaplains Gilles Joye (can. 1459–†1483) and Pierre Basin (1467–†1497) developed mostly in Bruges. Among the non-resident canons, there were the duke's *protocapellanus* Nicaise Dupuis (1446–47), Dufay's successor in the twenty-fourth prebend; Nicholas Boidin (1447–57), Dupuis's successor in the same prebend, who served the Burgundian and, later, the Savoyard chapel; Pierre Maillart (1440–48), who seems to have been the composer Petrus de Domarto (see p. 123 f.); Philippe Syron (1449–†1485), court singer from 1441 and *protocapellanus* from 1465.[54] Canonries were also held by Robert Auclou (1437–c.1473), a close associate of Dufay, and Antoine Haneron (1446–†1490, and provost from 1467), a privy councillor and ambassador of the duke, tutor of Charles de Charolais, archdeacon of Cambrai and professor of Louvain, where he founded the Collège de S. Donatien in 1484. The latter two were not active musicians, but important patrons of music.

The musical personnel
(see also Appendix A)

The actual musical offices at the collegiate church during this period were held by less well-known personalities. Some of the succentors were composers: Cornelius Heyns (1452–53 and 1463–65), Jean Boubert (1452–61) and perhaps Pierre Basin (1465). The organists included Petrus Paes (1432–39), Paulus Bloume (1439–47) and Rolandus de Wreede (1447–†1485).

Apart from the choirboys, the most important group of musicians were the *clerici installati*, normally lay-clerks, although the number of priests among them actually increased during the fifteenth century. In addition to their many other duties, they had to sing the discant; of the total number of eighteen clerks, about twelve seem to have been regularly available for polyphony from as early as *c.*1440. Known as the *socii de musica* or *ghezellen van der muzycke*, these clerks regarded themselves as a privileged group, and exploited their expertise to earn money in other churches, not always with the chapter's leave. Thus four of them – Olivierus, Clemens, Achilles (de Bleysere) and Johannes Luucx – were punished on 17 August 1414, because they had absented themselves from their duties on the feast of the Assumption, together with the organist, Johannes Zwinemersch. They were forbidden thenceforth to sing 'apud Droghenboome et alibi' on high feast-days without special permission; that is, the group had performed polyphony at the Franciscan convent before the wealthy confraternity of 'Our Lady of the Dry Tree', of which more will be said later (see pp. 70 – 73).

To this group of low-paid singer-clerks, the rivalry of other churches, who were prepared to pay handsomely for polyphony, always offered a temptation. This continuing conflict led to a dispute of wider dimensions in 1449.[55] Before Easter week that year, the chapter had to impose a fine on those who would not take part in the services on Palm Sunday. This angered the self-confident clerks and led to excited verbal exchanges with their spokesman, the chaplain Philippus Dullaert. Called to order by the *scholasticus* Beversluus, he retorted: 'This scholaster, this *coquin*, who can neither read nor sing – he calls us "pipers" and gets up to no good himself.' And: 'We'll see whether we're not just as free as the canons; you'll find out how strong we are.' He refused to take leave from a canon before going out to sing ('demonstrando pollicem'), and accused his colleague Thomas le Canu – evidently a supporter of the chapter – of keeping the scholaster's brothel in his house. It then became known that twelve or thirteen clerks, including the organist de Wreede, regularly met on Saturdays in the Franciscan convent and plotted revolt. This was certainly in connection with the singing of polyphonic masses there every Sunday for the 'Dry Tree' confraternity. Punishing twelve clerks, even by imprisonment in some cases, did not put an end to the chapter's problems in this respect. On 2 April 1449 it had to be admitted that singing for payment in St Basil's chapel, at least, could not be forbidden, since the chapel officially belonged to the collegiate church. There is mention in 1452 of a mass of the Holy Cross every Friday in St Basil's with 'socii de choro', i.e., discant singers.[56]

The archives of other churches in Bruges also reveal that the clerks of St Donatian's were engaged to sing polyphonic masses celebrated there: at Our Lady's from about the middle of the century at the latest, at St Walburga's and St James' in 1461, at St Saviour's in the 1480s and perhaps earlier, in the Abbey 'ten Eeckhout' from *c.*1470. In most cases the 'zanghers van Sinte Donaes' were rewarded with wine or an appropriate *pourboire* of up to 8s per person; usually between four and six singers were engaged, and often the organist as well. This practice spread even to the succentor and the choirboys from *c.*1458,[57] and had eventually to be tolerated by the chapter.

The chapter's concern was caused solely by the fear that the services of St Donatian's itself might suffer. The training and specialisation of the clerks in polyphony continued to be encouraged. The success of this policy is demonstrated not only by the engagements of the *socii de musica* of St Donatian's in other churches of Bruges, but even more by the positions which many of them found at court, in other towns, or even in the papal chapel. Those who stayed at home became chaplains and, sometimes, canons; the best of them, like Jean Cordier, Martinus Colins, Johannes de Vos, Pierre Basin, Nicholas Mayoul *junior*, and Philippe Paillet were requested by the dukes of Burgundy and their successors Maximilian of Habsburg and Philip the Fair. (See Appendix A.) Most of these musicians were either natives of Bruges or came from elsewhere in Flanders, but received their training at St Donatian's. The chapter was also prepared to appoint clerks trained in other centres, sometimes at short notice: when Colins, Amouret, Platea and Jacobus Luucx threatened to move to the service of the bishop of Liège in 1468, three other singers were quickly engaged, two of them from Antwerp. Only the best of them, Colins, was persuaded to stay with a considerable increase in salary.

The musical specialisation of the singers is often indicated in the chapter minutes. From *c.*1450 onwards, the denomination *tenorista* is given to about half of them – it must refer to both the singers of the tenor and the *contratenor bassus*. Johannes de Vos is called 'tenorista . . . habens vocem profundam' in 1484 and 'tenorista bassus' in 1485. In 1480, Johannes de Vico is described as 'habens vocem altam' and Johannes Bouchout as 'contratenor [altus?]' in 1480. Zelandrinus's voice is referred to in 1485 as 'vox supremi cantus' (which he lost, however, on arrival from Cambrai).

Gilles Joye

The self-confidence, lively intelligence and loose morals of these men are well illustrated in the career of one of the most gifted of them, Gilles Joye. He appears for the first time in the chapter minutes on 15 March 1451, then already in characteristic circumstances: during mass on the previous Christmas Day he and his friends Johannes Band and Jacobus Tayaert had concocted saucy verses about all their colleagues, which had then been recited at dinner ('fuerunt jocose recitata'). He was admonished on 19 August 1451 for his part in a street-fight, in which Tayaert and Comere were also involved. On 7 January 1452 Joye, Tayaert, Leonis and Cornelius Heyns were reprimanded for their express refusal to assist the succentor in motet-singing on the eve of Epiphany; they had done so as a protest against the chapter's decision (not for the first time) to cancel the popular 'Feast of Asses'; (see also p. 33 f.). (Succentor himself from 23 June 1452, Heyns was not the most dutiful servant of the chapter; on Ascension day 1452 he had absented himself from vespers in order to go and play ball games: 'ivit lusum in phala ad pilam'; as for Tayaert, he was accused on more than one occasion of spending his days in brothels.[58]) Joye himself had a concubine. When he (re-)applied for a *stallum* in the choir on 27 November 1454, he was told that, as a priest, he would first have to mend his ways, control his language ('abstinere ab oblocutionibus quibus habundare consuevit'[59]), and, above all get rid of the woman who lived with him and was known to the population at large as 'Rosabelle' ('vocatam in vulgo "Rosabelle" '). Though this was not necessarily the woman to whom the chanson *O rosa bella* (probably by Dunstable) was dedicated, Joye may have sung it to her sometimes.[60] Joye's immorality was harmless enough in comparison with that of some of the canons, who are known to have been guilty of seducing and even raping innocent young girls; the composer Jacobus de Clibano was involved in one such case as a procurer.[61]

Although Joye was awarded a prebend in Cleves in 1453 and the rich curateship of St Hippolytus in Delft at a later date, he spent most of his life in Bruges, from 1462 as a ducal chaplain. A canon of St Donatian's from 1459, he continued to influence the music of the collegiate church. He may have been instrumental in the appointment of the distinguished singers Jean Cordier and Pierre Basin in 1460, Martinus Colins and Christiaen Baelde in 1467; he acted several times as a musical referee, for example in the audition of choirboys and even of organists; he was part of the committee which induced the nobleman Johannes van der Coutre to make a huge new endowment for the choirboys in 1470; as *magister fabrice* 1467–69, he spent the largest amount ever on the copying of polyphonic music (see below), and in 1468, at least, he administered the funds of the ducal endowments. In 1481 and 1482, he was still in debt with the bookseller Jean de Clerc for parchment which had been provided for two splendid graduals in 1468. Joye died on 31 December 1483, and, in spite of some difficulties over paying his debts, received a handsome burial with the tolling of the bell 'Lenaerd' and a mass for his soul, for which he had left an endowment. The tombstone in the sacristy has been described by later historians; above it, there was probably displayed what is the only attributed portrait painting of a fifteenth-century composer that still survives:

Memling's portrait (dated 1472) of the forty-seven-year-old singer, poet and composer; a commemorative slab was appended near it.[62] Joye's life bore out his name, which is possibly one he gave himself – by no means unlikely in the case of a clerk who may have been of illegitimate birth.

Another vivid portrait of Joye is provided, of course, by his surviving chansons with their texts, particularly the well-known *Ce qu'on fait a quatrimini* (see also p. 126). It would be in character if Joye were the composer of two anonymous masses composed sometime in the 1450s on the tune *O rosa bella*.[63] There is a dialectical wit in the way the first mass takes the tenor of the chanson as its tenor and is in *tempus perfectum* throughout, while the other is entirely in *tempus imperfectum* and uses the chanson's *contratenor*.

Endowments and discant books

All the polyphonic choirbooks of St Donatian's were destroyed in the sixteenth century, it seems. Nevertheless, the church's account books, and the text of endowments, give some clues to the polyphonic repertory in the fifteenth century, although names of composers or works are rarely mentioned there (for the indirect evidence, see Chapter VI).

Up to about 1460 the endowments usually provided for motets and individual mass movements, apart from the chapter's foundation of the *Missa de Salve* and a few privately endowed mass cycles such as the Rapondi mass. One of the two daily masses founded by Philip the Good, and confirmed by his son in 1467, may have been a discant mass, but the original document seems to have been lost.[64] Polyphony was increasingly used for other liturgical forms: there was the *Salve regina* on Saturdays from 1434, followed by the *Alma redemptoris mater* in Lent from 1447 and the *Regina celi* (Easter to Whitsunday) from 1448; the sequence *Lauda Sion salvatorem* on Corpus Christi from 1454; also the *Deo gratias* after the greater hours seems to have been sung in discant from very early on. Polyphony for the Magnificat and the Te Deum is first mentioned in the account books of 1468, when already eighteen Magnificats and one Te Deum were notated in the choirbooks. Unspecified *moteti* and also some individual settings of the *Patrem* continued to be copied. In 1455, for the first time, a cyclic mass is mentioned by name in the account books: a *Missa de gratiarum actione*, perhaps for a public ceremony on the occasion of the suppression of the Ghent uprising, at which a Te Deum must also have been sung. This was entered by Thomas le Canu in the *magnus liber motetorum*, a parchment codex, to which a further large number of leaves was added in 1460.[65] Only after that do we note special mass codices, mostly of paper, and referred to as *libri discantus*. Nearly all of the polyphony from *c.*1468 to 1485 was notated by Martinus Colins. The following chart shows all the works that are individually mentioned in the account books as having been copied (the accounts from 1456 to 1462 are missing).[66]

	Complete masses	Magnificats	Other
1463/4	3		
1467/8	2 (one of which was '*L'homme armé*' by Ockeghem)		1 '*Patrem 3 regum*'
1468/9	16	18	1 Te Deum, 3 *Patrem*
1469/70	1		
1470/1	16		9 Te Deums, 1 *Patrem*
1471/2	8	2	
1472/3	2		[67]
1473/4	4	4	
1474/5	5		
1475/6	4 (two '*O Venus banden*', one '*de Mimi*', probably by Ockeghem; one for the '*crepelfeest*')	10	2 Te Deums, 1 '*Patrem de village*' by Ockeghem
1476/7	4 (one '*de cuiusvis tono*' probably by Ockeghem; one by Wreede; one by Balduin Mijs; one by Aliamus de Groote for the '*crepelfeest*', and from now on each year a new mass for this feast)		
1478/9	2	2 Magnificats '*de O Christi pietas*'	
1479/80	1		
1483/4	1		
1484/5	1		
1486/7	14		
1488/9	5		
1489/90	1		
1491/2	1 (by Obrecht).		

This list totalling ninety-one masses and thirty-six Magnificats is augmented, moreover, by a large number of works which are given summary entries. In 1472, 'diverse misse' were copied; in 1479/80, the costs of a new 'liber missarum et motetarum' on parchment, with miniatures and decorated initials, included £42 paid to Martinus Colins for the notation alone. Judging from the rate at which Colins was normally paid for copying, the codex must have consisted of 280 folios, which would have accommodated something like twenty-five masses and twenty-five motets. The twenty-one historiated initials or miniatures and a thousand other initials ('littere floreate') were the work of the illuminator Johannes de Vico (perhaps identical with the singer of that name). It was a true forerunner of the splendid choirbooks of the Habsburg-Netherlands court, written from *c.*1495, which have come down to us. Two new books of polyphonic Magnificats were written in

1498/9, and in 1499/1500, a 'liber discantus, missarum de Salve sancta parens et aliis' was made, in which the staves were drawn by Obrecht.

The sheer scale of the cultivation of music not only in Bruges alone but throughout the Low Countries in the fifteenth century has been underestimated. This area did not only provide the musical talents for the courts and churches of central and southern Europe, but its own establishments also fostered a vigorous musical practice second to none at the time.

The polyphonic repertory of St Donatian's must have been used not only in the services of the collegiate church itself. The *socii de musica* would have sung these works also in their many engagements in other churches of Bruges. Other copies probably existed in their hands before the chapter agreed in each case to pay for the production of the more formal choirbooks, at the instigation of such men as Gilles Joye and Jean Cordier.

Organists and organs

The organists of St Donatian's were undoubtedly learned musicians and experienced in polyphony. We know that discant singers like Coutreman, Colins and de Vico took over as organists for a time. Rolandus de Wreede, who was organist from 1447 to 1485, appears to have composed a mass in 1476/7.[68]

There are frequent references to the use of the organ in endowed polyphonic masses and motets. The organ also accompanied, or alternated with, the plainchant. Genres for which the participation of the organ is regularly mentioned are the Magnificat and the Te Deum, the Nunc dimittis, hymns and sequences, lessons and the Kyrie in the mass. Most of these genres are strophic and include choral recitation, so that the great organ on the loft would have alternated with the full choir. The verses of hymns, *cantica*, sequences, etc. which were played by the great organ must also have been sung, because it is unlikely that any text was left out, but the organist may have added extemporised embellishments over the plainchant, which was then performed by soloists. This can have been the practice which is recorded in the account books of the fourteenth century, where the organists were paid special gratuities for playing the Magnificat and Te Deum on the day of the Assumption and other high feasts. The introduction of written discant in these genres or, at first, some kind of extemporised polyphony such as *fauxbourdon*, gave the opportunity for three-sided exchanges between choral plainsong, organ verses and discant verses. We have to assume that the great organ was not used for the accompaniment of discant masses and motets – the organist on the loft could not see the choirbook anyway – but that at least the cantus firmus of these polyphonic genres was played on smaller organs which stood near the singers; such performances often took place in chapels, not in the choir.[69]

The organs cost the church a lot of money to run and required constant attention from the chapter. St Donatian's had a great organ as early as 1127, and certainly a salaried organist from the mid-thirteenth century.[70] For the fifteenth century, Alfons Dewitte has published most of the relevant documents, including a detailed description of the new great organ ordered in 1434 from Johannes Crane.[71] Building began in 1443; a model drawing ordered in that year placed the instrument on the west side of the nave above the font, whereas the old organ had stood on the choir screen. During the construction, the new organ was situated in the provost's palace; it was transferred to the church in 1454, and decorated with paintings by C. Muul and many sculptures by the wood-carver Jacob van Belle. Repairs and adaptations followed almost immediately; they were commissioned in 1454–63 from the Dominican friar Hugo; in 1471–73 from Marc Sproncholf; in 1479 from a certain 'magister guilelmus'. From 1482, the organ-builder Judocus Buus received an annual salary for looking after the organs of the church; in that year, also, an (apparently unsuccessful) attempt was made to enlist the old friar Hugo again for a major repair.[72] There was always at least one smaller organ available during these alterations, besides the one or two portatives used in the nave or in individual chapels. After major repairs or rebuildings of the great organ (in 1449, 1465 and 1467), trials were held with the participation of organists from Bruges itself and also from Veurne and Antwerp; one of these was a certain Theodor Spierinck. They were paid for their expenses, and for drinking parties afterwards ('bibalibus').

By 1482 it was time to find a successor for Rolandus de Wreede, who was then so old and frail that he could 'scarcely climb the steps to the organ loft'. On 21 January 1482 the chapter installed a certain Johannes Fernandis, who had come with his brother Carolus, as deputy organist. Although he was nearly blind ('non valens videre ut legat', 'semicecus'), he was regarded as 'habilis et ydoneus'. But he resigned as early as 4 March 1482, having been summoned to Rome by the bishop of Tournai. Johannes Fernandis, 'ludo organorum peritus', and his brother Carolus were no other than the blind brothers praised so highly by Tinctoris, who heard them play stringed instruments when he visited Bruges (see p. 88). It took much time to find a replacement for Rolandus. Three candidates were auditioned in 1482 by Gilles Joye and Pierre Basin (de Jonghe, de Vico, Crauweel); in 1483, the post was given to Eustacius de Paris.

Before 1483, there is no evidence for the use of other instruments in the church. The city minstrels who were hired by the chapter on St

Donatian's day assembled under the porch and then passed through the streets with the procession; their instruments (slide-trumpets and shawms) had to be borrowed from craft guilds.[73] On 16 April 1483, however, the chapter agreed to a request made by the citizen Jan de Blasere and the succentor Aliamus de Groote to allow the minstrels ('tubicentes et mimi hujus opidi Brugensis') to perform daily 'Salve' concerts after compline during the May Fair. This followed initiatives of the city fathers to entertain the population and the prominent visitors on market-days; the city paid for the concerts, which must have included polyphonic music (see p. 85f.).

Special ceremonies and feasts

The cultivation of music at St Donatian's was by no means confined to the church and the conventional liturgy. There were many festive occasions when plays and specially composed musical works were performed by clerks and boys under the guidance of succentor and schoolmaster – sometimes in the church or the refectory, sometimes publicly in the streets. The ceremonies on some of these 'clergy feasts', in their blend of liturgy, mystery play, procession and banquet, were a form of artistic life which was closer than anything else to our modern music theatre.[74]

Certainly by 1304, and probably earlier, the widely known festival of the 'boy bishop' was celebrated at St Donatian's. This had originated as a feast of St Nicholas (6 December), but it became customary in many places to combine it with Holy Innocent's day (28 December). Every year one of the schoolboys or the youngest clerk was elected the 'boy bishop', who had to give a great banquet for the boys on 28 December. The clerks led the boys to dinner in a ceremonial procession on horseback – presumably they paraded round the *Burg*.[75] In close proximity to this feast, and sometimes identified with it, there was the musically important feast of the 'Pope of the asses'. Its traditional day was New Year's day, but at St Donatian's it was celebrated, from 1409, in the week after Epiphany, ending with a great banquet on the day of the octave (13 January). There was a satirical, burlesque procession with the *papa asinorum*, who was the youngest chaplain, and all kinds of sacred and not so sacred songs were heard. The canons were often perturbed by the boisterous things that went on and forbade the feast from time to time, meeting with strong resistance from the younger clergy (see also p. 28). At other times, the chapter chose to defend this privileged tradition against pressure from outside: for example in 1484, when the burgomaster Willem Moreel had complained to the dean about riotous behaviour shown in the Christmas procession of 1483 by the company of the 'asses'. This was regarded by Moreel as unseemly in the presence of so many 'nobles and magnates', and apt to induce the population to similarly petulant behaviour ('et populus ad petulanciam potius exemplo cleri provocatur') – probably the 'asses' collected money from the congregation with great noise. The chapter only imposed a few restrictions on the *papa asinorum* of that year, Christiaen Baelde.[76] The musical components of the festal period were partly the chants, motets and polyphonic masses for the feast of the Three Kings (Epiphany); a mystery play for this event is recorded as early as 1346. The musical and theatrical components were rehearsed and directed by the succentor. He also received a gratuity each year after the banquet of 13 January, for seeing the boys safely to their dormitory, so that they did not roam the streets to spread the fun ('ne vagarent per plateas').

An Easter play was given at St Donatian's from 1365 (see p. 14), a Christmas play from 1375, a *ludus de Sacramento* (Corpus Christi) from 1458, and a Passion play from 1476 at the latest. The last-named was introduced by the succentor Aliamus de Groote. His plays (in Flemish) were so successful that he had to be given leave, in 1483, to take to the streets with the performance, which was acted by the schoolboys on a carriage ('super carrum per vicos'). Jean Cordier was a musician with theatrical leanings as well: in 1485, he directed the Easter play, acting as Jesus. The liturgical plays in Latin or Flemish, usually referred to as *moralitates*, had developed as an appendix to the divine office, or introduction to mass. In the later Middle Ages, their place was at the end of matins – as if the drama had grown spontaneously from the lessons and antiphons. Many late medieval office texts (called *legendae* or *historiae*) are of themselves narrative or semi-dramatic. *Alternatim* performance involved the schoolboys for the psalm verses and lessons. This could be elaborated into a dramatic distribution of parts, given to the boys.

A liturgical plainsong ceremony, which developed into a mystery play, is the *Missus* ceremony in Advent, recorded at St Donatian's from 1380 (see also p. 52 f.).[77] Another ceremony, never fully dramatic, but largely musical and laden with symbolic significance, was the *Mandatum*. This series of antiphons for Maundy Thursday recounts the incident of Christ washing the disciples' feet, often breaking into direct speech for dialogue taken from the Gospels. The *Mandatum* was known all over Europe around 1400, and included the washing of the feet of twelve (or more) paupers and the distribution of white bread amongst all those present. In Bruges, the ceremony was performed in at least three places: at St Donatian's, following an endowment of 1395; at Our Lady's from before 1445 (see p. 46); and in the Carmelite convent from 1428 (see p. 69). The loaves of white bread, known as *crakelinghen*, were distributed first and foremost among the poor, but the trend was increasingly to a great banquet for all, held in the refectory, where also the special Gospel and the antiphons were sung.[78] A high mass in the choir belonged to the feast as well. Another important feast-day with masses, offices and processions, when bread was distributed at a banquet, was Corpus Christi – with obvious and similar symbolic associations. Also the numerous charitable endowments to the churches which included a 'table of the poor', throughout the year, always had their special masses.

A festival of great local importance was the *beianenfeest* (perhaps analogous to the 'bean feast'). There is a mention of it at St Donatian's in 1402, when it seems to have been equated with the 'feast of the asses'. From 1407, it was celebrated on Easter Monday, and was essentially a banquet, given by the newcomers to the school – *beedjanen, béjaunes* – to their colleagues.[79] A secular variety of the feast in Bruges was celebrated on 2 September, when the newly appointed civic officers had to 'spend a round'. St Donatian's also commemorated this day: the same citizen, Johannes de Waghenare, who endowed the *Mandatum* ceremony in 1395, also endowed a mass for the day of the 'renewal of the magistrate' ('wetvernieuwing').[80] (For just such an occasion, Bach composed his *Ratswahlkantate!*)

The clergy of St Donatian's had a big share in the great public processions which took place each year on the three Rogation days before Ascension (see p. 54) and, on Thursday after Whitsunday, to the nearby town of Aardenburg for the 'Feast of the cripples' (*crepelenfeest, festum claudorum*). The latter procession was shared by the clergy of all the major churches of Bruges, and regularly involved the performance of polyphonic masses in the church of Our Lady in Aardenburg, with a banquet afterwards which may originally have been intended for the benefit of the cripples.[81] From 1475/6 at the latest, the succentors of St Donatian's had to compose a new mass for this feast each year. Also the 'Feast of the asses' had an annual mass in polyphony from 1489, and the *beianenfeest* had one from 1488 if not much earlier.[82] The *Patrem trium regum*, copied by Colins on 5 January 1468 (see above), may have been one of an annual series of such *Patrems* for Epiphany. As has been mentioned, St Donatian's had processionals and choirbooks for special offices. For example, a *liber episcopi innocentium*, which was continually enlarged, already contained several *officia episcoporum* by 1453, and a second book was started in 1478/9.[83] Books such as this must have contained also polyphonic, non-liturgical music – rhymed Latin *cantiones* at least, and perhaps even secular chansons.

There may have been a musical element in the tradition of the secular plays which were performed by the schoolboys each year. The succentor Aliamus de Groote (1475–85), in particular, developed this tradition. From 1480 onwards, he also put on a celebration called *refrein* – a gathering in the refectory at which poetry was recited, perhaps partly with music.[84] The gathering took its name from the usual form of these moral, political or religious poems, as we know them from the surviving works of the great Flemish rhetorician Anthuenis de Roovere of Bruges (for the *refrein* as a musical form, see also p. 107 f.). In the context of de Groote's *refrein* on Sunday before Christmas, 1482, the chapter recognised his artistic standing as that of a 'princeps rhetorum Flamingorum'; by that time, de Roovere was dead.

The efforts of the schoolmaster did not stay far behind, since he arranged, from 1484 at the latest, annual recitations in Latin on St Luke's day (18 October), and later also in Lent. What was recited by the schoolboys was, in 1484, the first book of the *Aeneid*! A '*comedia*' by Lucian is mentioned in 1486; those of Plautus and Terence were acted in 1524/5[85] – surely not a new humanist fashion, but an old tradition, since such books were available in the chapter library from as early as the fourteenth century (see p. 19).

The Habsburg era

Under the rule of Maximilian of Habsburg, who married Charles the Bold's daughter Mary of Burgundy on 19 August 1477, the political and economical situation of Bruges altered very much for the worse. The citizens' uprising against Maximilian and his brutal governors in the spring of 1488 not only drove many foreign merchants out of the town[86] but also had a profound effect on the collegiate church, which was, once again, torn between loyalty to the ruler and the calls of Flemish patriotism. Maximilian himself, his wife Mary and the guardians of his son Philip the Fair (1478–1506) continued to accord St Donatian's the privileges of a court church with a standing that only Our Lady's came now near to equalling. The strange thing is that in spite of the wars, famines (especially between 1488 and 1490) and the loss of trading supremacy to Antwerp, art and culture in Bruges enjoyed one more brilliant efflorescence in these years. What remained of the city's wealth was squandered on art, music and ceremony by a haughty clergy and a population that had been spoilt for too long.

Evidence of this is found in the enormous increase in endowments settled on the collegiate church, in which polyphonic music was now almost the rule. The choral foundation of the *Missa de Salve* was at last placed again on a firm financial footing from 1484 with the endowment of Johannes van der Coutre; the annuity of no less than £600 went largely to the keep of six choirboys and the succentor.[87] Chaplaincies and polyphonic masses were endowed,[88] for example, in 1470 by Jean Meurin, secretary to Charles the Bold (a mass to be sung 'solemniter et tractim cum discantu' on the Thursday before Septuagesima); in 1483 by the civic official Adriaen Caervoet; between 1485 and 1489 by the canon Pierre Basin (see below); other requests for discant masses came from benefactors such as Antoine Haneron, Raphael de Mercatellis (a natural son of Philip the Good), Bernardino de Salviati and Richard Visch de la Chapelle, all canons of the church. The feast-days that benefited were those of St Anthony, St Servatius, St Gertrud, St Macharius, St Jerome, St Catherine and the Name of Jesus. The burgomaster Louis Greffijnc (1485) and Maximilian's governor Pieter Lanchals (1488) divided their huge endowments between several churches of Bruges, for polyphonic masses in the Rogation processions and on the feast of the Presentation of the Virgin, respectively. Several bankers and foreign merchants founded chapels in St Donatian's; the chapel of the Three Kings, founded by the Spaniard Jean Loupes and his son-in-law Silvestro Pardo, was used for polyphonic performances, as was the chapel of St Thomas Apostle, founded by the banker Thomas Perrot, who was perhaps of English descent (his father, Richard Perrot, had come from Rouen). In connection with many of these endowments, altar paintings and other works of art were made, some of which are still extant (at least those for Mercatellis, Salviati, Visch and Pardo).[89]

The number of distinguished musicians who served the church, or held canonries *in absentia*, increased, if anything, during this period. (Details about their careers are to be found in Appendix A.) Pierre Basin, a court singer to Charles the Bold from 1467, lived most of his life in Bruges; he was a member of a very musical family of the town, and an intimate of Joye and Obrecht. Pasquier Desprez (Paschasius de Pratis) was also a native of Bruges; from Malines and Antwerp came Nicholas Mayoul *junior* and Léon de Saint-Vaast, both chaplains of Philip the Fair. Prebends were awarded at St Donatian's to the singers of the papal chapel Nicholas Rembert,[90] Johannes Margas (who held chaplaincies from 1472),[91] Gaspar van Weerbeke (canon 1495–98)[92] and Guillermus Rosa (who resided in Bruges and contributed to the musical life of St Donatian's from 1476 to 1489).

Jean Cordier, perhaps the most famous singer of his time, was a native of Bruges. His first appointment was that of a clerk (*tenorista*) at St Donatian's in 1460, not 1469 in Florence, as all writers have assumed.[93] He was probably connected with the noble family Cordier whose members Rolandus and Ghisbertus administered the endowment of van der Coutre. In 1467, Jean Cordier was recruited into the chapel of the Medici. The Medici agent in Bruges, Tommaso Portinari, wrote on 13 February 1467 to Piero de' Medici that he had engaged a 'tenore' in Bruges and given him money for the journey[94] – on 23 February, Cordier was given leave by the chapter to absent himself 'in negotiis suis', until next June. Cordier became the leader of a group of singers who had been recruited by Portinari in Bruges and by Dufay in Cambrai, but which already left Florence again in 1468, allegedly at Cordier's instigation. He then entered the papal chapel, and the letter of appointment from Pope Paul II (2 January 1469) arrived at St Donatian's just in time to prevent his losing both his vicarship and his chaplaincy on grounds of absenteeism. Cordier's further career led him to serve the Aragonese in Naples, the Sforzas in Milan and the Habsburg court. He often returned to Bruges, particularly from 1483, when he was given a canonry at St Donatian's. Many entries in the chapter minutes acknowledge his outstanding services to polyphonic music, and he was given generous terms of leave when he had to travel to Milan and elsewhere. He was a member of the Bruges confraternities of the 'Dry Tree' and of 'Our Lady of the Snow'; he died in Bruges in 1501 and was buried in the choir of St Donatian's, leaving the church an endowment worth an annuity of £13.[95]

Jean Cordier must have been incomparable as a singer. In spite of his Flemish origins he fascinated the young Lorenzo de' Medici with his improvised singing to the *lira da braccio* in Florence. His links with Obrecht are particularly close: he was almost certainly the unnamed 'friend' who prepared the ground for Obrecht's engagement in Bruges in 1485. Two years later, he persuaded the chapter to give Obrecht leave to visit Ferrara. He paid a personal visit to Obrecht in Bergen-op-Zoom in 1488, and he also arranged the official visit in 1493/4 of the singers of St Donatian's to Obrecht in Antwerp. Cordier, who must have performed the works of Dufay in Florence, Josquin and Weerbeke in Milan and Obrecht in Bruges and Ferrara, does not seem to have composed himself. Probably his artistic judgment prevented him from emulating composers whose superiority he understood so well.

Jacob Obrecht

The task of succentor, which Obrecht undertook on 13 October 1485,[96] was made more difficult than he might have expected by various circumstances. As his predecessor de Groote had resigned on 7 February 1485, and the interim succentor Rykelin had clearly been inadequate, the group of discant singers had to be rebuilt; the endowment of van der Coutre, which came into force in 1484 and which called for two more choirboys, provided more money but also much more work. The choirboys had to be taken care of personally, and they lived individually with the succentor and some of the canons, especially in the following years of dearth because of the wars. The competition between the European chapels for singers had become fierce by the 1480s; there was very little the chapter could do when excellent singers threatened to go elsewhere for more pay (Johannes de Vico considered joining the chapel of Mathias Corvinus of Hungary in 1483). Before Obrecht's appointment, the chapter had asked him to bring along good singers from Cambrai if possible – he could provide only Egidius Zelandrinus, who lost his voice on arrival. He also had to engage choirboys from elsewhere – he found one (Philippe Paillet?) in Courtrai in 1488. It must have been difficult for anyone to live a quiet life, dedicated to the arts, in a town lacerated by revolutions and wars, as Bruges was from 1487 to 1491.

On the other hand, the many new endowments and the activities of the industrious de Groote had raised everybody's expectations with regard to church music. Perhaps the most onerous commission had been negotiated by de Groote with the city magistrate in 1480: the daily *Salve* or *lof* ('praise') of the Virgin, sung after compline in St Donatian's by the succentor and the choirboys, with organ-playing and candle-light.[97] This was a concert entirely financed by the city for the musical entertainment of the population and the many important guests of Bruges; it had been tried out for ten days in 1480, but was, from 1481, extended over the whole year. As a consequence, the succentor had to reschedule the 1½ hours' daily teaching of music to the choirboys from the evening to the morning, so that he was now continually busy from matins until lunchtime, besides the actual *Salve* concert in the evening. Aliamus de Groote had also involved himself and his choirboys in so many other engagements, from mystery plays to discant masses in other churches, that he incurred the chapter's reproaches for neglecting the *Missa de Salve*. As early as 23 June 1480, he had been ordered also to educate other boys in discant besides the usual four, so that the latter were always available while the additional boys could sing in other churches.

Obrecht, who hardly possessed the organisational talents of de Groote, and who had been dismissed from the succentorship in Cambrai for administrative faults, clearly could not cope with the task in Bruges. That he left the rehearsing of the mystery plays to de Groote (who continued to serve as a chaplain) did not prove sufficient relief. His journey to Ferrara, where his music was so much appreciated, and the subsequent stay at home in Bergen-op-Zoom (2 October 1487 to 15 August 1488) must have been like a ten-month holiday for him. The chapter was generous with an artist of his reputation and gave him the chaplaincy of St Catherine on 2 May 1489, but then tactfully tried to get rid of him. The chapter minutes never spell out what exactly went wrong, but on 26 May 1490, the canons had already made up their minds to dismiss Obrecht, and now tried to persuade him to resign 'in order to preserve his own honour'. The matter was delayed, and Obrecht could still accept the honourable invitation to give a concert in Sluis for Count Philip of Cleves in October 1490, 'ad faciendum ibidem bonum vultum'. This was a delicate political issue as the count partly supported Bruges against Maximilian, but was now himself on the eve of defeat. Obrecht went with Petrus Zouburch and Christiaen Baelde, singers of his own choice.

Obrecht was 'graciously' dismissed on 22 January 1491. He had probably waited with his resignation because he was looking for another appointment – whether he immediately found it in Antwerp or not is not clear. Relationships with Bruges continued to be good; they were marked by the mass which Obrecht sent from Antwerp in 1491/2, by the visit of Cordier with the singers to Antwerp, and, of course, Obrecht's short return to the succentorship from 31 December 1498 to 3 September 1500. In this period, the chapter gave Obrecht a new chaplaincy and a seat in the upper row of the choir stalls, but could not keep him.

An attempt to identify some of the works which Jacob Obrecht composed in Bruges will be made in Chapter VI. It emerges that the only work which is demonstrably written for the church of St Donatian itself is not the *Missa de Sancto Donatiano*, but *the Missa de Sancto Martino*.

This was part of an endowment by Obrecht's colleague, Pierre Basin,[98] a musician who had, at the beginning of 1486, something like the usual problem, a concubine. As penance, he then announced that he was to go on a pilgrimage to Rome; he made his will and left an endowment for an anniversary mass in discant on the vigil of St Martin (10 November), with choirboys and organ. Should he die on the journey, his brothers Jean and Adrien were obliged to pay the donation for him. Pierre did not go to Rome, however, and he mended his ways, so that the chapter only ordered him to go to Aardenburg; but the endowment came into force, and was celebrated for the first time on 10 November 1486, with a *Missa de Sancto Martino* sung by the choirboys and clerks in the chapel of the saint. Basin added more money subsequently; the endowment had reached its full form (with an annuity of £7) on 17 August 1489, including the discant mass and two vespers motets on 10/11 November, another discant mass, a polyphonic sequence and a vespers motet on the day of the Translation of St Martin (4 July), and processions on both feasts of the saint. In 1495, Basin had to donate an additional annuity of £4 to finance the processions. The explicit terms of the endowment provided 10s for the succentor for the mass on 4 July. He had to assemble the choirboys and *socii de musica* who were to take part; the latter had to be two of the best singers ('illi duo quos secum assumet succentor ad cantandum missam erunt de melioribus'), and received 4s reach. The organist was employed for vespers, for the sequence after compline (!) and for the mass; he received a total of 5s. The bell-ringer had to 'triplicate' throughout the mass and was rewarded with 8s.

The unusual passage that the succentor had to choose the best singers strongly suggests that Basin expected a more personalised service from Obrecht. Although the latter is not named, it is also clear that he must have composed the new music which was necessary. Suitable motets, or a sequence, by Obrecht do not seem to survive; but I suggest that his *Missa de Sancto Martino*,[99] which is built on a number of chants for St Martin from the antiphonal, was composed to fit both feasts endowed by Basin. The work is almost a *historia* of St Martin, giving a musical survey of the saint's life. It should be noted that Obrecht combines several cantus firmi also in his St Donatian mass (see p. 146 f.) – a technique which characterises several works written by Obrecht in Bruges. The apparently unique case that one musician composed a mass on another musician's request, and for the safety of his soul, is no surprise in an environment where musical patronage, performance and composition changed hands between friends and colleagues.

CHAPTER THREE

Other Churches

The collegiate church of Our Lady

In the Middle Ages, Bruges had two collegiate churches. This slightly unusual situation may have been due to the rival claims of the bishops of Tournai and Utrecht: whereas the *burg* with St Donatian's was founded under the patronage of Tournai, the territory on which Our Lady's arose in the eighth century originally belonged to the chapter of Utrecht. Our Lady's was a parish church as early as 909, and elevated to the status of a collegiate church in 1091 by the bishop of Tournai. According to the legend, the church had been founded by St Boniface in 744; in any case, it later possessed some relics of this saint and of his companions Cyrobaldus and Hilarius, which were gifts of the abbey of Fulda.

The core of the present building,[1] one of the most significant architectural monuments of Flanders, was erected in the thirteenth century, and recalls many elements of the early gothic style of Tournai cathedral. To the three naves of that period, two others were added in the following two centuries, as well as a vast ambulatory, but no transept. The spire was raised to the dominating height of 123m. The main entrance porches are on the north and south sides; the west portal had to be closed in 1465, because the passage between it and the Hospital of St John on the other side proved too narrow for the busy traffic. In the later Middle Ages, the south aisle alone was used as the parish church, whilst the central aisle was reserved for the chapter; the many chapels were controlled by guilds and confraternities. The church still possesses fascinating works of art, such as the funeral monuments of Charles the Bold and his daughter Mary of Burgundy, the marble scuplture of a *Pietà* by Michelangelo, bought for the church in 1514 by the businessman Jean de Mouscron, and recently excavated frescoes in the tomb of the curate Petrus Calf, of 1295. The church enjoyed the support of many craft guilds and individual citizens, but also of the later Burgundian rulers, and of the noble family of Gruuthuse, who built their palace next to it. The house is connected with the church by the famous 'oratory' of 1472–73, a closed balcony leading from the first floor of the palace to the ambulatory, and providing a view through windows onto the high altar. Among the guilds and trade corporations connected with the church, there were the tanners, fullers, barbers, wine-merchants, dyers and money-lenders; and their special feast-days, with a strong emphasis on Marian devotion, coloured the liturgical life. The calendar included a feast of 'Our Lady of Piety' (first Friday in March); a 'recollectorium festorum' of Our Lady (1 September); the tailors' guild formed the confraternity of 'Our Lady of the Snow' (5 August), which was to become one of the most active groups (see below). A painting by Memling in Munich, representing the 'Seven Joys' of the Virgin, is said to have come from the chapel of the tanners behind the high altar.

Almost no research has been undertaken on musical life at Our Lady's.[2] The choirbooks have been destroyed; an inventory of 1115[3] mentions two graduals, one antiphonal and one *troparium*, and fifteenth-century lists reveal a rich store of music books. The clergy could dedicate much of their time to liturgy and music. The pastoral duties were shared between three curates (or their vicars); the large parish was subdivided into the so-called 'golden', 'silver' and 'leaden' portions. By *c*.1480 there were eleven canons, twenty-four chaplains, four vicars, and at least fourteen *clerici installati*. The clergy formed a *confraternitas chori*, founded in 1298 and dedicated to Our Lady.[4] Its statutes were altered in 1429, with the effect that not only clerks in minor orders, but also clerks from other churches and even laymen could join. This reorganisation was the work of the provost Richard Visch de la Chapelle *senior*, the curate Christiaen Moesin and the canons Edmond Boet and Robert Sandewin. They made the confraternity responsible for a Lady-mass, to be sung each Saturday; financial support came mainly from Agnes de Gruuthuse and her son Jean (father of Louis) who were members of the confraternity. Besides Sandewin himself, who had been a papal singer, many other members were musicians then working in the various churches of Bruges. Among them were Leonardus de Gladio, Thomas Fabri, Petrus Zoeteman, Jacobus Coutreman, Jacobus de Clibano, Petrus Paes, Paulus Bloume, Aliamus de Groote, Pasquier Desprez and others (see also Appendix A). Whether these musicians also held clerkships or chaplaincies at Our Lady's is not always clear.

Johannes de Wreede, a composer who later worked in Spain, was the son of the organist of St Donatian's, Rolandus. He was refused admission to a clerkship in that church in 1451, on the grounds that father and son were not allowed to serve the same institution; but by 1457, Johannes was a *clericus installatus* at Our Lady's, and a chaplain soon after, until 1460 when he probably left for Spain.[5] Nicasius Weyts, a *magister* of the University of Paris, divided his time between the churches of Our Lady and St Saviour, serving mainly as a schoolmaster. He is almost certainly the author of a treatise on counterpoint transcribed in the Italian circle of John Hothby in 1474 (see p. 66), where he is also described as a Carmelite friar. In 1463–4 we see him involved in a literary dispute with the schoolmaster and *magister cantus* of the town of Oudenburg, Jan de Veere, who criticised Weyts for his bad Latin prose (not good enough, at least, to emulate Lorenzo Valla's *De elegantiis*), but acknowledged his poetic talents.[6] In one letter of the correspondence, Weyts was defended by a certain Alanus, identifiable with Aliamus de Groote. This musician-poet and humanist started his career as a chaplain at Our Lady's before 1458, at first in the service of the confraternity of 'Our Lady of the Snow'. If not exactly a hotbed of humanism, the church certainly assembled many clerics with literary and musical interests, particularly under the provost Arnold de Lalaing (1461–83), who is known as a humanist in the entourage of Charles the Bold. A court chronicler and professor of the time, the Cistercian Adrien de But, was a nephew of Nicasius Weyts.

The office of *cantor scholarium* is mentioned in 1432 (see p. 45). A source of 1536 states that the office of *rector choralium* was normally held by the secretary of the chapter;[7] in 1474, this was apparently the func-tion of Cornelius Moerijnc, who also served as organist.[8] But also the schoolmaster Nicasius Weyts was a musician, and the composer Aliamus de Groote used the schoolboys for the performance of his plays, which are recorded from 1469. Aliamus became succentor at St Donatian's in 1475, but returned to Our Lady's in 1491–95 as suc-centor, which is the first time that the holder of this office is actually named in the records.[9] Before *c.*1480, a clear distinction between schoolboys and choirboys seems not to have been made.

The church had an organ long before the fifteenth century. Names of organists are recorded only from 1444/5, when 'Heer Andraes den orghelare' received a salary of £17 6s; the position was filled in 1462 by 'Heer Cornelis' – probably Moerijnc.[10] Shortly before 1450, a chaplaincy had been awarded to a certain Henricus de Zwolle.[11] It can-not be ruled out that this referred to Henricus Arnaut de Zwolle, the famous organ-builder of Philip the Good. The court chaplain Mathieu de Bracle, provost of Our Lady's in 1459–60, was an organ player him-self ('ludo organorum imbutus'); he pressed for the acquisition of a new great organ in 1459, after the old one had been repaired in 1450/1 by Boudin de Wroe. A contract for the building of the new organ was made in 1464 with Marc Sproncholf.[12]

With a large number of clerks and schoolboys, Our Lady's had approximately the same resources for the performance of plainsong as St Donatian's. Together with the great organ, which was used at least for mass, matins and vespers on high feasts, these singers could give variety and brilliance to special liturgies. Magnificat antiphons, for example, were sung in a specially elaborate manner on some feasts. In *c*.1430, the practice observed for the antiphon *O Christi pietas* (for St Donatian, 14 October) was this: after the intonation, the *cantores* (clerks) sang the two halves of the antiphon alternately after each verse of the Magnificat, so that the antiphon was performed six times with the twelve verses of the Magnificat. This scheme is described as 'vicissim et per partes cum Magnificat' in a reference (of *c*.1420) to an antiphon of the Assumption, *Ave gloriosa*. It may have applied to all Marian antiphons, as far as they were sung at vespers on high feasts throughout the year. The endowments of the provosts Richard Visch (*c*.1450) and Mathieu de Bracle (*c*.1459) required eighteen schoolboys who sang the nine *lectiones majores* ('Parce mihi domine . .') and the responsory verses 'secundum notam et tractim'.[13] The even more splendid endowment of Louis de Gruuthuse and his wife Anne van Borssele (12 February 1473) provided for four annual Requiems and vigils with nine lessons each; eighteen boys were employed in the lessons, four at mass.[14] There was an enormous number of processions, both inside and outside the church. Usually, the participants sang a responsory when leaving the choirstalls, and an antiphon when returning; the former was normally appropriate to the feast, the latter a Marian antiphon according to the season. The boys had to sing the responsory verses and the *Gloria Patri*; the other participants carried banners, torches, relics and images of the saints, mostly small statuettes of silver or gold. The biggest annual procession was that for the patron saint, St Boniface, which moved through the town centre. From 1460 at the latest, four city trumpeters walked in front of the relics of the saint. The feast of St Mark (25 March) and the Wednesday after Easter saw processions to the nearby parish church of St Saviour. During the Easter procession a station was held in the nave of Our Lady's, at which the organist played the *Regina celi letare* 'against the choir'; one choirboy carried the cross, two others torches, and 40 other children were rewarded with bread, simply for coming along.[15]

Mystery plays are among the earliest documented ceremonies. From 1330, there was a *mysterium trium regum* at Epiphany, in which the three kings, represented by boys, offered their gifts at the high altar, singing the antiphon *Hoc signum*; thereafter, the choir sang the antiphon *Tria sunt munera*.[16] A *mysterium resurrectionis* may have existed already in 1350; a document of 1432[17] lists the following actors, with their wages: Jesus (12d); Mary Magdalene (8d); 2 other women (6d each); 2 angels 'ad momumentum' (4d each); Pilate (6d); 3 Jews (4d each); Adam (6d); Eve (4d); John the Baptist (6d); Murderer (6d); Physician (6d); 2 Pilgrims (4d each); 2 *cantores* (6d each); Thomas (6d); 'Cantori scholarium (ordinanti et procuranti ut fiat misterium prenotatum)' (6d); 'Obedentiario ecclesie (pro labore distribuendi singula predicta)' (4s).

This must have been a very long and elaborate performance, including the pilgrimage to Emmaus as well as other sub-plots. The two extra *cantores* may have sung the narrative and the verses of the sequence *Victime paschali*, while the antiphons were sung by the full choir. The succentor who 'organised and rehearsed' the play received a much lower gratuity than the treasurer of the church (a canon) who distributed the money. The whole sum was an endowment of the citizen Franciscus Lootghietere. The play took place at the end of matins on Easter Sunday, and probably ended with the collective singing of the Te Deum.

The *Missus* ceremony in Advent (see p. 52 f.) was instituted, or enlarged, by the curate Judocus Berthilde in 1475, the *Mandatum* ceremony (see p. 34 f.) before 1445. In the latter year, the participants consumed 64 pints of mead, 8 pints of white wine and 925 *crakelinghen*.[18] The feast of the Holy Innocents (28 December) was mainly a banquet for the singers and choirboys, who received a special New Year's gratuity for it. There were also the feasts of St Nicholas (6 December), celebrated in collaboration with the Friars Minor from 1479, the 'Feast of the asses' and the *beianenfeest* on Easter Monday (see p. 000). From 1481, a confraternity seems to have existed for the ceremonies, perhaps with a mystery play, on the day of the *Apparitio Sancti Michaelis* (8 May).[19]

A regular polyphonic practice must have arisen in the first half of the fifteenth century. An endowment[20] of the curate Judocus de Liza of 1446 required organ-playing and discant-singing ('organizabitur et discantabitur') in a mass on St Josse's day (20 December). In 1451, the church received an endowment of £18 annually from Philip the Good himself. This was destined for an annual mass during his lifetime on St Arnulph's day (16 August), at the high altar, 'with organs, discant and bell-ringing during the mass'. The *cantores* had to sing in discant 'Kyrie, Et in terra, Patrem, Sanctus, Agnus, cum moteto post missam'. This may refer to a specially-composed cyclic mass, or even a 'mass-motet cycle' — a genre of which some examples seem to survive in sources of the time. The endowment was confirmed by Charles the Bold. Around 1455 three more endowments show the steady increase in the use of polyphonic music. The nobleman Egidius Boulet, driven by 'glowing veneration of the glorious archangel St Michael', raised his feast on 8 May to a *festum principale* and provided it with a mass with discant and organ, 'as on other principal feasts'. This attests a more widespread polyphonic practice than can actually be documented. The provost Walterus de Mandra and the city official Antonius Brouc endowed similar discant masses for the other feast of St Michael (29 September) and for the vigil of St Martin (10 November), respectively. For such masses, the *socii discantantes* and the organist received, between them,

8s or 13s for a performance. Endowments with polyphonic music multiplied in the next decades. Among the benefactors were Paul van Overtveld, a councillor of Charles the Bold, with a mass for St Catherine (25 November) from 1471; the citizen Simon Jansszuene with a polyphonic mass of the Holy Sacrament, which was sung every Thursday from 28 January 1472; the curate Judocus Berthilde, an enthusiastic supporter of liturgy and music, endowed together with his sister and her husband the feast-days of the Presentation (21 November), St Joseph (19 March), the Name of Jesus (15 January), St Martha (30 July) and the Holy Sisters of Mary (a new feast: 28 May) with a discant mass each in 1474. The last-named, for example, was to be sung by the *cantere*, his 'helpers' and the 'children', accompanied by the organist. Berthilde also erected a chapel of the Name of Jesus, which gained the protection of Maximilian of Habsburg.

In the early 1470s, an interesting development was initiated by the brothers Colaerd and Pieter de La Bie, members of a very rich family of moneylenders. They systematically endowed the feasts of St Mary Magdalene (22 August), St Catherine (25 November) and St Barbara (4 December) with motets and vespers processions (the processional antiphon was *Ave regina celorum* in all three cases). This led to the foundation, on 18 September 1474, of the confraternity of the 'Three Saints', i.e. Mary Magdalene, Catherine and Barbara, for which the La Bie family instituted a total of 24 plainsong masses as well. The *'Drie Saintinnen'* confraternity was actually a guild of rhetoricians – those literary associations which were at that time springing up all over Belgium. The first Bruges guild of *rederijkers*, of the Holy Ghost, had been founded in 1428 (see p. 68). The chapel of the *'Drie Saintinnen'*, which still exists in Our Lady's, was built in 1486 and decorated with an altar painting perhaps by the Master of the Legend of St Lucy.[21]

The confraternity which fostered music most actively in the third quarter of the century was that of 'Our Lady of the Snow'. The name refers to the miraculous foundation of the Roman basilica S. Maria Maggiore, whose feast of dedication (5 August) was observed in many Flemish churches. The confraternity had been formed, sometime before 1450, by the craft-guild of the tailors, and represented the religious interests of ordinary citizens in the parish. But by c.1470 it already had hundreds of members, many of whom belonged to other professions, and, indeed, to the nobility and the court.[22] Of these, we may mention only a few: Charles the Bold, his mother Isabella of Portugal, Count Philip of Cleves, and several members of the Gruuthuse family; there were foreign merchants and diplomats like Alexander Bonkil of Scotland, Giovanni and Michele Arnolfini of Lucca, along with artists such as Petrus Christus, Arnoud de Mol, Hans Memling and Willem Vrelant, and singers of the ducal chapel such as Pierre Basin, Robinet de la Magdalaine, Jacques Amouret, Antoine de Francavilla and Pasquier Desprez. The confraternity had an altar, founded in 1464, and a new chapel in the north ambulatory which was erected in 1473 according to the wishes of the ducal councillor Simon de Lalaing and the ducal *protocapellanus* Philippe Syron. This foundation followed a festive visit of Duke Charles and several members of his chapel to Our Lady's on 5 April 1472, during which also the new 'oratoire' of the Gruuthuse palace was visited. The confraternity celebrated its main feast-day on 5 August with mass, two vespers, processions and a banquet in the guild-house of the tailors for which new dramatic performances were staged almost every year. The play for 1475 was written by the famous *rederijker* Anthuenis de Roovere – those in other years mostly by Aliamus de Groote. The city minstrels, usually four pipers and one 'tambourin', played for entertainment at the banquet. In 1468, the cost of the banquet was £46 – more than a quarter of the annual budget. The ceremonies in church were no less magnificent. The mass on 5 August was sung by the succentor with the 'zanghers' and choirboys, and with the organ. There was a motet for each vespers service, and another discant mass, without organ, in the octave. The five city minstrels also played for mass and vespers on 5 August – possibly under the porch where people gathered before the services. The confraternity held several other annual feasts, for example of Corpus Christi and St Boniface's day (5 June). A special feast for the 'king' (alderman) of the guild probably included literary recitals as in some similar societies. Merry gatherings without a sacred excuse took place on the so-called 'verzwoeren maendaghe' (three Mondays in January, April and May) – these days were celebrated with banquets by other groups in Bruges also, such as the association of the city clerks.

All these customs had been instituted in the confraternity of 'Our Lady of the Snow' before 1467/8, the first year for which the account books are preserved. From 1468/9, another musical performance was added to the annual programme: a *lof* or *Salve* sung by the succentor and the boys after vespers on all Sundays and Marian feasts, with organ. For these concerts, the succentor usually hired two or three *socii* besides the choirboys; in 1471/2, they are specified as being from St Donatian's. He also arranged occasional performances, such as a mass for the well-being of Duke Charles on 2 August 1472, in which no fewer than ten discant singers took part, two of them from St Donatian's. About £40 was spent each year for polyphonic music alone, not including the discant books which the confraternity also owned, besides plainsong books with special offices for their main feast-days.[23]

The greatest patrons of music at Our Lady's in the later fifteenth century, however, were the princes. Charles the Bold already treated the church as a second court chapel. He held his feast of the Order of the Golden Fleece there in 1468. In charters of 1470 and 1477, respectively, he and his daughter Mary took the church under their special protection.[24] On 25 March 1477, Mary of Burgundy made an endowment of £72 annually for twelve solemn masses with discant on high feasts.[25] On her deathbed exactly five years later, she chose Our Lady's as her burial place – much to the disappointment of the clergy of St Donatian's – and endowed it with an annual revenue of £108 for the support of the succentor with four choirboys, and the organist. These musicians had to perform two daily masses, one Marian mass after matins in discant, and a Requiem. On Sundays, high feasts and during the octave of all Marian feast-days, the organ had to accompany the discant mass. This foundation of 1482 was confirmed in 1483 and 1492 by Mary's son Philip the Fair, and on 4 January 1496 by Maximilian as well, who ultimately fixed the annuity at no less than £813 for all services, with and without music. He also had the musical ceremonies classified into discant masses with organ (Sundays etc.), discant masses without organ, and plainsong masses: the high rank given to the organ reminds us of the important role which it played in Maximilian's own chapels in Innsbruck and Vienna. These were reorganised about the same time, possibly using Our Lady's in Bruges as a model.[26]

On the basis of this choral foundation, many other festive endowments could be carried out as well. One of them came from Pieter Lanchals, the governor of Maximilian, who had been tortured and executed by the rebellious citizens in March 1488. Although he was of humble origins, his will revealed gigantic riches in capital and estates all over the Low Countries. Lanchals allocated a total of £500 annually for services in churches in Bruges, including two discant masses in Our Lady's for his patron St Peter; he also endowed a burial chapel, daily requiems and a chaplaincy in that church.[27] Less magnificent, but interesting for other reasons, is an endowment of 1488 by the barber Jean Basin.[28] In collaboration with his brother Adrien – the composer – he founded an altar and a chaplaincy of St Adrian with an anniversary in discant; among the pittances, distributions which had to be given out on the day of the anniversary (4 March), Jean Basin allocated some money for each of his brothers, Adrien and Pierre.

With all this powerful support, the state of music-making at Our Lady's changed very much in the 1480s. Many new singers could be engaged in a relatively short time; the chaplaincies and choir-stalls awarded to them may have earned them the jealousy of many a non-musical colleague. Almost overnight, the music of Our Lady's could rival that of St Donatian's, from where Aliamus de Groote returned as succentor in 1491. High standards were also expected from the choirboys, who needed to have a 'vox angelica' and were auditioned in front of the whole chapter.[29] The adult singers and choirboys were sometimes hired by other churches (St Saviour's, for example) like those of St Donatian's before. The atmosphere of competition also led to conflicts and complaints concerning the music. It was perhaps due to resentment over low pay, when the organ blowers worked so badly in November 1487 that the organ could not be heard, or when the bell-ringers rang so loudly on 9 January 1488, that the organ could again not be heard. Most of the troubles were caused by the *socii de musica*, however: having been engaged in haste, many of them may have shown little loyalty to the church, in which they saw just an opportunity for a musical career. A relatively harmless transgression was that of Bernardinus Vale, who in 1486 drank all the wine which the group of singers had been given after a general procession; but there was much insult and violence between the musicians, sometimes involving Aliamus de Groote. Mutual jealousy seems to surround de Groote's sudden resignation on 3 September 1495, and the events in 1501, when the chapter apparently tried to engage the *tenorista* Jeronimus (de Clibano), although there was no vacancy. Clibano went with Philip the Fair to Spain later that year.

Privately endowed services were clearly not the only occasion on which polyphony was performed. On 16 November 1485, the chapter ordered the singers to sing discant at mass on all Sundays and all minor or major principal feasts of which there were about 50, 'whether endowed with polyphonic services or not'. All those normally receiving the gratuities of the musicians ('musicorum vel discantantium'), whether clerks, chaplains, vicars, or others, had to expect severe fines if they absented themselves from the performances without permission. This calls to mind the reference to polyphony for principal feasts in the endowment of Egidius Boulet in *c.*1455, and a similar document of St Donatian's of 1442 (see p. 22). It also shows that the performances on non-endowed feast-days were so unpopular with the singers that they could be enforced only by imposing fines. In view of the competition of other churches, which were prepared to pay high wages to hired discant singers, the main incentive for polyphonic singing had to come from endowments which ensured a fixed wage to the musicians for every service in which they participated.

The parish church of St Saviour

St Saviour's, which ranked third among the churches of Bruges in the Middle Ages, is the cathedral today. Its history[30] is as ancient as that of its rivals – a chapel certainly existed in the ninth century, and legend has it that St Eloy, bishop of Noyon, founded it in 640. Its patron saints are the Saviour, St Eloy and St Wulfram. The parish was established by the tenth century, and two other parishes, St James's and

St Walburga's, are said to have branched off from it in 1239. The present building goes back to a complete reconstruction after a fire in 1358. The very high nave and transept, unaltered since that time, form an architectural landmark of indisputable monumentality. The vast ambulatory was added in 1480. The art treasures of the church include a famous altar-painting by Thierry Bouts and Hugo van der Goes, as well as works of art (missals, paintings etc.) once belonging to St Donatian's. The fine choir stalls were completed in 1478, for the occasion of the feast of the Golden Fleece, which Maximilian of Habsburg held here in that year.[31]

The musical traditions of the church have not yet been investigated;[32] lack of sources prevents substantiation of the use of polyphony before *c.*1470. After that, an almost stormy development of polyphonic practice was initiated, and it continued throughout the sixteenth century. Obviously, this parish in the centre of the town was mainly supported by middle-class citizens and craft guilds. There were the chapels and altars of the painters and sadlers, roofers, metal-founders, cordwainers, beer-transporters, cabinet-makers, fullers, retailers of second-hand clothes (*oudekleerkopers*) and many others concerned with the textile industry and trade. They had confraternities of St Eloy, St Nicholas, St Catherine, St Barbara, SS. Peter and Paul, St Drogo, St Job, SS. Crispin and Crispinian, of the Holy Trinity and of Corpus Christi. The last-named was perhaps the most important; it owned, in 1523, not only its chapel with missals and other books, but also the organ in the loft. From 1397, the clergy was organised as a *confraternitas chori*, which was dedicated to the Assumption of Our Lady.[33] St Saviour's had its grammar school from 1293 at the latest; a *magister scholarum* is mentioned in 1325.[34] The schoolboys participated in all festal masses and in the greater hours, as well as processions.

One particularly important document for the development of the liturgico-musical practice is the *Liber Planarius* of the fourteenth and fifteenth centuries, which records obits and endowments over many generations, often with precise descriptions of the ceremonies.[35] Such *Planarii* are also preserved for other churches and convents of the time; in general, they are valuable sources for the social, economical and cultural history of these institutions. In St Saviour's, evidence from the *Planarius* is often confirmed by surviving funeral brasses or tombstones. The following are but a few examples drawn from the *Planarius*. The obit of the citizen Laurentius Keyt (14 January 1438) is connected with a vespers procession each Sunday, at which two boys had to sing the antiphon *Ave sponsa insponsata* when leaving the choir. The feast-day of St Anthony Abbot (17 January) required the antiphon *Alme redemptoris presul*, to be sung (no doubt to the melody of *Alma redemptoris mater*) in alternation with the verses of the Nunc dimittis at compline; at matins,

the hymn *O nimis felix preliator* was sung, and in the vespers procession
the antiphon *Confessor domini* and the responsory *Anthoni compar*. The
processions on the five major Marian feasts (*Purificatio*, 2 February;
Annuntiatio, 25 March; *Assumptio*, 15 August; *Nativitas*, 8 September;
Conceptio, 8 December) were endowed by the priest Judocus Troppeneel
in 1427; the antiphon *Beata dei genitrix* was sung when leaving the choir,
and the antiphon *Salve regina* in the nave, with psalm verses recited by
six schoolboys; bells had to be rung throughout the processions. On 1
May, a *Missa de S. Maria de Salve* was celebrated with organ and (two?)
scholares, who had to sing the Gloria trope *Spiritus et alme*. The priest
Guillermus de Wachtere (*c*.1440) instituted the feast of the Five Joys of
the Virgin (Saturday after Ascension), for which he presented special
chant-books to the church. In 1525, the proper chants for this feast
were replaced by the popular prosa *Inviolata* at first vespers, and the
Alma redemptoris mater at matins.[36] Hermannus de Zindbave endowed
(1438) the feast of SS. Peter and Paul (29 June) with a vespers procession containing the antiphons *Petrus Apostolus et Paulus Doctor* and
Gloriosi principes terre and the responsory *Tu es Petrus*. The schoolboys
were sometimes employed for the singing of the proper of the mass: in a
private requiem on 30 July, two boys sang the Gradual, whereas in a
mass for the chaplain Ghiselbertus Boye (*c*.1430), the Gradual was sung
by two *cantores*, and the Alleluja by two clerks, while the two *scholares*
assisted the celebrant. Organ music was already endowed by the city
treasurer Walter Coopman in 1387 (for 7 September and 7 December).
His devotion to Our Lady is expressed in the inscriptions on his funeral
brass: 'Maria mater gracie, mater misericordie, tu nos a morte protege,
in ora morte [*sic*] suscipe' and 'Averte faciam [*sic*] tuam a peccatis
meis'.[37] Another surviving funeral brass belonged to the grave of the
Portuguese merchant Jean Vaesque (†1467), who was secretary to
Isabella of Portugal and Charles the Bold. His house in the Zilverstraat
near the church still stands; its façade shows the year '1466' and the
device 'A bon compte avenir'. Vaesque's funeral inscription records his
endowment of two annual 'tables of the poor' and three requiems with
organ.[38] The chaplain Nicasius Weyts, who also worked at Our Lady's,
left an endowment in 1448 for the feast-day of his patron saint (14
December). The ceremonies included a procession at vigils with proper
antiphons and the peal of the bell 'Salvator', the hymn *Lux veni vita
premium* and the antiphon *Stella cujus claritas* at vespers – it seems that
Weyts had written these texts himself.[39] The *Planarius* also contains a
very detailed description of the ceremony of the 'Golden Mass' or
Missus, according to an endowment of 1425.[40] This ceremony, popular
all over Europe, always took place on the Wednesday of the Ember
days before Christmas, and represented in a more or less dramatic form
the Annunciation to the Virgin. Its name derived from the solemn

recitation of the gospel *Missus est Gabriel angelus* at the end of matins, around which much musical and theatrical display developed. At St Saviour's, there was no actual mystery play, but four to seven choirboys, clerics of different ranks, the organist and the bell-ringers were amply employed. The most prominent chants were the *Alma redemptoris*, the *Salve regina*, and the prosa *Inviolata, integra et casta*, which was sung both at matins and at high mass. The Kyrie and the prosa were sung with organ – 'in organis decantabuntur', i.e. perhaps 'sung in discant with organ'.

The mystery of the Holy Sacrament fascinated medieval men. Elaborate ceremonies accumulated around the subject, to which many altar paintings of the period are dedicated. At St Saviour's, the feast was promoted by the confraternity of the Holy Sacrament; individual benefactors were, among others, Jean Vaesque, and the courtier Hippolyte Berthoz, who commissioned the above-mentioned painting of his patron saint from Bouts and van der Goes.[41] About 1475, he endowed the singing of the antiphon *O salutaris hostia* in all masses (!) in the octave of Corpus Christi. There were also daily processions in the octave, on the day of the octave outside the church, when the responsory *Homo quidam*, the antiphon *O salutaris hostia* and the hymn *Veni creator spiritus* were sung in the streets.[42] An endowment of Lodewijk Clays (1473) extended the topic to other times of the year: on the five Marian feasts and eleven other high feast-days, the ceremony called *Letatus* was to take place, i.e. the recitation of the psalm *Letatus sum* during mass between the *Pater noster* and the *Agnus Dei*, while the sacred host was lying exposed on the high altar.[43]

The endowment of Lodewijk Clays also records the use of polyphony. A motet had to be performed by the 'cantere metten kinderen' on the feast of St Louis (25 August) in the procession at first vespers. Several similar motet endowments followed, mostly for processions: for St Joseph (1473), St Drogo (1476), the Name of Jesus (1479), St Catherine of Siena (1480), St Giles (1480s), and the Exaltation of the Cross (1489). Discant masses were required on the day of St George (23 April) from 1473, and at least three others from 1485 and 1489, which were sung by the 'cantor cum sociis' with organ accompaniment.[44] This must have been the period when a permanent body of discant singers, clerks and choirboys, started to be available. It was in the 1480s that the two feast-days of the patron saint Eloy (25 June and 1 December) began to be celebrated with a solemn procession, a motet at vespers and a discant mass each.[45] Apart from the succentor (*cantre*) and the choirboys, singers from outside were regularly hired until 1486 – then musicians of St Saviour's itself took over. On 1 December, the church also used to hire the city trumpeters to accompany the procession with the relics of the saint in the streets. The musicians of

St Saviour's were then also able to participate in the great processions on the *dies rogationum* with discant masses, founded in 1485 by the burgomaster Louis Greffijnc. On Monday to Wednesday before Ascension, the clergy of the three major churches of Bruges, together with city representatives, participated in three processions to the parish churches of the Holy Cross, St Catherine and St Mary Magdalene, respectively, all three outside the town walls. The singers of the churches were required to sing in turn one mass in discant at the place of arrival. This amounted to a kind of public musical competition, especially as the succentors of each church (St Donatian's, Our Lady's, St Saviour's) had to compose their respective masses every year.[46] The succentors had the same duty on the occasion of the annual *crepelenfeest* in Aardenburg (see p. 35). A regulation of the chapter of St Saviour's of 1506 records these usages, and also stipulates that the cantor of the church had to compose each year a new motet for the feast of St Eloy on 1 December, plus new songs for the feast-day of the Holy Innocents (28 December): 'et in die Innocentium nova carmina juxta antiquam consuetudinem componat et cantet'.[47] These polyphonic *carmina* must have been secular songs in Latin and French, which were recited at the banquet given to the choirboys and clerks on Holy Innocent's day; it is not certain whether this 'ancient custom' goes back much before 1491, when the feast of the 'Boy bishop' is first mentioned in the church's account books.

All the discant books of the church have been lost, but in 1482/3 seven new polyphonic masses were entered in a 'boeck van discante'. Other masses and motets followed; the copyist in the 1480s was one Claeys Frueyten, whereas in 1493 the *cantre* himself wrote out the music. The discant book and several plainchant books were bound by the famous Jean Guillebert and the chaplain Thomas van der Gavere, and illuminated by the chaplain Paschasius Claeysszuene. The schoolmaster Willelmus van Schoonhoven also copied plainsong books.[48]

The musical personnel of that time is recorded (incompletely, no doubt) in the church accounts, and in the *Liber confraternitatis chori* written about 1510.[49] The latter also contains the names of singers and composers who served other churches, such as Jacobus Tijcke (St James's) and Cornelius Moerijnc (Our Lady's), as well as the organists of St Donatian's, Petrus Paes and Paulus Bloume. Among the clergy of St Saviour's itself were the musicians Walterus de Raedt, Philippus Bollaert, Nicasius de Brauwere and several singers of whom we know only the first names (see Appendix A). The priest Jacobus Buus was succentor for three months in 1504/5; the organ-builder Judocus Buus looked after the organ from 1484. The organist received a salary of £24 – a considerable sum.

The *Liber confraternitatis chori* also records the name of the deceased member 'Anthonius Bunoys'.[50] He had held the office of cantor ('onus regendi cantoriam'), according to an entry in the lost chapter minutes, dated 6 November 1492.[51] At that time Busnois was dead, and his post was filled *interim* by 'Dominus Walterus' (*sc.* de Raedt). In April 1494, one 'Walter' and one 'Denys' (*sc.* van Spiere, *tenorista?*) were paid a total of £22 4s for their joint services for half a year; this may still have been the office of *cantor*[52] (the account books for 1492/3 are lost). On 12 January 1495, Petrus van Vineloo was appointed *magister cantus chori* – he was a discant singer, and employed as succentor at St Donatian's in 1504–1507. As *cantor chori* at St Saviour's, Vineloo was admonished on 21 December 1495 to instruct his boys more diligently ('ut pueros suos diligentius instruat').[53] Thus, the Latin term *cantor* is used at St Saviour's – differently from other churches – as the equivalent of the Flemish *cantre* or *cantre van den kinderen*, which appears in other records, and the holder of the position united the functions of the cantor, who ruled the plainsong, and of the succentor, who taught discant to the boys. If this was, in fact, the office which Busnois had held, then he cannot have obtained it before 1484/5, because, in that year, Nicasius de Brauwere is referred to as 'cantre van den kindren van Sint Salvator' in the account books of the city (he had composed motets for the city minstrels: see p. 86). Busnois had belonged to the chapel of Mary of Burgundy at the time of her death in 1482,[54] and may have participated in her funeral service at Our Lady's on 2 April 1482. One may suggest that he owed his position of cantor at St Saviour's, which was possibly provided with a prebend, to the protection of Maximilian of Habsburg, who also obtained a curateship for his court chaplain Nicholas Mayoul *junior* in 1486. Busnois was perhaps not permanently resident at St Saviour's – either the chaplain Nicasius de Brauwere or the copyist of the polyphonic masses, Claeys Frueyten, could have deputised for him. Nevertheless, it is exactly in those years from 1485 that the polyphonic practice of the church started to flourish, and that a proper body of discant singers was formed. Such initiatives must be partly due to Antoine Busnois.

Around 1500, the music of St Saviour's entered a new phase of expansion, partly because it was raised to the rank of a collegiate church in 1501. The musical practice of the other collegiate churches was imitated in a massive endowment of the draper Michiel van Hille in 1496. It concerned the daily performance of a *Salve* or *lof* in the evening, by the *zangmeester*, four choirboys, a *tenoriste* and two other *ghezellen*. In addition, the organist had to play a motet on the organ. Together with bell-ringing and candle-light, the total expenditure was £156 annually, of which the singers received £69 12s. The precise text of the endowment was carved into the tombstone of Michiel van Hille and his wife.[55]

Scholars have already discussed the confraternity of 'Our Lady of the Seven Sorrows', which was founded at St Saviour's in 1492 under the protection of Philip the Fair.[56] It was not the only such confraternity in the Low Countries at the time, nor even in Bruges: Margaret of Austria founded another in the convent of the *Annonciades* in 1514. A choirbook connected with this particular devotion, copied probably in Malines, still survives (see p. 149). The confraternity at St Saviour's paid the choirboys and clerks an annuity of £228 for performances on the main feast-days (first Sunday in September) and on many other days.[57] Although the seven founder-members belonged to the higher clergy, the confraternity was also connected with the craft guild of the *oudekleer-kopers*, whose confraternity included many priests and city notables, as well as the canon of St Donatian's, Pierre Basin (in 1486).[58]

In the first third of the sixteenth century, the musical practice was completely reorganised. The ceremonies with polyphony were now distributed almost schematically over the whole year, giving the feasts of Easter, Ascension, Whitsunday, Trinity, Corpus Christi, All Saints and Christmas the same kind of musical decoration. It normally consisted of a polyphonic hymn and two motets at vespers, a polyphonic Te Deum with organ at matins and discant with organ at high mass.[59] This systematic renewal marks the distance from the uninhibited and nearly chaotic flourishing of private endowments, so characteristic of the late Middle Ages.

St James's

Probably more than half of the population of Bruges in the later Middle Ages belonged to the four smaller parishes: St James's, St Giles's, St Walburga's and that of the Holy Cross. Culturally ambitious and wealthy citizens supported the musical life in these churches, but space forbids giving more than a few examples of their respective musical traditions.

St James's could draw on a particularly wealthy parish, where most of the foreign merchants lived; the ducal palace (the 'prinsenhoof') was situated close by, and rulers such as Charles the Bold used to hear mass and to confess in St James's when they resided in Bruges. The most important craft guild with a chapel in the church was that of the furriers, with its several subgroups (*grauwerkers, wiltwerkers, lamwerkers*) whose craft related directly to the trading interests of many foreign merchants. For the furriers, the Florentine Tommaso Portinari erected a chapel of St John the Baptist in 1474, and a merchant from Pisa, Giambattista dell' Agnello, was buried there in 1494. The furrier Willem Moreel *senior*, for a long time alderman of the guild, endowed a chaplaincy with masses; he also donated the magnificent altarpiece by

Memling for the altar of St Maurus, St Christopher and St Giles in 1484. Another leading member of the guild, Donaes de Moor,[60] and his wife Adriaene de Vos, endowed two masses in discant for their respective patron saints, two chaplaincies with daily masses, a 'table of the poor', a painted panel for the high altar (it was possibly the Deposition from the Cross painted by Hugo van der Goes in 1471) and an almshouse in the parish, erected in 1480, the buildings of which still exist. The discant mass for St Donatian is most likely to be the one composed by Jacob Obrecht (see p. 146 f.).

Giovanni Arnolfini of Lucca and his wife Giovanna Cenami also lived in the parish and had a pew in the church.[61] Other patricians connected with St James's included the Bave, Biese, van der Buerse (the founders of the stock-exchange), Dault, Cavalcanti, Macharis and de Gros families; chapels belonged to the craft guilds of the butchers, coopers and masons. The trade guild of the barbers, whose patrons were SS. Cosmas and Damian, was a major supporter of music. In an endowment of 28 August 1432,[62] the guild provided the following services for the patronal feast-day (26 September): at first and second vespers, the hymn and Magnificat were performed with organ; the procession to the altar of the saints (an altar painting or sculpture of the saints is mentioned) included a motet, sung by the *kinderen* according to the 'custom of the church'. Matins, compline and all the lesser hours were sung; at high mass, the 'great organ' played the Kyrie and the sequence. The mass was sung in discant by 'six or seven companions' (*ghezellen*) of the choir, with organ. This ceremony survived well into the sixteenth century. Continuing polyphonic practice is also shown in the endowment of a motet for the octave of Corpus Christi in 1454 by Jacob Bave, again referring to 'ancient custom'.[63]

Other interesting ceremonies in the calendar of the church[64] were the feasts of the Three Kings, of the 'Boy bishop' (from 1443), a special Whitsunday ceremony with a representation of the descent of the dove (from 1464), a play for the Purification of Our Lady, and the *Missus* ceremony, which from 1519 was an elaborate mystery play with polyphonic music.[65] From 1498, a confraternity of the 'Presentation of Our Lady' (21 November) commissioned much music, including, from 1508, a Te Deum in discant.[66] St James's day (25 July) was celebrated with a procession around the parish, and hired discant singers 'sang merrily', according to the account books of the 1460s. *Ghezellen* were also hired for Candlemas, on Shrove Tuesday and on Corpus Christi – no fewer than eighteen discant singers took part in the Corpus Christi procession in 1467. The church's own forces included about ten singers-clerks, the succentor (mentioned in 1424 as 'de cantre instrueerende de kindre in zanghe'), four choirboys and the organist. In 1461/2, the salaries of succentor and organist were £18 and £21, respectively. From the mid-fifteenth century, the church owned at least one discant book (for a list of the singers and copyists, see Appendix A.) There was a great organ in the loft and a small organ was tested in 1455/6. The organ-builders who worked for the church included Boudin de Wroe (mentioned 1458), Olivier (1473/4), Anthuenis Haghelsteen (1452), Judocus Buus (from 1489) and his son Jooris (from 1519), who were followed by Charles Waghe, head of a new dynasty of organ-builders.

St Giles's and St Walburga's; Hospitals

The church of St Giles, which still exists in its fifteenth-century form, had a large parish in the north of the town from 1386. The clergy were able to sing all seven hours of the divine office daily in Lent,[67] after the curate Bartholomaeus Niet (†1422) and Bartholomaeus Willaert, his successor, had attracted donations and endowments from citizens and noble families. A mass endowment of Count Louis de Male had existed since 1360. There was a salaried organist throughout the fifteenth century, while the position of succentor seems to have been established some time before 1463.[68] The existence of a group of singers-clerks is recorded in 1487/8, including one 'Heer Ghiselbrecht de tenoriste' and the succentor 'Jan de cantere'.[69] The *Missus* ceremony was founded in 1459 and enlarged by a new endowment in 1467.[70] A painter, Cornelius Bollaert, endowed what was probably the first polyphonic mass on 31 October 1477.[71]

St Walburga's had a number of musical services, and provided the singing of the canonical hours on higher feasts as early as the fourteenth century.[72] The city councillor Pieter van Campen *senior* (†1464), who seems to have been involved in the trade with the Mediterranean, was a churchwarden in the 1450s; in connection with an anniversary endowment of 1455, he gave the church seven 'new books': two antiphonals, two graduals, two psalters and one 'bouc van discante'.[73] The organist of the church played for most anniversaries and on all Marian feasts. Only the feast-day of the patroness (4 August), with procession and other ceremonies, seems to have regularly included polyphony. For this, singers were hired from outside, who are specified in 1461 as being from St Donatian's. There must have been four of them; their gratuity consisted of two pints of white wine each, at the value of 7s each.[74]

The hospitals of Bruges represent that peculiar mixture of religion and charity with business and art, which is so typical of medieval towns. These pious foundations were administered by the city, by churches or convents, and run by lay brothers and sisters. The largest and most ancient of them, the hospital of St John (founded 1188),[75] had not only a chapel, but also a very able choir of brothers, who sang on all higher feast-days. Endowed services – among them a daily mass for

Duke Philip the Good – provided a part of the large income; the annual budget of the hospital of c.£10,000 in 1467/8 was, of course, much greater than that of an average parish church – and more than £500 of this went to the services in the chapel.[76] Three splendid Memling altars were commissioned by members of the community in 1479 and 1480.[77] Forms of music other than the plainchant may have existed in the chapel. Due to a misreading of the account book of 1404/5, it was formerly believed that the hospital hired a 'clavecin' in 1404, but that entry does not refer to music.[78] In 1412/3, however, the brothers Johannes Wouters and Wellekin Spikinc were paid £7 to teach organ-playing and singing – probably to the other brothers and sisters.

Music in the other hospitals and almshouses of Bruges is absolute *terra incognita*. But some sources survive: the small hospital of St Josse received a manuscript with a full office and a plainsong-mass for their patron saint, specially composed by the schoolmaster of St Donatian's, Johannes de Cruninghe (c.1420).[79] The only antiphonal of Bruges of the later fifteenth century that still survives, comes from the ancient hospital of the 'Potterie'.[80] In the lepers' hospital of St Mary Magdalene, no fewer than 31 liturgical books were in use around 1500; two graduals of 1504 and 1506 are preserved.[81] They contain an impressive collection of sequences; the rite is not that of the town of Bruges, but of the diocese of Tournai in general.

CHAPTER FOUR

Convents and Confraternities

A 'lost' culture

No picture of the cultural life of a town like Bruges would be complete without some mention of its convents. Many monasteries and friaries of the Middle Ages have disappeared in the religious struggles of the sixteenth century; in Flanders as well as in England, radical reform movements were directed largely against those institutions from which many of their leaders had originally come. Both Erasmus and Luther had been educated in houses of mendicant orders – and what modern civilisation owes to these men, it indirectly owes to medieval monasticism. The mendicant orders, in particular, helped to form the spirit of the fifteenth century, and the culture of the cities. They not only took care of the spiritual needs of the townspeople by singing masses, praying for the dead, hearing confessions and preaching, but also provided social services in general: health service, burials, charity for the poor and elderly, and education for the young. Their lifestyle and business were integrated into the urban life; most upper– and middle-class families had sons and daughters in some of the town's convents.

For all this, the regulars were well supported by the population. A look at the panoramic map of Bruges drawn by Marc Gheeraert in 1562 (see jacket cover) reveals the splendour of the Dominican, Franciscan, Austin and Carmelite friaries, with large dwellings and chapels of the size of collegiate churches. All of these had been built in the thirteenth century, and were entirely destroyed by the reformers in the 1570s and 1580s. The same is true of other monastic houses: those of the Carthusians outside the walls, of the immensely rich abbey of the order of St Clare (the 'Rich Clares'), of the Augustinian abbey of St Bartholomew. Only the lay community of the Beguines, founded in 1245, a female order famous for its handicrafts, survives in the old buildings today. Bruges is still rich in smaller sister-houses, many of which were founded in the fifteenth century.

The economic basis for this kind of monastic life was not so much the feudalism of the earlier Middle Ages as the urban community of the thirteenth to fifteenth centuries. Musical and ceremonial life, too, was largely a result of collaboration between convents and citizens, the latter being organised in guilds and pious confraternities.

Bruges had developed without much influence from Benedictine houses. The nearest Benedictine abbey was that of St Andrew just outside the walls; it seems to have had a tradition of music, as one of its monks, Christian Sage (1410–1490) is reported to have been 'in vocali ac instrumentali musica expertissimus'.[1] He is the author of a treatise on mensural notation printed by Coussemaker.[2] The two great Cistercian abbeys of western Flanders, Ter Duinen (near Koksijde) and Ter Doest (at Lisseweghe), functioned as cultural centres in the twelfth and thirteenth centuries. The abbot of the latter had a palace in the town. The high attainment of these Cistercians in learning and liturgy can still be recognised from their manuscripts,[3] which are preserved in the libraries of Bruges – all extant codices of music theory in the area came from those two houses. Ter Doest also had a succentor for the musical instruction of the novices.[4] The Augustinian abbey of St Bartholomew, called 'ten Eeckhout', in the town, played a more important role in urban life. Its abbot was the highest ecclesiastical dignitary of Bruges, and presided over public ceremonies such as the procession of the Holy Blood. The canons of the 'Eeckhout' did not normally sing mass outside their community. Their most interesting cultural contribution rests on a confraternity which they housed: the association of booksellers and illuminators, called the 'ghilde' of St Luke and St John the Evangelist.[5] Manuscripts produced by its members survive in hundreds, if not thousands – they were sold on the open market or made on commission, and met a continuous demand of the lay population, including the nobility and the court. Woodcuts, and then printing with movable type, were introduced in Bruges by members of the guild such as Colaerd Mansion and Jan Brito. It is from them that William Caxton received the first encouragement for his own activities as a bookseller, translator and printer. Famous 'Burgundian' miniaturists and copyists were members: Philippe de Mazerolles, Jean Dreux, Jean le Tavernier, Willem Vrelant, Loyset Liedet, Morisses de Haec; the same is true of the bookbinders' families Bloc and van den Gavere.

The chapel of the confraterniy in the abbey was the place where the main feast-days of the patron saints St Luke and St John were celebrated: 18 October for St Luke, 6 May and 27 December for St John. These masses, and the many anniversaries endowed by members of the guild, were sung with organ. From 1457 at the latest, hired musicians were employed: the account book of 1469/71 specifies the singers as being from St Donatian's. The organist who accompanied these discant singers in the 1460s was the Minorite Jan de Pape. It seems that originally the musicians had to bring their own portative organ. A contract of 1499 between the abbey and the guild gives the latter the right to hire singers from St Donatian's or from other churches at their own convenience, but it also stipulates that the guild should now use the church organ, and its organist. The altar in the chapel, rebuilt in 1474, was decorated in 1478 with a new painting by Hans Memling. The panels were a gift of Willem Vrelant, the most productive bookseller-illuminator of the period in Flanders. In the contract of 1499, the panels ('by wilen meester Hans') are described as containing the portraits of Vrelant and his wife; there were four wings, and carved sculptures of St Luke and St John stood on top of them. Vrelant had died in June 1489, and had left an endowment for a mass in discant on St Boniface's day (5 June).

Various mendicant houses

For all kinds of civic ceremonies, and for the masses which regularly accompanied them, the town relied mostly on the mendicant orders. Dominican and Franciscan brothers were often requested to say mass in parish churches, chapels and hospitals. There existed rotational schemes by which priests from the four large friaries said mass in turn in the town hall on public occasions.[6] They also specialised in organising the numerous general processions of Bruges. These had often to be staged at short notice, whether it be for a military victory of the ducal army, the birth of a prince or princess, the illness or death of a ruler or of one of his family.[7] Among the recurring events, the annual festival of the Holy Blood (see p. 5) involved the largest processions. These were also organised by mendicants. The Beguines in particular, who were also known for their learning and probably ran a music school, had to sing the processional chants – in which, no doubt, all other participants could join. Two surviving chant-books with music for the Holy Blood procession (c.1510) come from the sister-house of the Beguines.[8] They were written and illuminated for them by professional scribes; but we also know that the Beguines themselves produced music manuscripts, and some sisters were members of the guild of illuminators. Another female convent, that of the Carmelite sisters (founded in 1488 with public subsidies), owned already dozens of chant-books by c.1505, many of them written by the sisters.[9] Similar musical interests were pursued by the 'Black Sisters' of St Augustine, or of Bethel, who also served as nurses in the Hospital of St John. One of their chant-books is preserved, an interesting miscellany of antiphons and other chants of 1506, which still belongs to the order.[10]

The 'Black Friars' of St Augustine (Austin friars) fall into a different category. As one of the larger houses, founded in 1250 in the middle of the trade quarter, the convent attracted many rich confraternities, including those of foreign merchants.[11] Daily masses and anniversaries with organ, cantor and choirboys were requested in the chapels of the merchants from Genoa, Lucca, Venice, Navarra and Nuremberg, and in those of the noble families Metteneye, Halewyn and Ruebs, among others. Marguerite van Nieuwenhove endowed an anniversary in 1466, which was to be sung by the cantor and four choirboys and supervised by the guild of the sailors.[12] Another endowment came in 1490 from Raphael de Mercatellis, the abbot of St Bavo's in Ghent, and a natural son of Philip the Good.[13] In the chapel of the Holy Cross of the merchants from Lucca, Giovanni Arnolfini (†11 September 1472) and his wife Giovanna Cenami endowed a daily mass and an anniversary for the annual revenue of £80. Giovanni's brother Michele Arnolfini endowed the convent with £70; he was buried in the chapel itself (†26 October 1473).[14] Some of the Austin friars seem to have been Englishmen. The prior of the convent in 1387 was called 'Jan van Inghelant', and in 1422, an English Austin friar was appointed confessor to the English 'Merchant Adventurers'[15] (see below).

There are few notices about music in the largest convent of Bruges, that of the Dominicans ('Jacobites', *Predicaren*), founded in 1234. We know of some rich endowments, one of which (1488) must have included polyphony, as a special amount of 7s was set aside for the *sanghers* – probably hired ones from St Donatian's.[16] Choirboys are not mentioned, but the boys of the convent school would have acted and sung in some of the civic festivities, to which the Dominicans often contributed 'living pictures' (see p. 82). They had an organist, of course; the Dominican friar Hugo rebuilt the great organ of St Donatian's in 1454–63.

The Carmelites and their foreign guests

A British Library exhibition in 1976, for the quincentenary of the introduction of printing into England,[17] drew my attention to the fact that William Caxton had spent many years of his life in Bruges, where he was a member, and from 1462 governor, of the 'Fellowship of the Merchant Adventurers'. This extremely important trade association[18] had come into being in 1296 as a sub-group of the London mercers, but had gained almost complete independence and royal privileges for the overseas trade by the fifteenth century. The English wool staple for the Netherlands had been transferred to Bruges by Edward III in 1340; despite growing rivalry and mutual trade embargos, the English trade in wool, silk, cloth and many other goods had its busiest foreign market and financial focus in Bruges. Here, the 'Merchant Adventurers' established their headquarters in 1344 (another existed in Middelburg in Zeeland) in the guise of a confraternity of St Thomas Becket. Like other merchant groups or 'nations' residing in the town, they had their own 'hotel', the *domus Anglorum*, and a private chapel in the Carmelite convent. The archive of the 'Ongheschoeide Karmelieten' in Bruges still contains two identical acts of foundation (dated 26 May and 12 June 1344 respectively) of the confraternity of St Thomas Becket, 'of the English merchants who frequent the staple of Bruges'.[19] A chapel of St Thomas was to be built in the conventual church, where a mass was to be sung every Tuesday (the special day of the saint); other services included burials and christenings. Later members of the confraternity added endowments, such as William Kyvir (Reynier?) in 1438, Lawrence Stevens in *c.*1444, Thomas Stevenson of Boston in *c.*1473 and John Pray (Bray?) in the 1480s.[20] A royal privilege granted to the Merchant Adventurers by Edward IV in 1462 sets aside a quarter of all forfeitures and confiscations received by the Fellowship for the maintenance of the two chapels in Bruges and Middelburg;[21] a sixteenth-century document says that the confraternity paid a half-yearly amount 'to the friars who sing in the chapel in Bruges'.[22]

The music which the 'White Friars' provided seems to have included polyphony from the early fifteenth century. In 1456, a legal case was brought by the governor, William Ouvray, against the Florentine merchant Jacopo Strozzi, who had insulted the honour of the English nation. As a fine, Strozzi had to pay for a 'messe solennelle du Saint Esprit en discant et à organes', to be celebrated 'en la chapelle des Anglais en l'église des Carmes'.[23]

For the English merchants, the convent was much more than a religious base. It was a centre and a meeting place for business encounters and festivities. The Merchant Adventurers took part in major ceremonies and processions in and near the convent, often by having their street (the *Carmersstrate*) decorated and illuminated. Important visitors from England could be lodged in the convent, such as Queen Margaret of Anjou during her flight from England in 1463, or the retinue of Margaret of York during her wedding celebrations in 1468.[24] Unlike other merchant nations, however, the English did not live permanently in Bruges (as they had the shortest way home), but normally only from the time of the May Fair to autumn. They inhabited rooms and houses rented from the Carmelites, and used the chapel and refectory to deposit their charters and valuables.

Perhaps nowhere in Europe were international trade relations as closely knit as in Bruges. On 28 October 1347, the Hanseatic merchants from Lübeck, Hamburg and Danzig established their head-quarters in the Carmelite convent, using the refectory for their meetings, and sharing the chapel of St Thomas with the Merchant Adventurers for their masses. The 'Easterlings' were the largest foreign community in Bruges. They were the ideal trading partners of the

English: they sold leather, furs, amber, metalware, etc., but had to buy wool and cloth. Business contacts were upheld in spite of worsening political relations. The Hanseatics also collaborated with craft guilds of Bruges, mainly the lacemakers and the 'paternoster-makers' (carvers of amber). Many German merchants became citizens of Bruges; some endowed their requiems in the convent, such as Willem Hempel (1423), Johannes Salborch (1472), Heinrich Terrax (1468) and Johannes van den Houtte (1480).[25]

On 6 July 1366, the Carmelite prior granted the use of a chapel of Our Lady and St Ninian to the Scottish merchants.[26] They made numerous donations to the convent: William Goupylt endowed an anniversary in 1383, in which the participation of the organist of the convent is called for; other endowments came from Johanna Karres (1416) and Andrew Bollys (1451). The chapel of St Ninian was maintained partly by subsidies from the city. As so many Scottish families settled in Bruges (more, indeed, than from any other nation), a Scottish chaplain was appointed in 1457 by the bishop of Whithorn. Two Bruges citizens of Scottish origin, Alexander Bonkil and Alexander Napier, led political and commercial negotiations between Burgundy and Scotland in the 1460s and '70s; other negotiators were the Flemish noblemen Clays van Nieuwenhove and Anselmo Adornes[27] – both of them benefactors of the Carmelite convent, where all those men must have met frequently. Adornes, who endowed a daily mass at the high altar in 1460,[28] was one of the most colourful political figures in Flanders. His family (of Genoese descent) had their private church 'of Jerusalem' in the town; members of the family were often mayors or magistrates. Anselmo Adornes served King James III of Scotland, who made him Lord of Corthuy and councillor in 1469; he died in Scotland in 1483, then being governor of the castle of Linlithgow. His diplomatic activity went hand in hand with his commercial and cultural interests. When the Hanseatics had captured, in 1473, a vessel owned by Tommaso Portinari and the Medici bank, which carried papal alum and also an altar painting by Memling, it was Adornes who led a delegation to Hamburg and Danzig to recover the ship.[29] In 1472, James III of Scotland sent his servant John Browne to Adornes in Bruges to receive lessons on the lute. Around that time, Adornes sold two silver trumpets for the guild of the crossbowmen of St George.[30] He owned two paintings by Jan van Eyck (see p. 73) and seems to have been a protector of Hugo van der Goes: the famous Edinburgh panels of this master, which were commissioned by Edward Bonkil of Trinity College, Edinburgh,[31] were most probably painted in the Carmelite convent and represent its organ or a similar one.

The fourth important merchant community to be established in the convent was that of Aragon. Their chapel, which must have' existed before 1400, received charters from King Alfonso V of Aragon in 1458 and from King Ferrante in 1483 and 1488.[32] Endowments of individual merchants included those of Andreas Pool (1456) and Petrus Andree (1482). The close trade relations between Aragon and Flanders must have led to cultural exchanges as well; Aragonese minstrels visited Bruges in the fourteenth century, and the court of Alfonso V is known for its imports of Flemish singers and works of art. Chansonniers from Aragonese circles in Naples, c.1460–1485, seem to draw directly on Flemish sources, also for English music (see p. 137 f.).

The 'Order of Our Lady of Mount Carmel' itself had a tradition of learning and music. The Bruges house was one of the twelve *studia generalia* of the order in 1345. Connections across the channel were close: the English *magister* Thomas de Illedia joined the Bruges house in 1293 and was its prior from 1314 to 1320.[33] A number of friars in the fifteenth century were also Englishmen.[34] The study of music was widespread in the order. Although the general chapter of 1324 adopted the terms of the notorious papal bull of 1322 against polyphony, several Carmelites are known as composers after that: Bartolino da Padova (*fl.* 1385–1400), the Englishman John Hothby (see p. 122 f.) and the Fleming Johannes Bonadies, the teacher of Gafurius. Carmelite manuscripts of polyphonic music include an early fifteenth-century fragment in Dijon, containing mass music, motets and a monophonic *lai*, and the largest collection of early keyboard music, the 'Faenza codex' (*FZ 117*), which originated in the Ferrara house c.1420.[35] Around fifty years later, this codex went through the hands of Johannes Bonadies (Godendach) and other Carmelites of the circle of John Hothby, who added some compositions and treatises on counterpoint and proportion. One of the treatises is attributed to 'Nicasius Weyts Carmelita' – surely the same man as the chaplain of Our Lady's in Bruges. He is actually mentioned in a document from the Bruges house[36] and may have taught music to the boys in the convent school. The additions to the 'Faenza codex' may have been made when Italian Carmelites had visited Bruges, perhaps in connection with the trip of Bishop Stefanò Trenta of Lucca in 1467 (see p. 122 f.).

The musical personnel of the friary itself is unknown. I believe that English musicians were active there, at least intermittently. The German poet and singer Johann von Soest reports in his autobiography that he was invited to Bruges, in the early 1460s, by 'der meister tzwen uss Engellant' – English masters or *magistri*; from them, he learnt 'contreyn und fauberdon' as well as 'proporcion vil mancherley'.[37] If the English musicians were based in Bruges, they could have been connected with the Carmelite convent.

The Carmelites seem to have hired discant singers from outside for some of their ceremonies, probably in 1476 and certainly in connection with an endowment of 1485 (see below). The latter document shows that they had discant singers inside the convent as well. The main musical forces, however, consisted of the 'full choir', the cantor and the choirboys. All of them were employed in specified roles, for example, in a celebration of the Holy Sacrament every Thursday from 1423, which also involved the sounding of cymbals in the church. In 1444, the citizen Jan van den Vagheviere founded an altar of Our Lady with daily masses, and an anniversary mass in which the organ and the *jonghen broederkins* (boys who were novices) took part. After mass, the boys had to sing the *Salve regina* 'as they do on high feasts'. This mass is mentioned, with another endowed by the same benefactor, in a charter of 1474 as 'deux messes à notes', which under the circumstances must mean 'discant masses'. The *kinderen* of the convent are also mentioned as singers in documents of 1447, 1458 and several others.[38]

At least for part of the fourteenth century, the Bruges Carmelites were also connected with minstrels. In 1318, the city paid a subsidy to the minstrels who held their annual school in Lent (see p. 78) 'behind the Carmers' convent' – a locality near the ancient site of the convent which is still known by the name of '*Speelmansstrate*'. The minstrels probably rented the ground from the friars, and may have been paying guests of their refectory. Aragonese minstrels who came to Bruges in the fourteenth century can have met their fellow-countrymen in the convent; English musicians in the retinue of visitors like the bishops of London and Winchester, the earl of Derby and the duke of Lancaster, would obviously use the house of the 'White Friars' for their lodgings.

Confraternities in the Carmelite convent

Among the local craft guilds which supported the convent were the sailors, brewers, 'paternoster-makers', lacemakers, chandlers and dyers; other benefactors were the noble families Gruuthuse, Nieuwenhove, Adornes, Goossin and van den Vagheviere as well as the Spaniard Gondisalve de Vargas, a physician of Charles the Bold. Besides the merchant groups, there were three major religious confraternities in the convent: of the Immaculate Conception, of Our Lady of Roosebeke and of the Holy Ghost. The first of these was founded in 1429, probably as an association of the friars themselves with lay people who supported the dogma of the Immaculate Conception, for whose acceptance in the church the Carmelite order had long been campaigning. From 1457, the confraternity had an altar containing a painted panel on this specific subject; a Lady-mass was sung every Saturday.[39]

Roosebeke, a village half-way between Bruges and Courtrai, was the site of the battle of 1382, when Count Louis de Male defeated the Flemish towns (see p. 104). According to oral tradition, an annual pilgrimage to the chapel of Our Lady in Westrosebeke originated around that time – a procession is still held in the village every year. The confraternity of Bruges, in collaboration with others of Menin and Bourbourg, organised the procession from 1452 at the latest, when the courtier Jean de Wavrin made his will in favour of the Carmelites. He gave £840 for daily masses in the chapel of St John the Baptist 'or of Roosebeke', where he was also buried in 1453.[40] Two of his ancestors had been killed in the battle of Agincourt in Burgundian service, and one had already fought for Louis de Male at Roosebeke. The purpose of the endowment, and of the confraternity itself, may therefore have been to commemorate Flemish nobles killed in the military service of the rulers. Another Jean de Wavrin (probably a nephew) was a courtier of Charles the Bold and author of the well-known *Chroniques d'Angleterre* (finished in 1471); some of the information in this book may have been supplied by Englishmen whom Wavrin met in the Carmelite convent.

The annual pilgrimage to Roosebeke was a major musical festival.[41] According to a description of 1545, it began on the Saturday before 22 July with a *Salve regina* in the convent, in which city minstrels took part; a banquet with music followed. On the way to Roosebeke, the pilgrims lodged in a hostel of the church of Torhout, where the city trumpeters played for supper. On Sunday, there was a solemn procession through Roosebeke with trumpeters and other minstrels from Bruges, Bourbourg and Menin. At home in Bruges, the Carmelites sang masses on Sunday, Monday and Thursday of that week. This programme had developed from the Wavrin endowment, and those of the citizen Jacob van den Weghe (1453), the German merchant Heinrich Terrax (1468) and the Florentine Carlo Cavalcanti, nicknamed 'Kaerle Stros', who was the sole exporter of silk for the Medici in the 1460s. Terrax endowed six annual Lady-masses in the Roosebeke chapel, and one anniversary for himself during the week of the pilgrimage. It is interesting that during these services the doors of the chapel had to be closed, so that only members of the confraternity could attend.

The confraternity of the Holy Ghost was none other than the famous 'Chambre de Rhétorique du Saint Esprit' of Bruges,[42] founded in 1428 by Jan van Hulst, and one of the most ancient literary societies of Belgium. These *rederijkerskamers* were in a sense the heirs of the *trouvères*, and of the middle-class guilds in Flanders and France who organised processions, miracle plays, literary and musical festivals. They were analogous to the later *Minnesinger* and to the *Meistersinger* in Germany. The Bruges guild of rhetoricians seems to stem from loose associations of citizens and clergymen who performed plays and music on religious feasts and other occasions. One such association is referred to in 1422 as 'ghesellen van der kercke'; another, which cultivated poetry in the native tongue, was called 'Het penseken' or 'La pensée'. A certain Jan van Hulst directed plays in Bruges for the Duchess Marguerite as early as 1394, and a miracle play of the twelve apostles which was performed in 1396 in the Holy Blood procession.[43] He may be identical with the Jan van Hulst who was a miniaturist of Philip the Bold,[44] and certainly is one of the poets of Flemish songs in the famous 'Gruuthuse manuscript' of the late fourteenth century (see p. 108). From the texts of these monophonic songs, Karel Heeroma has rightly concluded that the circle in which they originated was acquainted with polyphonic singing as well.[45] An account book of the city of 1410/11 records a payment to 'Jan van Hulst and others who sang mass on behalf of the confraternity of the Dry Tree for our lord the duke'.[46] The mass must have been sung in discant, as there would otherwise be no need for specially paid singers in a mass, and as the 'Dry Tree' already had a tradition of performing polyphonic masses (see p. 71). Another Jan van Hulst, if not indeed the same, founded the *rederijkerskamer* of the Holy Ghost in 1428, during a meeting of thirteen members of 'Het penseken' in his house on Maundy Thursday. As the men were commemorating the Passion of Our Lord and the Last Supper, a white dove flew into the room, carrying a scroll with the inscription 'Mijn werck es hemelijck' ('My work is heavenly'), which was adopted as the motto of the new confraternity of the Holy Ghost. This foundation legend, as told in the seventeenth century by Antonius Sanderus, elaborates on some historical facts: the symbolic number of thirteen founder-members (Christ and the disciples) is to be connected with the miracle plays of the twelve apostles which had been staged by Jan van Hulst (the Elder?) and others; the custom of the guild of celebrating the *Mandatum* ceremony on Maundy Thursday is documented.[47] The celebration also included a Passion play and the recitation of vernacular poetry. The other annual feast-day was that of the Holy Trinity, which had been the emblem of 'Het penseken'. The new guild appears in city records of 1458/9 as 'ghezelscepe van den helighen gheeste' who performed a play of St Silvester in the *burg*; they also appeared in other towns in theatrical competitions between various guilds, festivals which were later called *landjuweelen*.[48]

The true story of the foundation of the Bruges guild involves the patronage of the Gruuthuse family. The nobleman Jean de Gruuthuse, grandfather of Louis, is mentioned in one of the poems of the 'Gruuthuse manuscript' as 'king' of the society of the 'White Bear' who organised jousting tournaments in 1392. It is possible that part of the manuscript was dedicated to him; the whole compound codex later belonged to his grandson Louis, who may have inherited it.[49] The widow of Jean, Agnès de Mortaigne, was a benefactor of the Carmelite friary, where she founded a chapel of the Holy Ghost, with an altar dedicated to the Trinity, on 31 August 1426. Another charter relating to this endowment was signed in her presence on 15 April 1428. She died on 23 July 1438 and was buried in the Holy Ghost chapel.[50] The rhetoricians must have been allowed by her to use this chapel; in 1466, Louis de Gruuthuse handed over its full use to them 'according to the wishes of his grandmother'. This is mentioned in a charter of the confraternity of 1485, which also describes some of its customs.[51] Their principal feast – probably Trinity Sunday – was called 'de cueninc feeste van refrein daghe', i.e. the feast of the 'king' of the guild with the recitation of *refreins*. For the masses in the chapel, the Carmelite organist was paid 2s, but extra gratuities were available for the singers 'whether hired from inside or from outside' the convent. All this is said to have been in accordance with 'ancient custom'. For their dramatic performances and for the *refreins*, the rhetoricians used the convent's refectory, as did the younger guild of Bruges rhetoricians, the 'Drie Saintinnen', which had been established at Our Lady's in 1474. A contract of 1495 between the two related guilds, in which the *ancienneté* of the 'Holy Ghost' is confirmed, was signed on behalf of the latter by the members Adriaen Drabbe, Rombaut de Doppere and Aliamus de Groote, among others.[52] De Groote, who was a chaplain of Our Lady's in 1474, may have helped found the 'Drie Saintinnen' as a break-away group from the 'Holy Ghost' – just as Jan van Hulst had founded the latter as a break-away group from 'Het penseken' with the encouragement of Agnès de Mortaigne. All these societies had similar artistic goals, and their members included amateurs – wealthy citizens – as well as professional musicians.

The Franciscans and the 'Dry Tree'

Franciscan devotion in its various forms was represented in Bruges by several convents. There were the communities of the third order of St Francis, such as the Beguines, the *Bogaerds* and the 'Grey Sisters' of St Elizabeth. Newer, reformed houses were those of the *Staelijzers* of St Martin, of the Observants and of the 'Poor Clares' or *Colettinen*. Unlike these reformed communities who shunned all modern luxuries such as polyphonic music, the two largest, long-established houses participated actively in the cultural life of the town: the abbey of the *Clarisses* or 'Rich Clares', founded in 1266, which had become a kind of boarding-house for unmarried daughters of the nobility, and the main male convent, that of the Friars Minor (*Fremineuren*), founded in 1245 on the *Braemberch* in the town centre.[53] The Friars Minor specialised in public preaching, processions and other civic ceremonies. They were supported by guilds such as the carpenters, who had a chapel of St Louis in the convent's church, and the guild of the archers of St Sebastian, whose chapel is mentioned in 1396.[54] The city subsidised building works, and Duke Philip the Good paid for the repair of stained-glass windows with his coat of arms in 1451.[55] The local nobility (the *Franc de Bruges*) paid for a new organ in 1425/6; Isabella van der Coutre endowed a daily mass in the chapel of St Francis, which was controlled by the guild of the leather-dyers.[56] The most important benefactors, however, were the Florentine and Castilian merchant communities.[57] The Spaniards erected their chapel of the Holy Cross in 1414, which seems to have been shared by the Florentines from 1418.

Foreign merchants united with local nobles and citizens in the 'ghilde van Onzer Lieve Vrauwe van den Droghen Boome' (of 'Our Lady of the Dry Tree').[58] Before the religious radicalisation of the sixteenth century, this confraternity was a rather worldly club of wealthy people, who very much wanted to display their devotion. Their chosen name points to Marian symbolism: the 'Dry Tree' was a symbol of the Immaculate Conception, an idea supported not only by the Carmelites but also the Franciscans. The confraternity existed before 1396 and had its own chapel. Florentines were among its early leading members and dominated the organisation throughout the fifteenth century, although there were also other Italians and Spaniards. It seems as if the 'Dry Tree' had originated as a group of supporters of the Immaculate Conception like that in the Carmelite convent. Another theory draws a connection with a group of lay brothers in the 'Eeckhout' abbey, the so-called *fratres ad succurrendum* of the early fifteenth century; among its members were Duke John de Berry, Sir Henry Percy of Northumberland and also a certain Jan van Hulst. Besides, there is a foundation legend which involves Philip the Good and the battle of Hal in 1422. But the confraternity of the 'Dry Tree' existed well before that, as is shown in their earliest charter,[59] dated 20 December 1396. At that time, the members promised to pay the Friars Minor for a daily mass in their chapel and sermons on all Marian feasts – but every Sunday, the mass was to be sung in discant. The singers were all friars – either members of the 'ghilde' or other friars who were to supplement them (*helpen discanterene*) for a gratuity of 2s each. The discant mass was always a Lady-mass, and there were also special ceremonies on Marian feasts.

The confraternity soon began to hire singers also from outside the convent. In 1410/11 it was the turn of Jan van Hulst and his *ghesellen* to sing a mass for the duke,[60] but in 1414 four discant singers and the organist of St Donatian's were lured away on the feast of the Assumption, and in 1449 twelve or thirteen singers from St Donatian's defected to the Sunday services in the friary (see p. 26). The 'Dry Tree' had started to become an aristocratic and merchant club which employed musical specialists – although it still counted many artists among its own members. Petrus Christus, who painted the altar panel of the confraternity (showing the Virgin and Child appearing in the 'Dry Tree'), is registered in the membership book (c.1462–65)[61] along with Arnoud de Mol, another painter; several other members belonged to the guild of the booksellers and illuminators, for example a certain Jan van Hulst – perhaps the same as a friar of this name who is mentioned in the account-books of the guild of 1495–1497. Professional artists, middle-class amateurs and wealthy patrons must have prayed side by side in the chapel; many women and children were members in their own right. The approximately 200 members in the 1460s, and later, included Philip the Good and Isabella of Portugal, Charles of Charolais and Isabelle de Bourbon, Louis de Gruuthuse, the Lords of Archy, Ghistel, Dixmuide, Varssenare, the bastards Anton and Balduin of Burgundy, many abbots, curates and canons, the patricians Pieter Lanchals, Pieter van Campen, Louis Greffijnc, Colaert Dault, Anthonis Goossin, the Italian merchants Carlo Cavalcanti, Tommaso Portinari, Paul Meliaen, Giovanni and Michele Arnolfini with their wives, the Spaniards Alonso Pardo, Alvaro de Castro, Martin Gonsales, the Englishman William Bray, the naturalised Englishman(?) Thomas Perrot, the ducal singers Robert Pelé, Adrien Basin and Jean Cordier, and several Friars Minor and ladies of the abbey of the 'Rich Clares'. The leading organisers at that time, however, can be discerned in the sixteen signatories to a new contract[62] made with the convent in 1469 (which specifically refers to the contract of 1396 and now mentions the organ in the chapel, but no longer the discant singers, as these were now regularly hired from outside the friary): among them were Paul van Overtveld (dean), Anselmo Adornes, Giovanni Arnolfini, Joos Berthilde, Jan van Nieuwenhove, Donaes de Beer, Tommaso Portinari and Petrus Christus.

The accounts of the confraternity are preserved from 1495 onwards.[63] Around that time, the annual membership fee was 24s, the total budget about £240. Of this amount no less than £78 was paid (in 1496/7) to the singers and the organist for the discant masses sung every Sunday and on high feasts; the singers usually came from St Donatian's. The friars received around £50 for preaching, low masses and requiems. Besides, the four city minstrels played in the chapel – which is unusual – on certain feasts; they received a total of £24. The organists Claeys Grape and Jacob Honie were members and may have lent their professional services. The organ-builder Judocus Buus was regularly paid for looking after the organs.

The end of the splendid cultural life of the 'Dry Tree' was foreshadowed in 1466–68, when Tommaso Portinari, Isabella of Portugal and then also Margaret of York began to divert their protection to the reformed branch of the Franciscans, the Friars Observant (*Recolletten*). A convent and church was rebuilt for them outside the *Ezelpoort*, on land donated by Portinari; the duchess laid the first stone.[64] The

Observants soon surpassed the *Fremineuren* in number and popularity, so that in 1518 the two houses had to be merged under the new rule. The community moved into the buildings on the *Braemberch*; the confraternity of the 'Dry Tree' was faced with an ultimatum either to move out or to accept the new rules, which excluded all luxuries, and forbade women to enter the convent. After much litigation, they accepted.

We witness the end of an era: the liberal, even enlightened co-operation between lay people and friars succumbed to religious radicalism in a polarised society. The friar Cornelius van Dordrecht became known as the 'hammer of the heretics' – and the Protestant reformers destroyed the convent altogether in the 1580s. Zegher van Male still records the existence of the 'ghilde van den Droghen Boome' in the Franciscan friary in 1578. Later, the 'ghilde' moved into the Dominican convent, and finally into the church of St Walburga, where they acquired a new altar painting by Pieter Claeyssens *junior* in 1620.

Several works of art had by then passed into other hands. A panel of the 'Deipara Virgo', painted *c.*1520 by the Master of the Holy Blood, seems to have belonged to the 'Dry Tree', as it represents the theologically connected image of the 'Tree of Jesse'; it was originally in the Franciscan convent and is now in St James's in Bruges. There is also a panel by Petrus Christus with Our Lady, St Francis and St Jerome, dated 1457, which may have belonged to the convent on the *Braemberch*.[65] The will of Anselmo Adornes (1470), a leading member of the confraternity, mentions two small pictures of the Stigmatisation of St Francis, by Jan van Eyck, which Adornes left to his two daughters, both nuns. Two such panels do indeed survive (in Turin and Philadelphia), although their authenticity has been questioned.[66] It has also been asked why the Franciscan habits worn in the pictures are brown, denoting the reformed branch of the order, which was not introduced in the Low Countries until after van Eyck's lifetime. The answer may be that he painted the original panel for Isabella of Portugal; when she began to favour the Friars Observant in the 1460s, she commissioned a larger copy (with brown habits) from Petrus Christus, for the new church of the Observants, through Adornes. This copy would be the larger of the two surviving panels, now in Turin. Adornes kept the original and had another copy made, also by Christus and in the original size, so that he could give the two small panels to his daughters. One of these (the copy) would be the small panel in Philadelphia, while the original is lost.

Eight leaves of an antiphonal, which may have belonged to the *Fremineuren* of Bruges, appear to be the only extant source of their music. As regards the polyphonic Lady masses of the 'Dry Tree', however, one or more of them may have found their way into the Lucca choirbook, written in Bruges *c.*1470 (see p. 120 ff.).

———— ◆◆◆◆ ————

CHAPTER FIVE

The City and the Court

The minstrels

Professional musicians of the later Middle Ages who were neither clerics nor employed by the church are usually referred to as 'minstrels'.[1] Although society needed them for many different purposes, and although their skills were as varied as were their lifestyles and aesthetic views, it is essentially correct to use a common name for all these people. In the historical sources, the following terms are, on the whole, interchangeable: *ménestrel* (*ministruel, ministrer,* etc.); *jongleur* (*gokelare, joculator, juglar*); *spilman* (*speelman, gleoman*); *histrio*; *mimus.* As the profession always had to struggle for social recognition, which the church, in particular, denied to it, the terminology sometimes reflected social differentiation. There could be a wide gap between a travelling minstrel without regular employment – the *histrio* – and the courtly *valet de chambre* or *faiseur* (a creative poet and composer). But over longer periods of time, and wider areas, the terminology is not consistent; it rather depends, in each document, on the social status of the writer himself, the language used, and on the function of the document (church and court accounts, city registers, narrative sources, poetry, and so on).

If we define the late medieval minstrel as a musical entertainer with a basically secular education, this does not imply that he could not serve individual churchmen, such as bishops, as well as nobles or burghers, or that sacred music was outside his reach. He was by no means limited to a certain repertory or musical style. Among his skills, singing was always important; the '*ménestrel de bouche*' is a standard denomination in Burgundian records, and some convents of Bruges may even have hired minstrels for the singing of polyphonic masses. Court minstrels of the highest artistic rank like Baude Cordier of Burgundy or Jacomí Sentluc and Mossèn Borra of Aragon were composers who mastered the extreme intricacies of the *ars subtilior.*

The task of the minstrel encompassed many non-musical activities. According to the circumstances, he could appear as an actor, fool (*zot, nar*), poet or circus artist; if a chamber valet at court, he could be employed as messenger, diplomat and spy; the town musician served as wait or bellringer on the town's belfry, or as a member of the forces of law and order. Every political legation, and every army, in particular, included professional trumpeters. The high responsibility of such jobs, which could help save or destroy lives, was rewarded by society with a high social status. In the medieval cities, the integration of some professional musicians with the middle classes reflects the need for music as a useful punctuation and accentuation of daily life.

Civic and political functions

We know of the regular employment of city waits and war trumpeters in Bruges from the beginning of the fourteenth century, whilst earlier records do not survive.[2] It is actually surprising that the specific function of the city wait was reserved to professional musicians. Was it necessary to be a musical specialist in order to give horn or trumpet signals from the town belfry at agreed times? What must have mattered even more was the personal integrity and reliability of those who had to spend night and day on the tower to warn their fellow citizens of fires or approaching armies. Were the city waits originally travelling minstrels who found a niche in urban professional life, or were they citizens who had specialised in the musical craft? The question must remain open. We do know, however, that the earliest city waits of Bruges known by name were regarded as real musicians, and used as such. In 1310, the 'wachters up de halle' (i.e. on the belfry) Fierkin de Trompere, Henric de Gartere and Lammekin Spetaerd were paid for playing in festivities ('te hooghetiden'). This combination of signalling and entertaining functions fulfilled by the waits was to last, in Bruges as in many other towns, well into the eighteenth century. From as early as 1331, and regularly thereafter, four *wachters* received annual salaries, wore liveries, and were socially equated with city officials and clerks of the magistrate.

An apparently different group of *ministruelen* accompanied the civic militia on military expeditions, such as those in 1302 (the battle of the 'Golden Spurs' at Courtrai, a glorious victory of the Flemish cities against the French army) and in 1336/7 (the sea-battle of Sluis, won by Edward III of England against the French, with Flemish support). In the latter expedition, three 'trompers ende blasers' were allocated to the company of the Bruges crossbowmen (*scotters*), and another three to the captains of the urban militia (*hoofdmannen van den poorters*). This basic performance unit consisted of trumpets and shawms. Each musician received a salary of 2s 8d per day. They travelled on wagons or on horseback, and served individual battalions, such as the crossbowmen, in small groups of one or two trumpeters and two to four pipers. In the war between Bruges and the duke of Burgundy in 1436–37, trumpeters were also paid as individuals with different itineraries, probably in the function of messengers. They received no less than 12s per day each. These trumpeters were representatives of the city, and their instruments were decorated with banners of the city's coat of arms. They played straight *trompettes de guerre*, often of silver, which were normally owned by the captains of the militia or the crossbowmen. This type of instrument was, therefore, not restricted to royal or ducal armies, but was used also by the urban middle class for representative purposes. Trumpeters accompanied civic legations and welcomed prominent visitors on horseback outside the city gates. When a prominent guest, with his retinue, proceeded through the streets, a city trumpeter or wait had to herald the arrival and to contain the crowd, giving signals to withdraw into the side streets ('achter strate te vertrekkene'). Trumpeters and pipers also gave signals to clear the way for processions, sometimes in co-operation with the urban police (*scarewetters*), who had to make space for scenic performances. A trumpeter was usually assigned to the troup of *roecaproenen* (red coats), another special military unit of the town.

Public entertainment

The same men who fulfilled such 'signal' and military functions were also able to play music for entertainment. As early as 1331/2, the four city waits Fierkin de Trompere, Coppin Zeghaerd, Hannekin van der Porte and Jan van der Piete joined with four other musicians to play for a courtly banquet in the castle of Male on trumpets, organs and fiddles – a mixture or rather alternation of loud and soft music, *haute* and *basse musique*.

The main public occasion for music was the annual procession of the Holy Blood (3 May), and the May Fair, which lasted fifteen or eighteen days from the beginning of May until Whit–Sunday. The procession on 3 May was instituted in 1305 or earlier; it was accompanied by trumpeters from 1315 at the latest.[3] Processions, carried out mainly by the religious orders, were held on almost every day of the May Fair in the mid-fourteenth century. On three specified days, the town square was especially busy with merchants, as buying and selling was then tax-free. On these days ('vrije tooghedaghen'), the magistrate entertained the crowd with music from the belfry, or from the corner of the old town hall, where a special estrade for the minstrels was built in 1466/7. During the reign of Philip the Bold (1384–1404), the city also paid for the processional music played by the city waits and many additional minstrels who accompanied the two guilds of crossbowmen and the six city captains in the great procession on 3 May. Each captain, representing one of the town's districts, had his own group of two trumpets and one shawm. The latter instrument is often referred to as 'riethoorn' or 'rietpijpe', its player as 'piper'. It was thus not a horn, but a curved reedcap instrument, also occasionally called 'kromme scalmeye' – a forerunner of the Renaissance crumhorn.[4] The eighteen minstrels for the city captains were sometimes hired from elsewhere. Between 1391 and 1407, reference is made in the city accounts to minstrels from Sluis, Eeklo and Ghent; from the service of the lords of Ghistel, Halewyn and Huutkerke; of the count of Namur and Saint-Pol and the duke of Britanny. From c.1409, however, the number of players for the captains was reduced to a total of two trumpeters and one piper, all from Bruges itself.

The musicians who played for the district captains and the crossbowmen in the procession must have served them also in war. One wonders how much the music differed on either occasion. The instruments were the same – they were owned by the captains and the crossbowmen – and the march movement of the procession, with all the banners and crossbows, may have recalled military advances on the battlefield.

The *ommegang* of the Holy Blood offered opportunities for more relaxed music-making, too. During the great procession, a banquet was normally given to prominent visitors or prelates in the hospital of St Julian or private houses, where minstrels had to entertain. At one such banquet in 1391, given by the receiver-general of Flanders, Pieter Adornes, several 'zanghers ende vedelaers' performed. In 1393, a 'tumelare' (i.e. *thymelicus*, minstrel) from England and other 'diversen zanghers ende menestruelen' were rewarded after the banquet.

Foreign and court minstrels

When Edward III of England campaigned in Flanders at the beginning of the Anglo-French war, the city made gifts to his minstrels almost every year between 1341 and 1347. In 1344 the English minstrels are specified as those of the royal sailors ('sconinx sciplieden'). Minstrels from ships are also mentioned in the city accounts of 1404 and of 1445/ 6 (the latter were those of the Florentine galleys).[5] The city often paid for the lodgings of the foreign musicians, for example in 1341, when English minstrels were put up together with soldiers and squires from Brabant and Germany. Minstrels came in the retinue, or as messengers, of Count Heinrich of Holstein (1369/70), of the bishop of Cologne (1371), of Count William of Namur (1388/9), of the duchess of Cleves (1429/30), of the towns of Arras (1425), Lille (1434) and Valenciennes (1455/6). In 1447, Duke Philip the Good rewarded four trumpeters of the city of Florence who had played for him in Bruges.[6] Players of soft instruments were also welcome in the town: the city rewarded André Dester, a gitternist of Queen Philippa of England, who was himself from Bruges, in 1363;[7] Parrin Thierry, the harper of the count of Charolais, in 1446/7; Mahienet, the lutenist of the 'wife and children of the chancellor of Flanders', in 1473/4; and two lutenists of Maximilian of Habsburg, in 1485/6.[8]

The city also subsidised the 'minstrels' schools'. These were large gatherings of musicians from different towns and countries, held annually in Lent in several towns of Flanders.[9] They were organised by the profession itself, in order to exchange ideas and new skills between singers and instrumentalists, performers and composers. In the fourteenth century, musicians from Aragon and Navarra visited the schools in Flanders and Germany, and probably vice versa. The famous Jacomí Sentluc (Senleches) from Aragon attended the school in Flanders at least in 1378/9. In 1318, the city subsidised the school which was held behind the Carmelite convent;[10] but there are no other references to such subsidies in the later city accounts, probably because they were taken over by other bodies. The tradition of the minstrels' schools seems to have died out rather soon in Bruges, where many other opportunities for meetings of local and foreign minstrels existed.

Some of the most splendid gatherings took place during the peace negotiations between France and England, held in Bruges in 1375 and 1376. The accounts of Duke Philip the Bold alone (researched by Craig Wright)[11] reveal enormous expenditures on music, although he was at the time neither the ruler of Flanders nor a main negotiating party. He rewarded the minstrels of the king of England, King Henry of Castile, Duke Albert of Bavaria, the counts of Namur and Blois, the king of Scotland, Count Louis of Flanders and the duke of Brabant. There were also gifts to minstrels who sang for Duke Philip, to players of gitterns, harps and the 'eschiquier', to Philip's harper Gauthier 'l'Anglois', to 'maistre Jean, narcarin du duc de Lencastre', to the minstrels of Duke Philip who went to England with the duke of Lancaster, to two children 'ménestriers de bouche', to Claux, the *tambourin* of the count of Flanders, and – interestingly – to a 'faiseur de rondeaux demeurant à Bruges'. Was he a minstrel, a clergyman or perhaps one of the amateur poets who contributed monophonic songs to the 'Gruuthuse manuscript' of the 1390s (see p. 108)? Obviously, new sacred and secular music must have been created during these magnificent feasts; some of it may have been taken abroad by foreign musicians, for example the motet '*Rex Karole*' (see p. 103). The musical exchanges between Bruges and England may account for the transfer of some French *Ars Nova* works to England during this period. Also in the fifteenth century, English prelates and nobles regularly visited the town: we know of visits of the bishops of London and Salisbury, of

Henry Beaufort, bishop of Winchester, and many others, who often came for the May festivals and the Holy Blood procession.[12] Visitors from the Mediterranean area were also numerous, and musicians in their retinue may have collected music in Bruges. A case in point may be that of Cardinal Niccolò Albergati of Bologna, who attended the May festivals in 1432[13] and was then portrayed by Jan van Eyck.

The minstrels of the Burgundian court were almost at home in Bruges. The city paid them a regular New Year's gift of £72 from 1413, because they played so often in the town.[14] As early as 1315, a minstrel of Count Lodewijk of Flanders ('Coppin den spelman') had been rewarded by the city with 30s. Many musicians from Bruges entered the service of the counts and dukes, either for occasional performances elsewhere, or more permanently. Louis de Male awarded pensions, in 1356, to the Bruges minstrels Hannekin Pipen and Loenkin Pipen, and to a certain Nicholas de Hampon (Hampton?).[15] Guillaume de Hucorgne and Guillaume de Strivere, minstrels of Philip the Bold, were given pensions in Bruges in 1404; a certain 'Stroman, minstrel of my lord the duke of Bourbon' played for Philip the Bold in Bruges in 1390;[16] he must be the Willem Stromanne who performed with others for the guild of the 'young' crossbowmen in the Holy Blood procession of 1393. Josse du Jardin, nicknamed 'de pipere' was at the court of Philip the Bold[17] from the early 1380s until 1404, when he returned to Flanders. He and his companions participated in the Bruges procession of 1399 as 'pipers of my lord of Ghistel', and Josse himself played in the procession of 1425. His personal medallion has survived, and it shows what must have been his main instrument, the bagpipe. Later, we encounter a certain Pieter le Brun, son of Nicholas, in the Burgundian service in 1441, who may be identical with a city minstrel mentioned in 1475. Names of ducal musicians such as Pavillon, Willemart and Buekel point strongly to musical families of Bruges.

Pageants, jousting and dancing

The cultural relationships between the court of Burgundy and the city of Bruges were clearly reciprocal. This is true with regard not only to personnel, but also to sponsorship of the arts. Whenever the rulers paid a stately visit to one of their towns, it was the duty of the town, not of the ruler, to provide the ceremonial framework. In Bruges, the city fathers hired minstrels locally and from elsewhere for stately visits, or they paid the court musicians for their services on the occasion. The minstrels had to play on top of the city gate through which the visitors entered, in the *burg*, in the market square or in front of the ducal palace. When Philip the Bold first visited Bruges in 1369, the city paid £12 16s to the ducal minstrels and £15 to those of the town, who included trumpeters. At a visit of King Charles VI of France in 1387, £48 was paid to the royal minstrels. At the first visit of Marguerite de Male as new duchess on 20 July 1389, the ceremonies included performances by 23 trumpeters and pipers in the market square; the pipers of the duchess received extra gifts from the magistrate. There is a long list of such public visits (*inkomsten*) throughout the fifteenth century and into the time of Charles V of Habsburg; the procedures were all similar. Although the number of players varied from four to over a hundred, there was always a mixture of natural trumpets, often of silver and decorated with banners, of minstrels' trumpets (slide trumpets) and of various instruments of the shawm family. In 1405 (visit of John the Fearless) the account books distinguish between six pipers, four 'trompers' and two 'trompetten'. The 'riethoorn' is mentioned, for example, in 1408 and 1413. When Philip the Good returned from his journey to Germany in 1455, together with the newly-wed Charles of Charolais and Isabelle de Bourbon, the instruments used to welcome them are referred to as 'trompetten ende claroenen' – long and short natural trumpets. In one of the biggest of these events, the entry of Philip the Good and Isabella of Portugal following their wedding in Sluis on 8 January 1430, contemporary chroniclers disagree as to whether the number of trumpets alone was 120 or 164. They also mention 'joueurs d'orgues, harpes et aultres instrumens'. The city wait Jan van der Woestine and his companions had to play from the old town hall during the whole of the festivities on 10 January. Probably the soft instruments were employed in connection with 'living pictures', as was the case in 1440 (see below). On 4 April 1457, Duke Philip had the Dauphin Louis in his train, and French and Flemish minstrels played together – some of them, according to Chastellain, 'all night'.[18]

Bruges took enormous pride in the staging of ceremonies and had its own historiographers to record them. It was felt necessary to outdo the rivalling towns in their efforts to celebrate a visiting ruler, and spies were sent to other places to report what had been done there. In 1494/5, the city paid Aliamus de Groote and Jooris Jooris (significantly, two members of the *rederijkerskamer* of the Holy Ghost) for a trip to Antwerp to take a written record of the pageants given to Maximilian of Habsburg.[19] After the 'tryumphante et sollemnelle entrée' of the young Charles V as the new King of the Romans in Bruges on 18 April 1515, an exhaustive report was printed with many woodcuts showing the pageants and the musicians.[20]

The pageants for the 'blijde inkomst' (happy entry) of Philip the Good into Bruges in 1440 may be described in more detail, on the basis of a contemporary manuscript chronicle.[21] It was a festivity of political significance: the citizens had rebelled against the duke and the nobility in an attempt to defend their privileges in 1436–37. In the latter year, the ducal fieldmarshal and a whole battalion had been killed in an uprising in the streets of the town. The ensuing war led to the defeat of the city; the magistrate had to beg for mercy and to endow a solemn requiem for the fieldmarshal, Count Jean Villiers de l'Isle-Adam, and his companions.[22] In his first visit after these events, on 11 December 1440, the duke confirmed his pardon to the city. In his train were the duchess and many members of the court, but most importantly Duke Charles of Orléans, whom Philip the Good had bought free, in 1439, from his long English captivity.

When the visitors arrived outside the Holy Cross gate, all the city notables − mayors, captains, magistrate, bailiff, clerks, etc., 1300 people altogether, bare-foot and bare-headed − went to meet them in a solemn procession. They all knelt down before the duke and presented him with the keys of the town. They were joined by the officers of the craft guilds, the order of the Beguines in procession with relics, three abbots and hundreds of foreign merchants who stood by in well-ordered parade. As soon as the duke had pronounced the pardon, everyone sang the Te Deum, and the procession entered the town through the gate, on which 80 trumpeters and 6 *claroenen* played. (They then left by a side street to re-assemble in other places for the next welcoming fanfares.) All church bells were sounded throughout the whole procession; the houses along the road were decorated with ducal and city banners. The pageants were among the most elaborate Bruges had ever seen. At every corner along the street up to the *burg*, there was a 'living picture', prepared by the town's musical and dramatic specialists. All of them were, of course, symbolical. The first one, on the gate, was a green wood with the figure of St John the Baptist and the inscription 'Ecce vox clamantis in deserto: parate viam domino'. Next to this, a stage displayed the 'hystoire' of St Job, with his words 'Dominus dedit dominus abstulit domino placuit ita factum est', accompanied by two harpers. At the first street-corner four prophets sat on a stage, holding scrolls (inscription 'Hec est dies quam fecit dominus . . .') and singing each time a group of nobles stopped in front of them. Near the St Obrecht hospital, the story of Abraham and Isaac with the angel was displayed; three minstrels performed on harp, lute and dulcian. Further on, another platform with prophets as before. The 'Tree of Jesse' followed: Jesse in bed, with a tree growing from his body, and many small children in white dresses on the branches. At the next corner, another stage with four singing prophets, acted by the 'beste zanghers van der kercke'. The next picture showed the story of Esther, with living people who 'stood motionless as if they were a picture'; three minstrels performed on organ, harp and lute. A similar stage with the story of Esther followed − the symbolic meaning of this was the intercession of the duchess Isabella for 'her' people − accompanied by harp, lute and dulcian. The same instruments were used on the next stage with St Mary Magdalene ('Dimittuntur tibi peccata multa . . .'), also of living persons who 'stood in countenance as if they were a picture'. Next to the Dominican convent, an angel announced the birth of Christ to the shepherds, singing from the top of the building, and accompanied by lute, harp and dulcian. The friars also provided a story of Our Lady and St Dominic, this time with lute, harp and organ. Zacheus in the Tree followed, particularly fitting in its symbolic content, and then a large podium with the City of Jerusalem – symbolizing Bruges – all painted. King David played the harp, and the musicians around him had organs, lutes, harps and dulcians; the girls of Jerusalem welcomed the duke with the cry 'Noel! Noel!'. Further on, there were four interrelated pictures showing the seven deeds of mercy, with many instruments. The gate of the *burg* was decorated with the story of Joachim and Anna, with many children sitting on the gate, singing and playing on organs, harps, lutes, as a symbol of the Immaculate Conception: the pardon of the duke had been given on 8 December. In the *burg* there was a stone pillar and a castle, with the statue of a nude woman who squirted wine from her breasts. In front of the city prison, the liberation of St Peter from prison was shown, referring to the duke of Orléans. In the market square there were many stages and living pictures including statues giving milk and wine, and six little stages with children who sang all the time while the train crossed the square. Finally, in front of, and above the palace gate, there were several structures with living pictures, for example of the Transfiguration, with music, or of a wild man on a camel in Saracen dress. On the gate itself, many minstrels trumpeted to the sound of the church bells for the whole time while the train entered the palace, that is, from two to five o'clock in the afternoon.

We owe the description of these pageants to a city chronicler, almost certainly a member of the organising committee itself. His report seems to have been written on the basis of a program which had been produced beforehand, and may therefore be more systematic and comprehensive than accurate in detail. A court chronicler,[23] for instance, is much shorter, but seems to remember, as an eye-witness, some things that actually happened but are not included in the city chronicle. He quotes the use of a psaltery in the living picture of the City of Jerusalem (which he identifies with the city of Bruges), and he combines minstrels' trumpets, harps and lutes in several instances.

The festivities continued in the evening of 11 December and on the following days with public dancing, with other living pictures in the streets, made by the inhabitants in a prize-winning competition, with illumination, music (pipers and 'trompers'), two great balls – one in the palace and one in the town hall – and several jousting tournaments in

the market square. Most amazingly, the whole series of pageants is said
to have been exactly repeated for Charles of Charolais when he visited
the town two months later. The list of expenses of the city for all these
ceremonies would fill a separate publication.

The artists who contributed to these events are unknown.[24] It is
possible that Jan van Eyck was involved in his role as an almost official
city painter; the theatre specialists will have included some of the
rhetoricians of the Holy Ghost. The singing prophets, twelve of them
altogether, and the singing children, were clerks and choirboys of St
Donatian's, no doubt.

On some of the later occasions, the names of organisers of the
pageants are known.[25] It is no surprise that several of these were also
members of music-loving confraternities such as the 'Dry Tree' or 'Our
Lady of the Snow'. During the royal visit of the fugitive Margaret of
Anjou, queen of Henry VI, in 1463, living pictures were provided by
Colaert Dault, Janne Tsolle, Pieter van Bouchoute, Anthuenis Damast
and Petrus Christus, all leading members of the 'Dry Tree'; the last-
named constructed a 'Tree of Jesse' of metal in the street, together with
another professional artist, Pieter Nachtegale. Other pictures were the
'Judgment of Paris' with Venus, Pallas and Juno, and a castle of
'Vrauw Venus' built upon the river. The former was the work of the
famous rhetorician Anthuenis de Roovere, the latter of the businessman
Colaert Dault. Christus and Nachtegale also built a 'City of Jerusalem'
which was traditional, but the preference given to classical *histoires* is
remarkable. For the *inkomst* of Duke Charles the Bold on 9 April 1468,
Anthuenis de Roovere and the 'Dry Tree' members Olivier d'Haze and
Anselmo Adornes organised pageants and other festivities; Charles's
majordomo Olivier de la Marche (also a member of the 'Dry Tree') and
de Roovere were the leading spirits in the wedding festivities of
Margaret of York in July 1468 (see p. 98 f.).

Besides such spectacular single events, the city of Bruges staged
festive ceremonies almost every year to coincide with the regular visits
of the court – between 1440 and 1467 usually three times a year – and
with the occasions offered by the calendar: carnival time and the May
festival. Many of the celebrations were banquets, balls, jousts and
tourneys. The jousting was organised by the noble 'Society of the White
Bear' whose leaders were often the lords of Gruuthuse and Ghistel.
These large gatherings attracted the nobility from far and wide, but
also the townsfolk and, of course, many musicians. Everyone was under
the spell of chivalry: the city put together its own group of combatants
for the big tourneys (*steicspele*), mainly from the guilds of crossbowmen
and archers. The tourneys with 100 and more men required a
correspondingly large number of trumpeters and other minstrels; on
one occasion (the visit of the Dauphin on 1 May 1457), the magistrate

paid £24 to the minstrels alone. They had to welcome the participants in the jousting from the city gates, and also to herald each combat in the market square. Softer music accompanied the festivals, too: in 1407, a gratuity was given to a 'scoonincx dichtere', i.e. to a singer-poet in the service of the 'king' of the 'Society of the White Bear'. The 'Gruuthuse manuscript' of Flemish songs and poems (see p. 108) is partly related to the jousts on Shrove Tuesday 1392 under Jean de Gruuthuse as 'king' of the 'White Bear' society. Flemish songs and French rondeaux were probably recited at the banquets following the tournaments, before a large audience. It is not only in the secluded atmosphere of princely chambers that secular songs were performed, but also in places like the great reception room of the town hall, where the magistrate covered all expenses, including the music.

Another civic and aristocratic festival with music was the annual target shooting of the 'parrot', with crossbows and longbows. It was the main annual feast of the crossbowmen and archers, and took place on Trinity Sunday, in the *burg* or outside the Holy Cross gate. Music was provided by trumpets and shawms, on instruments belonging to these guilds themselves. Originally a citizens' sport, the 'parrot' shooting became more and more gentrified in the fifteenth century, when the 'White Bear' society took over its organisation. Maximilian of Habsburg attended several contests in Bruges.

The famous dancing festivities of the Burgundian court, which often took place in connection with jousting tournaments, were also arranged partly by the city.[26] Besides the 'open' ball in the palace, to which the duke or the count of Charolais invited the women of the town, there were balls in the reception room of the new town hall in the *burg*. This room had a balcony for the musicians, of just the kind illustrated in many Burgundian manuscripts, which was called 'paradisekin' ('little paradise').[27] According to the miniatures, three players were normally active at a time, but a city payment of 1434 to 'two pairs' of minstrels shows that there were four of them, so that each player could have a break, in turn. These minstrels of the city – not to be confused with the courtly dancing master on the ballroom floor with flute and tabor – played dance music from their own repertory. Its style must have been quite distinct from that of other festal music; different metres had also to be observed from the slow, serious *basse danse*, the merry round and the pantomimic morris dance, which was executed by specialist dancers. The largest surviving collection of fifteenth-century *basses danses*, a manuscript which once belonged to Margaret of Austria, may be said to reflect the dance repertory of Bruges (see p. 115). The monophonic tunes were performed with extemporised or, at least, non-written counterpoint. The basic tune was treated like a cantus firmus in notes of equal length; each note corresponded to one step of the *basse danse.*[28] This style has influenced the polyphonic works of masters such as Obrecht; several others used dance tunes as cantus firmi in sacred music. Binchois's chanson *Filles à marier* uses a popular tune as cantus firmus, and has as its text a dance-song which addresses a civic audience – the girls of the town.[29]

The invitation of the local women and girls to the balls was a special ceremony, paid for by the city. A herald and several pipers went around the town to invite the women to the ball in the palace; in 1394, the pipers received a total of £48 'for going to court with the women on the occasion of the duke's masked ball, the evening after the jousting'. Balls on Shrove Tuesday were normally masked balls (*mommeries*). For one of these in 1436, the duke paid for the minstrels and their liveries, for torches, 'faux visages' and the material used for the disguises. For a ball given by Duke John in 1406, it was the city which spent £120 on wine, mead, fruit, sweets, candle-light, doorkeepers and other personnel, including minstrels. Similar expenses amounted to £206 in 1450 at the first *mommerie* of Charles of Charolais. These balls must have been regarded as important opportunities for fraternisation between the court and the town – with music as a powerful messenger.

With similar considerations in mind, the city fathers used music and related entertainments regularly for the reception of ambassadors and trade delegations. The visitors would be offered at least one great banquet in the town hall, at which musicians and fools entertained. Masses were celebrated on such occasions as well; they were said by mendicant friars in the town hall itself, which had a chapel. It is probably for such purposes that the old town hall under the belfry had an organ. This was built in 1299 by a 'Walterus orghelmakere'; in 1300, a Petrus de Dam played it.

The earliest public concerts

The expenses of the city for military, ceremonial and processional music reached their peak in the decades around 1400. During the following century, however, the emphasis shifted toward the use of music for the mere sake of listening – a typical development, as the emancipation of individual arts from previously ancillary functions in a homogeneous society often accompanies the political and economical decline of these societies. In Bruges, this was a slow process, originating with such musical entertainments as those given by the city waits on the day of the Holy Blood procession and on the free-market days. These 'serenades' still went together with collective activities. But in addition to them, special performances arose in the later fifteenth century to which people went purely to listen to music. The city government sponsored these performances in its desire to keep the citizens in a good

mood, and to preserve the sympathies of the rulers and foreign merchants, against the gloomy economical background. From 1480, the
chapter of St Donatian's was paid £2 daily for performances of the *lof* or
Salve in the church (see p. 39). These took place immediately after
compline, but were not religious services in the strict sense. From May
1483, the city then began to pay its minstrels for giving an instrumental
Salve performance after the singing on each of the free-market days; the
chapter of St Donatian's agreed on 16 April 1483 that the 'tubicentes et
mimi' were allowed to play after the 'laudes Beate Marie' – in the
church.[30] Four, and later five, city minstrels received £1 each for the
instrumental *Salve* concerts on every free-market day; for the traditional
serenades in the market square which took place on the same days,
each player got £2. The serenades were regarded as the harder work,
and probably lasted longer; but the *Salve* concerts included mensural
polyphony: they were, indeed, deliberately juxtaposed with the polyphonic *Salve* singing of the succentor and the choirboys. Some 'motets'
were expressly composed, in 1484/5, by Nicasius de Brauwere, the succentor of St Saviour's, for the *Salve* concerts of the minstrels.[31] We may
speculate that the repertory of these concerts focussed on sacred tunes
of wide popularity, such as the *Salve regina* itself, but that it also comprised polyphony over well-known secular tunes as cantus firmi. The
style of these pieces may have reflected improvisatory practices known
to the performers from their engagements in balls and other festivities.[32]
I suggest that some of the pieces heard in the *Salve* concerts actually
survive among the works of Obrecht (see p. 144 f.). The minstrels played
to an audience which was familiar with their art from other occasions,
such as the feasts of confraternities, but which also knew the most
advanced sacred polyphony of the time. Admittance to the concerts
seems to have been free, so that this art now also reached the less privileged people. Not all of the salaried minstrels of the city had specialised
in polyphonic playing: the city trumpeter Dieric van Esschen, for
example, continued to occur on the payrolls only in connection with
ceremonial music and signals of the traditional kind.

Het Boeck

Various functions and skills of Bruges minstrels are mentioned in an
anonymous city chronicle[33] for the years 1477 to 1491. The references to
music are valuable, although clearly not written by a specialist. His
work reports, under 1 January 1483, the proclamation of the marriage
between Maximilian's daughter Margaret and the Dauphin (Charles
VIII): '. . . the town hall was decorated with tapestries . . . the alder-
men of the city were assembled in front of it . . . the city minstrels stood
by and the great bell of the belfry was tolled. At each stroke of the bell,

the minstrels played, interrupted by the sound of two 'trompetten' and a trumpet with the banner of the city'. On 1 July 1486, the rebuilt top storey of the belfry was inaugurated; a statue of St Michael had been placed on top of it. 'From the upper storey of the belfry, the minstrels of the town played a motet fine and merry, as is the custom, in honour of God and the holy angel St Michael.' After Maximilian had been imprisoned by the citizens in 1488, a truce was celebrated on 5 April 1488. In front of the town hall 'the city minstrels stood in their usual place for such performances, and they played in honour of Our Lady *Ave regina celorum*, as well as *Salve regina*, and several other pieces of music'. When Maximilian had to sign his oath to the privileges of Bruges on 16 May 1488, a large platform had been erected in the market square, 'and there was sung *Te Deum laudamus* in a solemn, exquisite and excellent manner, and the minstrels of the town stood in the square in their liveries, playing *Ave regina celorum*, followed by several other musical songs' ('liedekins van muzycke'). The following day, the minstrels were again in the square and played 'sweet and beautiful music, and money was thrown among the crowd'. At a general procession on 7 April 1489, prominent guests were assembled at the window of the town hall, and 'in another window above, the city minstrels played in honour of God and Our Lady *Ave regina celorum*'. Later on, the procession entered St Donatian's, where the Te Deum was sung with organ. Count Engelbert of Nassau celebrated the Treaty of Tours in Bruges on 6 December 1490: ' . . . on the town hall were the minstrels of the town, who played *Ave regina celorum*, first on this side [of the belfry], and then on the other, and all church bells were pealed.' A triumph for Emperor Frederick on 2 January 1491 was accompanied by two silver trumpets and two clarions, among other music. 'In the Spaniards' street, the merchants from Spain had provided two barrels of wine, from which everyone was allowed to drink freely, as long as it lasted. They had also made a big fire of large and heavy logs of oak, and they had hired two minstrels, one *tullul* and one shawm, to make the people dance'. Music and musicians must have been popular in Bruges.

We have to restore a balance, however: the years from 1477 to 1491 were among the darkest in the history of Bruges, and were chosen by the chronicler for that reason. He reports more crimes and executions than festivities. One of the delinquents was a musician 'called Anthuenis, and he was known as a soothsayer, who used to play the bagpipes, and he was put to death for things that are better not reported' – black magic, perhaps. On 27 April 1484, two thieves were executed, and one of them had been a choirboy of St Donatian's.

Conditions of life

The amazing diversity of conditions under which musicians lived was, at the same time, perhaps the one thing they all had in common. The 'wheels of Fortune' seemed to turn faster for musicians – had they not always been fond of the symbol? Notices about the various fortunes of a musician are sometimes so contradictory between themselves that they do not seem to fit one and the same biography. One example concerns Jean Carbonnier (Carbonerii), who was a choirboy of the Burgundian chapel from 1406 to 1412, *valet de chambre* from 1415, secretary and messenger to Philip the Good in 1424 and secretary to Henry VI of England in 1431.[34] He was also a composer and is mentioned in Binchois's motet *Nove cantum melodie* of 1431. A close colleague of his was Cardinet de Crepon, who controlled the gaming tables of Ypres; a quittance, signed by both Carbonnier and Crepon – in this context? – is dated 1 July 1419.[35] In 1418/9, a messenger of the duke brought sealed letters to Bruges, which concerned the lottery in the town; city accounts call him 'Janne Coolman, mijns heeren pipre'[36] – 'Coolman' is the precise Flemish translation of 'Carbonnier'. There was, however, also a Johannes Carbonerii who held a canonicate of St Donatian's from 1417 to 1438, when he was succeeded in the same benefice by the court singer Estienne Petault, and a priest named Johannes Carbonerii is mentioned in court records of 1419. Janne Coolman, on the other hand, is mentioned as a ducal messenger in Alost 1405 and Oudenaarde 1410,[37] but no Coolman ('piper' or other minstrel) occurs in court records of that time, while Carbonnier is often mentioned. Even if two or three different people are involved – John the Fearless employed two musicians with the same name at the same time as messengers, one a minstrel, the other a clergyman. One of them apparently drew profit from gambling.

Another example concerns the blind organist Jean Fernandes who worked at St Donatian's in 1482 (see p. 32). Tinctoris heard him and his blind brother Carolus in Bruges as virtuosi on the vielle, and he reports that they were also learned men.[38] Carolus and Johannes Fernandes were, indeed, professors of the University of Paris;[39] Trithemius calls Johannes 'virum . . . doctissimum, Philosophum, Oratorem et Poetam celeberrimum, Regis musicum' – Carolus was also a *musicus regius* in 1487, and the two brothers were rectors of the University in 1485. Johannes, whose name occurs (from 1478) in the university records as 'Johannes Citharoedi' or 'Le Herpeur', retired from his chair of ethics in 1491 and died in 1496. A blind player of vielle, lute and other *bas instrumens* – this is exactly the condition of Jean Ferrandes, who with his blind companion Jean Cordoval was employed by the Burgundian court from 1433 until at least 1456; the two men astonished the court, and all Europe, with their virtuosity. Martin le Franc dedicated to them some famous lines, in which he makes Dufay and Binchois blush with envy of the blind men.[40] Tinctoris calls Johannes and Carolus 'natione Flamingos', while the university records speak of Johannes once as 'Brugensis', once as 'Normannus'. The blind men of the Burgundian court were Castilians – but Johannes's country of origin was perhaps no longer known after he had lived so long in the north. Jean Ferrandes could, as a minstrel, have started his career early in life, with Cordoval as a senior partner; later, he associated himself with his own blind brother Carolus. Is such a career at all imaginable? The life of such musicians is itself a vision, which the eye of the historian is reluctant to confirm.

Stable and harmonious partnerships were vital for minstrels; most forms of music required a group of individuals who had formed a common practice together. The usual trio of the city waits or of the military musicians must have functioned in a strict distribution of roles and tasks, whether they played in alternation, in unison or poly-phonically. Collective extemporising needs a common internal and external rhythm. The minstrels did not perform from written music – but even those musicians who did, the succentor and the choirboys of the church, used to touch each other's shoulders to communicate rhythm, as can be seen in contemporary pictures.

The four or five city minstrels of Bruges were a very close group of men who were responsible for each other. From the time when they acquired the right of an annual pension (1336), they held an official and highly-paid position (the salary around 1467–1475 was £72 per annum), for which they had to take an oath of allegiance to the city. They had to guarantee for their own new colleagues, whom they chose themselves, often from far away and after long searches. The city minstrel Anthuenis Pavillon travelled, in 1479/80, to Namur, Utrecht and Cologne (all at the city's expense) to find a replacement for his own deceased brother Gillis. Gillis Pavillon had taken the oath in 1456, at the same time as the brothers Gillis and Pieter de Donckere. These city musicians were also admitted to full citizenship – a privilege which by no means all working people in Bruges possessed.

All the minstrels in the town were members of the same guild; the membership fee was 36s a year from 1431, and only the paying members were allowed to work as minstrels in Bruges.[41] This system of the 'closed shop', although normal with medieval guilds, ran almost to absurdity in 1466, when the barber Jean Basin was charged with having encouraged his little nephew of eleven, Jan Huussin, to play instruments at public feasts and masked balls: Jan was neither a citizen nor a member of the guild! The uncle pointed out that this was impossible because the nephew had not yet reached the minimum age for membership, fifteen. It was agreed in the end that Basin should pay the membership fee for the musical lad and should make him enter the guild as soon as he was old enough. This probably also satisfied Jan Huussin's other two uncles, the musicians Adrien and Pierre Basin.

Family bonds inside the profession were of even higher practical value for music than for other trades. The musical practice often extended to women. Many minstrels were married to a singer or dancer or instrumentalist with whom they could perform together; the children learned the craft at home. Musical dynasties flourished in Bruges: there were the families van den Piete – city minstrels from *c.*1330 to *c.*1450; de Buus – cantors, organists and organ-builders from *c.*1480; the minstrel families Pavillon, Willemart, van der Schuere, and many others. The families supported each other: Gillis Pavillon became, in 1466, the tutor of the young children of his deceased colleague Nicasius Willemart.

The minstrels of Bruges also formed a confraternity with a chapel. This tradition goes back to the thirteenth century, when they held common pilgrimages to the Holy Candle of Arras; the city subsidised these pilgrimages from 1292 at the latest. (In this context, we find the earliest record of a named Bruges minstrel: 'Pimpernel'.) In the four-teenth century, the minstrels had their chapel in St Basil's – one of the most respected locations in the town, where the city clerks also had their chapel. City clerks and minstrels held their annual secular feasts on the same days – the three 'verzwoeren maendaghe' (see p. 48), on which they held publicly subsidised banquets and processions.[42] In 1421, they started to build their own chapel, which still stands near the Wulfhagen bridge. This 'speelliedenkapel' once contained a fresco of the *Volto Santo* of Lucca – identified in popular tradition with a spurious St Wilgefortis or St Kümmernis, a bearded female saint who had been adopted as patroness by the minstrels.[43] The confraternity of the minstrels continued to exist in Bruges until 1795.

Musical instruction and instruments

The city of Bruges employed only four, later five musicians as official 'menestruelen van der stede' – all the others had to find day-to-day work. It was to the benefit of all minstrels in Bruges, however, that the city also subsidised musical instruction on a relatively large scale. From 1482 to 1489, at least, various payments are recorded to Adriaen Willemart and Anthuenis Pavillon for teaching several children to play the flute, the trumpet and probably other instruments, which seem to have been bought for them at the expense of the magistrate. The children lived in the houses of their teachers.

Most of the musical instruction must have been received within the families, however. A witness to this is the *Livre des mestiers de Bruges* of *c.*1370, one of the loveliest documents on life in the late medieval town.[44] It is itself an educational tool, being written by a Bruges schoolmaster for the education of children in the two languages, French and Flemish. It enumerates all things noteworthy in the environment synoptically in both languages, and had to be memorised by the children. The middle part of this 'poem' follows the alphabet, each letter being dedicated to a different craft. The stanza under 'T' reads:

Tierris, le jougleur	Tierrin, de gokelare,
et ses fieus, li tromperes	ende sijn sone, de trompere,
ses fillastres, li viellerres,	zijn stiefkind, de vedelare,
et ses serouges, le ghisterneur,	ende sijn swagher, die ghitternere,
ont mout de boins	hebben vele goeder
instrument; il ont	instrument; si hebben
ghisternes, herpes,	ghitteernen, herpen,
salterions, orghenes,	salterien, orghelen,
rebebes, trompes, chiphonies,	rebeben, trompen, chiphonien,
chalemies, bombares,	scalemeyen, bombaren,
muses, fleutes, douchaines,	cornemusen, floyten, douchaïnen
et nacaires.	ende nacaren.

It is the only stanza which emphasises family bonds in a craft so strongly, and implies that this wide range of instruments could all be owned by the same musical clan. Although this is a humorous and ironical piece of literature, the children will have noticed the insinuation that no instrument of the time was too 'high' or too 'low' for being taken up by a young person. Slightly didactical is also the rough division between stringed and wind instruments. The loud percussion, the nakers, are effectively placed at the end. The 'chiphonie' (*organistrum,* hurdy-gurdy) looks a little out of place amongst the *haute musique* of trumpets and shawms; the author does not yet differentiate between the slide-trumpet of the minstrels and the natural instrument, the *trompette*.[45] But neither the selection nor the order of the instruments have to be taken too seriously.

To comment on every single instrument that was used in Bruges would be beyond the scope of this book. We do have to add a note, however, on the activity of instrument-makers, and the instrument trade. Of the many organ-builders[46] who were working in Bruges in the fifteenth century, some have been mentioned in connection with the churches. Two significant masters had come from Delft, Rogerus de Noorthende, who was active at St Donatian's in 1411, and Adriaen Pietersseune, who became a citizen in 1446. Organs were also exported from Bruges, for example in 1385/6 to Arras on behalf of the court – the court organist Jean Visée supervised the transport.[47] Bruges craftsmen had a reputation which they shared with those of Sluis, for brass instruments. The representative silver trumpets were produced by local silversmiths, such as Victor Wieric in 1398/9. In the 1480s, we know of one 'Victor de trompetmakere', a parishioner of Our Lady's, and of Eewoud Wittebrood, who supplied the city with trumpets for the minstrels. Five wind-players of Duke John the Fearless got new instruments made in Bruges in 1407 – four of these must have been shawms, for which local turners were responsible.[48] Pierre de Prost was a turner and merchant who supplied the court in 1407, 1423 and 1425; he made flutes, shawms, bombards and *douchaines*.[49] Loys Willay made four 'grans instrumens de ménestrels' (possibly bombards), four flutes and four *douchaines* for the Marquis of Ferrara in 1426, on behalf of Philip the Good. Parrin Thierry, the lutenist of Isabella of Portugal, made two lutes for Charles of Charolais in 1441 and 1442; he seems to have lived mainly in Bruges, as did Nicholas Rakeman, mentioned in 1449/50 as 'facteur de luths'.[50] It is not always clear whether the instruments in question were made in Bruges or only passed through the hands of merchants there; the latter is probably the case with the 36 'cournez d'Angleterre' and another 100 (!) 'cors Anglais' sold to the court in 1375 and 1377 by 'Gillequin l'Angloiz, demeurant a Bruges'.[51] They must have been hunting horns. Jacques van den Castiele despatched 24 'cors de chasse' from Bruges to Burgundy in 1415; he was a merchant and probably not an instrument-maker.[52] Instruments went through many hands in Bruges, like other luxury goods. In 1470, the Florentine merchant Girolamo Strozzi sold two flutes to the city minstrel Adriaen Willemart.[53] There was no need to import instruments from abroad, so we can assume that Strozzi owned the flutes only in the course of a business transaction. Bruges was a place where musical instruments were at all times available on the market, and the population was neither too poor nor too uneducated to use them.

The music of the court in Bruges

Despite the model studies of Jeanne Marix and Craig Wright, a new history of music at the Burgundian court could be written: a history focussed on the local, regional and dynastic traditions which altogether formed what modern historians have abstracted to the notion of a 'Burgundian' culture. It may be true that music and fine arts, liturgy and literature would not have flourished in Brussels, Antwerp, Ghent, Bruges and Lille as they did in the fifteenth century, had the respective territories not been under one rule; but it is also true that the Valois dukes of Burgundy, on acquisition of Flanders, Hainaut, Brabant, Holland and Luxembourg from their French– and Flemish-speaking predecessors, harvested what they had not sown.

Their own dynastic tradition was French; John the Fearless (1404–

1419) fostered a courtly culture not essentially different from that of his uncles Charles V of France and Jean de Berry, and Paris was the preferred theatre of his political and cultural ambitions. The interests of Philip the Good, however, centred on the Netherlands. The duchy of Burgundy itself with its ancient capital, Dijon, was on a periphery rarely visited by Philip or his court, and even more rarely by his son. There were also new political and cultural links – those with England, and even more those with the German speaking duchies of Cleves and Guelders. But it is the Flemish component – the dominant component, I believe – in the courtly culture of Philip the Good, which deserves a reassessment: not in the slightly chauvinist manner in which Besseler has attempted it, but with more sensitivity for its own regional traditions.

Henry Leland Clarke, in his enlightening article on the 'Musicians of the Northern Renaissance', is a little harsh in saying that 'the flamboyant and itinerant Burgundian court was no wellspring of serious education. The Duke of Burgundy was a consumer of musicians . . .,'[54] but he is right in stressing the importance of the great choir-schools of the North for the cultivation of vocal polyphony (he is unaware, of course, of St Donatian's in Bruges). Sacred polyphony – not to speak of plainsong and secular monody – was quantitatively much more important than the genre of the polyphonic chanson; motets, masses and other liturgical compositions, besides organ music, originated in many collegiate churches and cities, proud of their individual traditions. And even the great chanson composers of the age were nearly all clergymen (the one exception may be Heyne van Ghizeghem), who owed their education and most of their income to the churches of the Netherlands and Cambrai.

It may be suggested here that 'Burgundian court music' did exist over and above the partial traditions, but as a rather thin layer. It arose from what may be called the 'unifying patronage' of the dukes, who drew artists and intellectuals together from all their territories. The famous library of the dukes is perhaps a better example of this patronage than the chanson repertory around Binchois and Dufay, which has a more complex ancestry, and was largely composed at a time (the 1420s), when neither composer is recorded as having served the duke.

The Burgundian court was not only peripatetic, it was a multitude of princely and noble households, each with its own musicians, which were rarely in the same place at the same time. Isabella of Portugal, Charles of Charolais, the lords of Croy, the Count of Estampes – not to speak of the many other princes or the several bishops who were relatives of the duke – did not always reside with the duke. The ducal chapel itself included musicians who appear to have lived more permanently in the places where their prebends were. Philip the Good used the churchly benefices in his lands, for which he had a right of collation, in such a way that he had different servants to attend him wherever he went, besides the relatively small core of chaplains, sommeliers, valets de chambre, etc. who normally travelled with him.

In Bruges, Philip the Good had the right of collating thirty canonical prebends *de privilegio* at St Donatian's during his lifetime; only the holders of these benefices were *eo ipso* exempt from the duty of residence at the church. Among these, there were Binchois, Pierre Godefroy, Philippe Syron, Pierre Maillart and Mathieu de Bracle. Other musicians resided at St Donatian's whilst at the same time serving the ruler – for example Jean Ondanch, Estienne Petault, Gilles Joye, Pierre Basin and (after 1477) Pasquier Desprez and Jean Cordier. Others came and went with the duke or on their own. This guaranteed a continuous exchange of the musical repertory of the court with that of the town.

It is apparently not yet understood why choirboys do not appear in the rolls of the ducal chapel after *c.*1430. John the Fearless had an arrangement with Notre-Dame of Paris for the education of his choirboys, and later with St Peter's in Lille; but the choirboys travelled with the court quite often. As late as 1426 and 1428, the boys were led to Bruges each time to appear at court (once under the supervision of the canon of St Donatian's, Jean de Masures).[55] Even trips of this kind seem not to have taken place after 1430. The reason must be that Philip the Good had made two rich endowments, in 1425, to St Peter's in Lille and to the Sainte-Chapelle in Dijon for the support of four choirboys each[56] – a close imitation of the choral foundation of St Donatian's of 1421. In Dijon, the choirboys had to sing a Lady-mass with organ every Saturday, and the endowment for Lille seems to have been similar. The boys were, therefore, occupied all the time, and the court was effectively deprived of choirboys for parts of the year. This may account for some sacred works which are written for low voices only.

The notion of 'Burgundian court music' should be put to the test with sacred works. Much of the liturgical music by Binchois may have been written for the ducal chapel, especially if for low voices only. Binchois must have composed, however, also for local churches such as St Donatian's, St Waudru in Mons or St Vincent in Soignies. The genre of the ceremonial motet was surprisingly rare at the Burgundian court. The only straightforward example of this is Binchois's incompletely preserved motet *Nove cantum melodie*, written for the christening of the first son of Isabella of Portugal, Antoine, in Brussels on 18 January 1431.[57] The text has been used as a historical source, as it mentions the ducal singers by name, according to the tradition of the 'musicians' motets' of the fourteenth century. I suggest that also

Binchois's *Domitor Hectoris*, copied *c.*1440 into the 'Aosta codex', is a ceremonial motet for the Burgundian court.[58] Its text ends with a praise of the Holy Cross, but the beginning alludes to classical mythology: the 'slayer of Hector, slain by Paris' is, of course, Achilles, and his spear which wounded Telephus also cured the wound. This connects Achilles with the Holy Lance and the Cross of Christ. The Burgundian 'Achilles' was John the Fearless, who had assassinated the Dauphin Louis of Orléans in 1408, and died himself as a victim of assassination – arranged by Charles, brother of Louis – in Montereau on 10 September 1419. His remains were buried a few days later in Dijon, probably just on the day of the Exaltation of the Cross (14 September). Binchois's work must be a funeral motet for John the Fearless, not necessarily written in 1419, but in a later year, to celebrate the anniversary of the funeral, sometime in the 1420s. Even then, the motet appears to be the earliest work that connects Binchois with the Burgundian court.

We do not have a single cyclic mass that was composed with certainty for the ducal chapel. It would be mere speculation to interpret Busnois's *Missa 'L'homme armé'* as such a work. A particular courtly group for which polyphonic masses were written, was the Order of the Golden Fleece, founded by Philip the Good in Bruges on 10 January 1430. Three chapter meetings of the Order (1432, 1468 and 1478) were held in Bruges in the churches of St Donatian, Our Lady and St Saviour, respectively. It is possible that composers of Bruges wrote masses for the Order of the Golden Fleece. A court manuscript once existed with several 'Messes de la Toison d'Or',[59] and John Hothby says that the teacher of Arnolfo Giliardi wrote a 'Missa de Panno Aureo' for the 'Dux Belgarum', which was really a Lady-mass.[60] Philip the Good endowed a daily mass in discant in the official seat of the Order, the Sainte-Chapelle in Dijon, in 1432. The first chapter meeting took place in St Donatian's on 30 November 1432, i.e. on the feast-day of St Andrew, who was the patron saint of the Valois and of the Order of the Golden Fleece as well.[61] A surviving mass in the 'Lucca choirbook' (see p. 126 f.) may have been dedicated to St Andrew and could be by a Flemish/Burgundian composer, as it was certainly known in Bruges.

The ducal palace in the town (the *prinsenhoof*) had a chapel where mass seems to have been said even if the court was not present. Services for the duke, or for any event concerning him that seemed important, were held daily or annually in many churches of Bruges. As far as polyphonic music was involved, as at Our Lady's from 1451, this could then be called 'courtly' polyphony in a wider sense, although provided by the local musicians. When in Bruges, the duke and members of his family often went to church outside the palace. Their official parish church was St Donatian's, but Our Lady's also claimed that Philip the

Good often heard mass there; Charles the Bold is reported to have liked to go to St James's; he and his daughter Mary were special protectors of Our Lady's. Isabella of Portugal and Margaret of York favoured the Carthusian and Franciscan convents of Bruges. The annual requiem for Jean de L'Isle-Adam (see p. 81) on 22 May was transferred, in 1455, from a chapel in the *Bouveriepoort* to the chapel of the painters' guild, because this was closer to the *prinsenhoof*, and the courtiers did not have so far to walk.

Requiem services for a member of the ducal family or household were often magnificent, even when the actual burial had taken place elsewhere. This was the case with the service for Marguerite de Male in St Donatian's on 28 March 1405, and with that for John the Fearless on 15 December 1419. The latter was celebrated with polyphony – four choirboys are mentioned – and the gratuity for the music, made by the chapter, went not to its own succentor but to one Jacobus Feskin (i.e. Jacques Fescamp, an ex-chaplain of Philip the Bold?).[62] Most of the ducal chaplains, however, were then in Dijon, where they sang requiems for the duke every day. The death of Philip the Good's sister Anne of Burgundy, wife of John of Bedford, in Paris in 1432, occasioned a splendid requiem service in St Donatian's on 30 November 1432; the court chaplains must have sung in this service, as it coincided with the feast of the Order of the Golden Fleece.[63] When Petrus de Portugalia, brother of Isabella, died in Bruges in 1449, three masses were sung at his funeral on 18 July: two of them – one of the Holy Ghost and one Lady-mass – by the clergy of St Donatian's, and the requiem by the 'cappellani cappelle domini ducis'. The duke himself, the duchess and the count of Charolais were present.[64] In January 1458, the court was in Bruges for the requiems for Jehan de Coimbre, a nephew of Isabella, and of 'Lancelot' of Hungary (i.e. Ladislas Postumus) in St Donatian's. The first chaplain of the duke, Nicaise Dupuis, received a total of £623 – probably for distribution among the ducal chapel and the singers of St Donatian's. When Philip the Good's own burial was staged in St Donatian's on 22 June 1467, the court chapel was, of course, present.[65] Charles the Bold's personal friend Jacques de Bourbon died in 1468 in Bruges (at the age of 23) during the feast of the Golden Fleece; he was buried in Our Lady's on 25 May with great pomp. In the case of Isabella of Portugal, who also died in Bruges, we know positively that the ducal chapel was not present at the burial in St Donatian's on 3 January – it is possible that she had forbidden too much luxury out of devotion. At the burial of Mary of Burgundy in Our Lady's on 2 April 1482, however, two chapels worked together, that of the church, and the court chapel – the latter probably including Antoine Busnois. It was Charles the Bold who did not receive the usual requiem service, because he died on the battlefield (5 January 1477), and the news was initially not believed everywhere. His remains were transferred to Our Lady's of Bruges only in the sixteenth century.

The marriage of Philip the Good and Isabella of Portugal was celebrated in splendour in Bruges on 10 January 1430, in conjunction with the proclamation of the Order of the Golden Fleece. The secular festival in the palace and in the streets almost overshadowed the solemn mass in St Donatian's, where the bishop of Tournai said mass and the ducal chapel sang 'en grand nombre'.[66] Binchois, who had received his canonicate at St Donatian's personally on 7 January, must have been present. The sacred ceremonies for the wedding of Charles the Bold in 1468 all but disappear in comparison with the other festivities (see below). Sometimes, even weddings celebrated elsewhere were commemorated at St Donatian's: its clergy sang a Te Deum in 1440 for the wedding of Duke Charles of Orléans in St Omer.[67]

Sacred ceremonies for christenings were perhaps of greater importance than those for weddings, as Holy Baptism was accepted as a sacrament. Molinet reports the christening of Philip the Fair on 28 June 1478 in Bruges[68] – an occasion for particular joy in Flanders, where his father Maximilian was very unpopular, and the country now had its 'own' prince again. Besides processions and much music in the streets, members of the court chapel were present in St Donatian's and sang a Te Deum. This seems to have been the usual polyphonic genre for such events, which was also represented in the choirbooks of St Donatian's.

This was also the church where every new ruler of Flanders had to take the traditional oath on the privileges of the country in the most solemn manner. The stereotyped ceremony described for 1384 (see p. 18) was repeated at the accessions of John the Fearless (30 April 1405), Philip the Good (22 September 1419) and Charles the Bold (9 April 1468). Besides the responsory *Honor virtus* and polyphonic organ music, no other music seems to have been unusually performed; but much of the splendour consisted in the decoration of the choir with purple velvet and in the peal of all the church bells.

Many other private or political events concerning the court of Burgundy were, of course, celebrated in the churches of Bruges – ducal victories, peace treaties, births or recoveries in the ducal family, and so on – but they were arranged by the local clergy in their own traditional ways.

The major and minor public festivities of Bruges, which are amply documented, give us the only opportunity to investigate what secular and instrumental music of the Burgundian court could be heard in the town. But this is part of a much more general problem: very little indeed is known about the actual occasions on which 'Burgundian court music' was composed and performed. Whether a polyphonic love-song, for example, originated in the palaces of Brussels, or Lille, or

Bruges, is almost impossible to determine − if it matters at all. The intimate character of this music, which could be sung and played by a soloist who accompanied himself (or herself?) on the lute or harp, or by only two or three musicians, seems to defy attempts at dating and localising. But the ceremoniousness with which a ruler like Philip the Good organised his days suggests that even performances of this kind were not completely independent of time, place and occasion. If we turn our attention to the documented, more elaborate occasions on which audiences were present, we discover at least some of the conditions in which this repertory originated.

The often-quoted 'Banquet of the Pheasant' ('banquet du voeu') in Lille, on 17 February 1454, is an example of the conflation of sacred and secular elements which was typical for these feasts.[69] The religious purpose or pretext of the feast was a crusade against the Turks, called for by the several laments on the fall on Constantinople (May 1453) which seem to have been recited. Dufay himself composed one such lament, the *Lamentatio Sancte Matris Ecclesie Constantinopolitane*, which may or may not have been performed at the feast. The *entremets* at the dinner table centred on a fully built church with glass windows, in which the bell was tolled, followed by the performance of a chanson by three boys and a tenor − the whole in lieu of the benediction before the meal. Later, the singing alternated several times with organ-playing, and also with secular tunes on bagpipes, lutes and dulcians. Two chansons are explicitly mentioned: *Je ne vis oncques la pareille* by Binchois or Dufay, and the lost *La sauvegarde de ma vie*. More Burgundian chansons can perhaps be dated and localised if one compares their texts with contemporary descriptions of courtly feasts.[70] The musical personnel at the 'banquet du voeu' must have included minstrels, court chaplains and also church musicians of St Peter's in Lille.

Local musicians were also used in the wedding celebrations of Charles the Bold and Margaret of York in 1468 in Bruges.[71] The minstrels and court singers of the town worked side by side with the court minstrels and those of the English delegation. When the princess entered the town on 3 July through the *Speyepoort*, she was welcomed by 'clarions, ménetriers, et trompettes, tant Anglois, comme Bourgongnons' according to Olivier de la Marche. After the customary procession through the streets with pageants and music (it was here, for example, that the singers of St Donatian's must have come in), the festivities continued for ten days in the palace and in the market square: a close succession of banquets, tournaments and balls. Every detail was fitted into a large-scale program, worked out by Olivier de la Marche in collaboration with other members of the confraternity of the 'Dry Tree' and the rhetorician Anthuenis de Roovere. At the daily suppers, a series of *entremets* showing the labours of Hercules was offered; it was planned and constructed by local craftsmen. The ruling idea about the music at the suppers was that it was all performed by musicians disguised as animals: lions, billy–goats, hares, donkeys, apes, wolves, boars. A dromedary was present, too, but did not actually sing. The music alternated between trumpet fanfares, soloistic chansons for two or four voices and motets, either sung or played entirely on instruments. Pantomimic morris dances were performed by seven monkeys led by a dancing master with tambourin and flageolet, and by 'chevaliers de mer' accompanied by the 'strange' singing of two sirens with tambourins and other instruments. Of the chansons for the *entremets*, one (*Bien venue la belle bergère*) was sung for the bride by Madame de Beaugrant, the governess of Charles's daughter Mary, riding a lion who sang the tenor. The other was in four parts, 'composed for the occasion' and sung by four donkeys: *Faictes vous l'asne, ma maistresse?*. The two-part chansons were always sung or played by an unequal pair of performers: singer and instrumentalist, human being and animal. No three-part music is reported; the four-part motets and chansons were either sung or played by homogeneous groups of performers in the same disguise, the instruments being of the same family: *haute musique* with shawms and sackbut, *basse musique* with flutes. The naive imagery of the whole feast is clearly reminiscent of the animal musicians in the *drôleries* of illuminated manuscripts, which were an old tradition. A more modern trait is the use of classical topics such as the labours of Hercules, or the sirens. These, again, are presented in a similarly anachronistic manner in Burgundian court literature – on the destruction of Troy, for example. The classical-mythological chivalry was, of course, suffused with heraldic symbolism, in which the ruler is identified variously as Hercules, Jason or Theseus, Flanders as the lion, England as the leopard, and so on. There was also symbolic play with the flower 'Marguerite' for the bride, and a touch of courtly pastoral. Chanson texts in the preserved repertory may give away more about their original destinations when scrutinised for symbolic references: Binchois's (earlier) chanson *Marguerite, fleur de valeur* may refer to Philip the Good's sister Marguerite, wife of Earl Arthur of Richemont, who was often in Bruges in the 1420s and was known as a jousting champion – the chanson could be a homage to the lady in whose name the 'valorous' joust was undertaken.

Too much attention has hitherto been paid to the extraordinary (and extraordinarily odd) court festivities like the 'banquet du voeu' and the wedding of 1468, and too little to the regular, recurrent feasts sponsored by the court. Those which took place in Bruges, among other towns, were, above all, the carnival and May festivals, and those for the New Year.

The carnival and May festivities had in common that they were held in honour of the ladies, and that their fitting framework consisted of jousting tournaments and balls; chansons on the theme of love were also newly composed and performed. The festivities drew on many traditions, including those of Philip the Bold's and Charles VI's *Cour d'amour* in Paris, as well as the local usage of May Fair and Holy Blood procession. The *Cour d'amour*[72] had originated in 1401 as an association of the French nobility, including musicians, which held its annual feast on St Valentine's day (14 February), but which also met monthly in all those towns where a local 'chapter' of the association existed – perhaps also in Bruges. Their music and poetry had expressly to protect and praise the honour of the ladies, and drew much of its imagery from the *Roman de la Rose* – which was suitable for the May festival, when dancing and jousting were imbued with the sweet gallantry of stylised courtly love. All this was, of course, a transposition of the age-old rustic or civic May dances into the courtly atmosphere. The girls of the town who would have gone dancing in the inns or the houses of some rich burghers or noblemen, were now invited to the balls in the *prinsenhoof* or the town hall. Binchois's dance-song *Filles a marier* is addressed to them. The rondeaux which were composed for the May festival can easily be recognised because they mention the month. Many of them are by Dufay and other notable composers; the tradition of these texts seems to start in Bruges in the reign of Philip the Bold. The succentor of St Donatian's, Thomas Fabri, has contributed a Flemish song to the genre, *Die mey so lieflic wol ghebloyt* (see p. 109 and music ex. 2), and the 'Gruuthuse manuscript' contains several May songs.[73]

A somewhat strange sub-group of the Burgundian chanson repertory seems to have originated with ceremonies of the *Cour d'amour*, as a kind of musico-poetic exercise in the art of courtly love: the *rondels de refus*. Several chanson texts form a chain of dialogue in which, alternately, the ladies rebuke their over-pretentious lovers, and vice versa. The earliest setting of such a text dates from the 1420s, but another group of four is connected with the court of Charles of Charolais – his chaplain Robert Morton and his Bruges servant Adrien Basin both contributed a setting.[74]

The festival of the 'Jour de l'an' united religious and secular ceremonies. The Burgundian court imitated the clerical feasts of the 'Boy bishop' and 'Pope of the asses' with its own feast of the 'Abbé des fous',[75] a function to which a ducal chaplain (normally the youngest) was elected every year. He had to direct satirical processions and plays, and pay for the banquet. The singers Pierre Fontaine, Guillaume Ruby, Mathieu de Bracle, Estienne Petault and Mathias Cocquiel were all 'abbés des fous' in turn. The chaplains and chamber valets participated in theatrical performances, and sometimes presided over rhetoricians' contests; like the month of May, the 'Jour de l'an' was welcomed with musico-poetic creations, and gifts (*estrennes*) were presented to the ladies. Several chansons for the New Year are preserved.[76] The tradition goes back to Baude Cordier, but Dufay wrote so many rondeaux for the New Year (as well as for May), that one can assume that he sent a new pair of such songs each year to the court, even in times when he was abroad. Again, the 'Gruuthuse manuscript' also contains several New Year songs; such songs were exchanged, according to the manuscript, between the poet Jan Moritoen and his ladyfriend Marguerite. Rhetoricians like Anthuenis de Roovere wrote poems for the New Year, and 'nova carmina' were sung in the church of St Saviour on 28 December or 1 January. The courtly 'fête des fous' took place in Bruges at least in 1457, but probably more often, as Philip the Good was sometimes in the town at the beginning of the year. This was also the time when the city presented its annual gift to the ducal minstrels, so that we may conjecture some public instrumental performances as well.

CHAPTER SIX

The Musical Repertory

The music which was produced and performed in Bruges in the late Middle Ages was a cross-section of the major trends in European music as a whole. For music as well as for the other arts, Bruges was a centre of production and even more of consumption and distribution. Its trade supremacy provided not only an economic foundation, but also specific opportunities for cultural exchanges with other regions and countries. While the contribution of Bruges to the development of the visual arts is widely appreciated, its music is almost unknown today. No attempt can be made here to fill this gap once and for all; but a surprising number of musical works and manuscripts, some of which have been discovered recently, can now be examined – enough material to put Bruges back on the musical map of late medieval Europe.

Mass and motet in the fourteenth century

That Flanders in general had its share of the musical realm of the *Ars Nova* is clearly documented by the famous 'Mass of Tournai' of the earlier fourteenth century. Although two movements of this mass cycle (the Credo and the concluding motet on the chant of the *Ite missa est*) seem to have been imported from the great centre of sacred music, Avignon, there is no reason to doubt that the manuscript in which all the movements were assembled, and which includes two further polyphonic mass movements, originated in Tournai itself.[1] Flemish musicians must have been involved, if not in the composition, then at least in the performance of the work, which may have been used for the daily Lady-mass endowed by Bishop Jean des Prets in 1349, sung at the altar of Our Lady in the transept of Tournai cathedral.[2] The endowment seems to be the one to which the Bruges choral foundation of 1421 (see p. 22 f.). refers when quoting the practice of a daily *Missa de Salve* in Tournai and other churches of the area.

St Donatian's in Bruges, too, had a *Missa de Salve* from 1312 at the latest. The use of discant for this ceremony may have begun in the later fourteenth century, when the church had a *liber motetorum* (before 1377) and when polyphony was adopted for the feast-days of St Machutius, St

Leonard and St Donatian. The earliest identifiable polyphonic work of Bruges origin is, however, not a mass but a ceremonial motet – no doubt an important genre for a collegiate church which enjoyed courtly patronage. According to Ursula Günther, the motet *Rex Karole, Johannis genite* was composed for the peace negotiations of 1375–76 in Bruges.[3] Its text celebrates King Charles V of France as a peacemaker. Although the name of its composer, Philippus Royllart, has not so far been found in Bruges documents, it certainly has a Flemish ring. The composer may have been a member of the musical entourage of one of the princes who visited Bruges in those years – but the most likely place for the performance of the motet is St Donatian's. It is a sacred work, whose motetus text is addressed to the Virgin, ending with the quotation 'virgo prius ac posterius' from the antiphon *Alma redemptoris mater*. That *Rex Karole* was copied into the discant books of the confraternity of Our Lady at 'sHertogenbosch in 1423/4[4] attests to its lasting popularity in the Low Countries; the musicians of that confraternity had connections with Bruges and may have received the work (with three others) directly from St Donatian's, where it may have been copied on one of the folios added to the *liber motetorum* in 1377.

A work which was certainly composed for St Donatian's is the hitherto unedited ceremonial motet *Comes Flandrie, flos victoris* (music ex. 1).[5] Its text alludes to a victory of the count of Flanders, Louis, which is celebrated in 'brugis', the 'urbs Ludowyci'. The triplum text emphasizes the contribution of the art of music to the triumph of the ruler, who governs according to lasting pacts and is destined to enter heaven. Boethius, the perfect harmonist, delights the hearts of the *studiosi* with the sound of 'unequal' bells (*cymbala*), which he uses to praise the Lord. With such sound is the city of Ludowycus decorated. The motetus text speaks of the heavenly Lord who wishes to be venerated with sound and the art of the musicians, who imitate the angels' choirs (*columnas celices*); to unite the jubilation of many, *cymbala* have to be employed. The Lord incites the artist (*architectum*) to praise Him; combining sound with sound, a grateful Bruges resounds with *melos* for its saviour. *Melos* has to adopt mode, as it excites the panegyrist of wisdom; he does not take revenge against violence (*gladium*), but has ordered this music for his maker. The text of the tenor is partly borrowed from a common antiphon at lauds: 'Praise the Lord with well-sounding *cymbala*, together with all the exulting angels, supported by their protection. Thus your souls will be free from the corruptions of crime, and you will enjoy the remedies of your illness here. Resist the lion-like seductions and their blades and missiles, and you will be steered through the flood of dangers with safe sails.'

This remarkable homogeneous picture is as much the description of a specific political situation as a recipe for the performance of the motet.

The political allusions fit the atmosphere of Bruges at the time of the
Flemish rebellions against Count Louis de Male in 1381–82. They were
led by the craft-guilds of Ghent under Philip van Artevelde, but only
partly supported in Bruges, where the nobility, and the higher clergy of
St Donatian's, were faithful to the count with his French allies. Louis
de Male obtained a first victory over the Ghenters at Nevele (eastern
Flanders), after which he was received in Bruges (1381) with celebrations including the tolling of all the church bells, as attested by the
account books of St Donatian's for 1380/81. Another, and more decisive
victory for the count followed on 27 November 1382 in the battle of
Rosebeke, in which Artevelde was killed. After this event, too, there
was a great thanksgiving procession with the ringing of all church
bells.[6] Either of the two events could have been the occasion for the
performance of the motet, whose text stresses the faithfulness of the
'urbs Ludovici' during dangers and seductions; 1381 is somewhat more
likely. The insistent references to the *cymbala* may point to the use of
chime-bells in the performance itself. Even more attractive is the idea
that the music actually depicts the soundscape of Bruges, with the
pealing of all the church bells while the motet was sung; the composition makes great play with the pitches of the hexachords on f and c',
mingling them in close succession and in lively rhythms; Boethius had
defined the hexachords with series of bells of unequal size. From documents of 1383 and 1387, we know the names and pitches of the bells of
St Donatian's: they were Donaes (*ut*), Lenaerd (*re*), Bernaerd (*mi*),
Agatha (*fa*), Benigne (*sol*) and Inghelant (*la*).[7]

Apart from the unusual acoustic realism, the work belongs to a genre
of 'motets about music' also because of its citation of a musical authority, Boethius, and of elements of music theory. In other works of this
genre, authorities like Boethius or Pythagoras are often mentioned,
sometimes together with more modern musicians. Close textual similarities connect *Comes Flandrie* with the widely distributed work *Apollinis
eclipsatur*, where a certain 'Petrus de Brugis' is mentioned among the
modern singers, and with *Musicalis scientia*, where 'Petrus de Burces' (?)
joins the ranks of many musicians from northern France and French
Flanders.[8] We may identify him with Petrus Vinderhout, a composer of
St Donatian's in 1381–82 – perhaps *Comes Flandrie* is his work.

The motet also belongs to a group of French/Flemish works which
found their way to South Germany and Austria. It was contained in the
lost Strasbourg codex *Sm 222* (see below) and in fragments of a choirbook once used at St Stephen's, Vienna (*c.* 1400).[9] This codex (see pl. 4)
seems to have included more music originally collected in Flanders: fragments of Glorias and Credos, Machaut's ballade *De petit peu*, an
untexted piece in the form of a virelai (provided with the German
rubric 'bobik blazen') and the two-part motet(?) *Deo gratias papales*. Its

text, a trope of the liturgical *Deo gratias*,[10] has enough similarities with *Comes Flandrie* to suggest a Bruges origin as well. While the upper voice invites papal officers, cardinals, abbots, etc. to praise the Lord, the tenor runs as follows (words concordant with *Comes Flandrie* in italics):

'Deo gratias fidelis quisque solvat, qui in celis fovet suos satrapas, cuius nos a *corruptelis* mundavit et Sathan *telis* protexit benignitas.
Hic nos saginat *medelis* sue carnis et *tutelis* ut credat fidelitas.
Ergo si gaudere velis et transire *tutis velis* ad sanctas celicolas, dicas deo gratias.'

This work was also once contained in a manuscript in Gdánsk (Danzig)[11] – a place not as remote as it may seem for music, considering the cultural interests of the Hanseatic merchants from the Baltic who settled in Bruges. Similar connections, and also the travels of Netherlandish musicians, may account for the distribution of some other *Ars Nova* compositions to Germany. Among them is the motet *Degentis vita*,[12] found in *Sm 222* and in the Viennese choirbook, but also in a set of fragments which come from St Gudule's in Brussels. Gilbert Reaney has reported[13] the discovery of these and several other fragmentary manuscripts in Brussels and Leiden, which confirm an active participation of the great Netherlandish choir-schools in the *Ars Nova*. One fragment in particular, from a choirbook with mass movements, motets and secular songs, in the University Library of Utrecht (*Uu 37^I*), may have been written in Bruges, or even be identical with one of the *libri motetorum* of St Donatian's of the late fourteenth and early fifteenth centuries.

Uu 37^I contains some Credos, unfortunately erased, and eight Glorias – including three with the Marian trope *Spiritus et alme* and two with the trope *Armonizabit* for the feast of the Assumption. There are also three Marian motets. One has the text *Ave Jesse stirps regalis* (an *Ave Maria* paraphrase which alludes to the 'Tree of Jesse'); another quotes from the text of the responsory *Veni sponsa Christi*, for the Assumption; a third has the tenor *Salve sancta parens*, the introit of the *Missa de Salve*. This repertory corresponds well with what we know about musical practices at St Donatian's: special performances for the feast of the Assumption (15 August) are documented in the fourteenth century, and it is this feast for which the discant singers and the organist were required, in more than one place, in 1414 (see p. 26). In one of the Glorias *Armonizabit*, the trope is sung by two high voices alone[14] – and the practice of using boys' voices alone for such tropes is confirmed in records of several churches of Bruges. Another Gloria has a trope which mentions the Great Schism (the almost illegible fragment yields the words 'adoretque non dubium' . . . 'scisma' . . . 'nos sub veri pape' . . .). Bruges was a battlefield of 'Urbanists' and 'Clementists' in this period.

Uu 37^I also transmits a French rondeau and four Flemish songs. One of the latter is a fascinating *quodlibet* of street-cries which depicts the soundscape of a busy market place, where fresh mussels, herrings and fruit are sold, money-changers offer their services and the public baths (in the 'Duinestrate') are advertised. The text spellings are Flemish rather than Dutch, and the market was obviously near the sea. The town involved may be Sluis or Damme in the vicinity of Bruges.[15]

The pieces in *Uu 37^I* are all unica except one. This work, an isorhythmic Gloria,[16] recurs in a manuscript from Padua, where it is attributed to (Magister) 'Egardus' – to be identified with the succentor of St Donatian's in 1370–71, Johannes Ecghaerd (see below).

The Utrecht fragments include two further sets of isolated leaves. One of them, *Uu 37^II*, is from a chansonnier and contains 17 French and one Dutch song, which may have come from a circle of *rhétoriqueurs* attached to a court in the Low Countries; the only named composer, 'clericus de landis bone memorie', must have been from Landen in Brabant. The third fragment (*Uu 37^III*) stems from an antiphonal written in the Low Countries, and contains a very elaborate set of chants for the Invention of the Cross (3 May), the highest feast-day of Bruges.

Secular song and the contribution of Thomas Fabri

The 'faiseur de rondeaux demeurant a Bruges' of 1376 (see p. 78) was surely not the only one in the town. The tradition of secular poetry and song can be traced back to the trouvère Jocelyn (i.e. Josse, Jossekin) de Bruges,[17] and Louis de Gruuthuse owned a manuscript in which a trouvère song was added at the end; and he or one of his ancestors had acquired a manuscript of Machaut's musical works (*MachA*).[18] The courtly, secular music of Bruges was, in this period, embedded in French culture. The poets living in the town used the Picard dialect spoken in the area, which, it is true, can be found in almost all sources of secular *Ars Nova* music. Rather more characteristic of the music of Flanders are the pieces connected with the great festivals of the 'jour de l'an' and May. They seem to have become a topic for polyphonic chansons at the court of Burgundy under Philip the Bold (1384–1404), and two significant early contributions to the genre are by the Burgundian court composer Baude Cordier – one of them being the ballade *Belle, bonne et sage* which, according to some, was written by the composer himself on the first page of the famous Chantilly Codex.[19] Songs for May and the New Year figure prominently in some Burgundian and North Italian collections of the early fifteenth century, which can be linked with Bruges in other ways (see below).

Still within the French repertory, there is the very popular rondeau

Jour à jour la vie whose tenor is identified in a German manuscript as 'comitis de flandorum jorlavie'.[20] It was composed some time before 1376, and the count referred to would thus be Louis de Male (1346–84), who normally resided in Bruges or in his nearby family seat of Male. Perhaps *Jour la vie* was his favourite song and was known as such.

There is at present no special bibliography of the 30–40 polyphonic songs in the Flemish language which were written before 1400 and which survive today, scattered through collections all over Europe.[21] Whilst the four songs in *Uu 37¹* can be traced to Bruges, this is not so clearly the case with the two largest collections of Flemish songs, the manuscripts of Strasbourg (*Sm 222*) and Prague (*Pr*),[22] which both originated in the area along the Upper Rhine. The lost codex *Sm 222* contained at least six Flemish songs (in germanised spelling), as well as the Bruges works *Rex Karole*, *Comes Flandrie* and *Jour la vie*, a chanson *Bon jour tres bon an*, an untexted piece *Schack melodye* which seems to refer to the *exchiquier d'Angleterre*, the keyboard instrument used at the court of Philip the Bold, and the anonymous ballade *Or me veult*, which was composed over an English tune,[23] although it is here erroneously attributed to Dufay. The codex *Pr* contains ten Flemish songs, among them a contrafactum of a French chanson, and the song *Ich sach den mey met bloemen bevaen*; in its entirety, this collection strongly suggests Flemish-Burgundian origin, although it was transcribed partly in a monastery of Clarisses in Strasbourg. In the latter area, music from various parts of Europe was available; the trade connections along the Rhine may have supplied pieces also from Bruges, and the Clarisses could well have received music from their sisters there, the 'Rich Clares', who participated in the musical patronage of the confraternity of the 'Dry Tree' (see p. 71 f.).

Two songs from Flanders turn up in an even less expected place at this time: in the 'Reina Codex' (*Pn 6771*), a large collection copied in Venice or Padua shortly after 1400.[24] One of the main copyists of this manuscript, who was either a Frenchman or, more probably, an Italian, took the trouble of writing out no less than 30 lines of the text of a Flemish ballade *En wiiflijc beildt ghestadt van sinne*, and the delightful macaronic song *En ties, en latim, en romans*. In the many French chansons which he also copied, Picard spellings are prominent; obviously, Bruges was the very place where an Italian – perhaps associated with some of the Venetian merchants there – could learn not only the Picard dialect but also some Flemish. This person may also have collected some of the French works in Bruges. He copied one Italian song, the ballata *Omay çascun se doglia* by the Carmelite friar Bartolino da Padova.

Een wiiflijc beildt is a *refrein* in the usual three sections, with a one-line refrain at the end of each stanza, and is clearly the work of a Flemish *rederijker*. In order to confirm this, we have only to browse through the songs of the 'Gruuthuse manuscript', the collection written in Bruges (*c.*1390–1400) in the circle of Jan van Hulst and the churchwarden of St Giles's, Jan Moritoen.[25] Song no. 30 in Heeroma's edition, *Lucht des edels wivelics aert* has exactly the same poetic form and is concerned with a similar subject. Different in form, but related in contents and diction, are songs no. 11 (*Een wijflic wijf vul reinicheden*), no. 53 (*Een wijf van reinen zeden*), no. 109 (*Mi heift ghevaen een wijflic beild*) and no. 124 (*Trauwe ende steide, scaemte, ootmoet*), among others. These are, of course, monodic songs, whose melodies are quite incomparable with the mensural elaboration found in the ballade of *Pn 6771*. The 'stroke notation' in which they are written does not even permit an easy interpretation in the regular trochaic rhythm found in the upper voice of *Een wiiflijc beildt*. A common element between most of the Gruuthuse songs and the polyphonic repertory, however, is the use of long melismas at the beginning and end of lines.

The Gruuthuse songs deserve much more investigation by musicologists: one is hoping for new attempts at a rhythmic transcription.[26] Their interpretation could also lead to a better understanding of the polyphonic repertory of the time, French and Flemish. To start with, the Gruuthuse manuscript has many songs for the New Year and for May – the tradition of presenting gifts to a lady for the New Year or May, whether a new song, or flowers, or one's own heart, seems to have been celebrated by the Bruges *rederijkers* with particular fondness. Is it from here that the genre of songs about this custom spread into the Franco-Burgundian chanson repertory under Philip the Good, where it is so well represented in the works of Dufay? There are other striking similarities between the Gruuthuse texts and those of the courtly chansons: the imagery of flowers and birds, the mannerism of acrostics and abbreviated names (for example, no. 44: *Een M. die nye van mi ne sciet*), the addresses to 'Vrauw Venus' (*amour*) and 'Vrauw Hope' (*espérance*), the occasional *pastourelle*, satire or drinking song, as well as the *déploration* on the death of a friend (the famous no. 98: *Egidius, waer bestu bleven?*) – all these elements appear on both sides of the artificial barriers between monody and polyphony, French and Flemish, which we are so used to.

The contacts of Bruges with the mainstream of European music are illustrated in the person of Thomas Fabri, who was succentor at St Donatian's from 1412 to 1415. One of his four surviving compositions is attributed to 'Tomas Fabri scolaris Tapissier': he was a student of the Burgundian court composer Jean de Noyers, called Tapissier, who apparently ran a music school in Paris which was frequented in *c.*1406–1408 by ducal choirboys. Fabri may have studied with him some time before that; the work in question, a Gloria, is in the extremely simple style in duple metre sometimes found in the Avignon repertory, and forms, in fact, a 'mass pair' with a Credo by Tapissier which also survives in a manuscript from Avignon.[27] Fabri appears in Bruges documents for the first time on 29 March 1412 as a clerk. Around that time, many appointments at St Donatian's were made on the basis of recommendations of Pope Alexander V and his successor John XXIII – Robert Sandewin and Jacques Vide both owed their prebends to these popes. If there is a connection between Fabri and Sandewin, this could explain why the former disappeared from Bruges in 1415: he may have gone to the Council of Constance, as did Sandewin, and have found other employment there. A manuscript containing his three other attributed works is now in the Cistercian abbey of Heiligenkreuz near Vienna(*HEI*; see pl. 5).[28] It dates from about 1410 – 1420; the text hand may be French or German, whilst the illumination shows strong Italian influence. The copyist mastered French, Flemish and Latin in almost impeccable spelling, but adopts German for three tiny subscriptions at the end of three pieces: 'Nw well got', 'hin ist hin' and 'es ist ge[tan?]'. Two of the six pieces in *HEI* are incomplete at the beginning: a rondeau (first line perhaps 'Mon seul penser') and a Flemish ballade (beginning of the second stanza: 'In vruechden gaet [?] al miin'). Another piece is complete, but anonymous: the two-part rondeau *Par un regart et un vis amoureux*, also known from the manuscript *Ox 213* (see below). The three attributions to Fabri (the 'Fa' being expressed as a solmisation symbol) concern one Latin and two Flemish songs,[29] which exhibit a striking variety of techniques.

The rondeau-refrain *Die mey so lieflic wol ghebloit* (music ex. 2) is obviously written for one of the May festivals. The text is an invitation to join a merry boat party of the kind illustrated in later Flemish calendar miniatures for May; a *schepelkin* (boat) is being ordered. The music has features which are progressive for the time around 1410, such as declamatory imitation at the beginning of lines and the smooth triple metre of the *tempus perfectum*. On the other hand, the piece has an untexted triplum above the texted voice, an arrangement rarely used outside church music after 1400. The range is extremely low and requires three male voices or transposition. The ballade *Ach Vlaendre vrie* (music ex. 3) is a much more ambitious setting. The intricate '$\frac{6}{8}$ rhythm' (*prolatio maior*), typical of the so-called *Ars Subtilior* around 1400, is softened by running melismas in semiquavers; passages in syllabic declamation are inserted, the first with imitation in all three voices, the second ('Ach Vlaendre, Vlaendre') in almost chordal declamation, although the lower voices are not texted. This emphatic and somehow moving line introduces the unexpected E^b chord into the basically Dorian piece; the cry 'Oh, Flanders' has to be performed with improvised embellishments of each note, indicated by pauses (*cantus coronatus*),[30] a device which is otherwise found in passages of high religious or political importance in motets and mass compositions. The whole work, a *refrein*, is extraordinary for its text:

'Oh, Flanders, free and noble, widely renowned of old; you could still be like this, but many a serpent carries envy against you. You have long been vilified: defend yourself by heart (. . .). Oh Flanders, Flanders, what hinders you?

Oh Flanders, how is it that you are being so hated, as you never did any harm to good people who came to you, but they received stately honours whatever the case, whether they came from far away or near. Oh Flanders . . .

Oh, Flanders, from now on be united in your land, and serve your just lord; truly, he is a fine prince. So you shall be without pain at all times. Oh, Flanders . . .

Oh, Flanders, joyful country, you must conserve all your goods, and God may protect your widely renowned count from the forces of hell, so that nobody may ever have reason to exclaim woefully:

Oh, Flanders, Flanders, what hinders you?'

The internal divisions of Flanders – Ghent against Bruges, middle class against aristocracy, Urbanists against Clementists – and the rebellions against the counts Louis de Male and Philip the Bold, had been disastrous indeed for the economic and political climate, even without the aggravation of the Anglo-French war; foreign merchants were driven away, despite the efforts of Bruges to make every possible concession to them. The poet was a Flemish patriot who was deeply concerned about all this, and who saw the only way forward in the submission to the house of Burgundy – a political alignment from which the clergy and the nobles benefited more than the urban middle class. It is significant, however, that the poem is in Flemish, and in the native form of the *refrein* (the three-section ballade where only the last section is repeated after the stanzas). The Gruuthuse songs no. 1 (*Here God, wie mach hem des beclaghen*) and no. 2 (*Wit ende zwart, dat es een snede*) have exactly the same number of lines, rhyme-scheme and literary diction. *Ach Vlaendre vrie* may therefore be by one of the Bruges *rederijkers*, although its political explicitness is unmatched even in the Gruuthuse collection.

The third work by Thomas Fabri, *Sinceram salutem care*, is radically different again. It is a puzzle canon, albeit with an easy solution, as the third verse asserts: 'everybody can investigate this under scrutiny, as the written notes show clearly enough'. The three sections of the piece, labelled [1°], 2° and 3°, look like consecutive lines of one voice of a ballade, but they can be sung all three together, or in any combination of two parts. (Music ex. 4 gives them in the three-part combination.) Two of the possible combinations (1+2+3 and 2+3) require only the small adjustment of exchanging the last two notes (given as version 'A' in the example). The simple *rondellus* technique found here also occurs in a slightly earlier piece, the song *He hula hu* in a manuscript in Leiden, which is a collection of Dutch and French songs, probably from the Wittelsbach court of Hainaut, Holland and Zeeland.[31] The use of this and other forms of strict canon – the present piece can be sung in the manner of a round – was popular at the time. The compositional task here consists in the avoidance of structural dissonances, including fourths, between any pair of voices (non-quartal harmony), which is in fact achieved except in bars 16 and 20. But the counterpoint is quite sophisticated; passing and even accented dissonances on short notes are not eschewed, and there is much melodic and rhythmic interest in all voices.

The text discloses that the piece is a witty message to a musician colleague. He is being challenged to 'harmonise' the piece, i.e. to put the parts together, 'for love of *gamautare*' – the musical practice of the gamut; the author himself wishes to join him in Bruges, open a bottle together (*'Bachum lacerare'*, a humorous classical allusion), and sing: 'ut-re-mi-fa-sol-la-re'. The name of the addressee is Buclarus; he is planning a flight to the sea (or overseas?), whilst he should rather (continue to?) teach the composer and his schoolmates the alphabet, and how to put songs together ('carmina grammare'). The spirit of the piece is quite unreligious, even a little blasphemous, when Bacchus is implored to send his 'dew' over the poet ('O ros Bachi me rorare'), an oblique allusion to the Advent introit, *Rorate celi desuper*. Bacchus's influence is so inspiring, indeed, that the poet manages only one rhyme for the whole poem, on -*are*. As a composer, however, he has enough wit to hide a lot of references to the 'ut-re-mi-fa-sol-la' in the texture.

Fabri's canon has a companion piece. It is preserved in a North Italian source (*Mod A*), in a section which is normally associated with the chapels of Popes Alexander V and John XXIII in Pisa and Bologna.[32] Like another work in this codex, a Gloria, the canon *Furnos reliquisti quare?* is attributed to a certain Magister Egardus. The music of this piece, which makes great play on the notes of the hexachord, and still more the text, leaves no doubt that it is a twin of Fabri's piece. A few extracts from the text must suffice here:

[Cantus]
Furnos reliquisti quare?
Quaeso: frater, dic, Buclare!
Optabam tecum cantare,
Ut-re-mi-re-fa-sol-la-re . . .

Set audivi garrulare
quod mansisti super mare
novi Pontus, ubi stare
tibi placet . . .

[Tenor]
Equum est et salutare
in primis te salutare.
Salve, vale, frater care
Pedibus qui super mare
ambulavit se purgare . . .

Precor hanc fugam cantare
dulciter et non amare.
Namque nosti me amare
diligenter gamautare,
ex quo scimus satis clare
cunctam Musam emanare . . .

Apart from the ostensible address to a common friend, frater Buclarus, Egardus and Fabri know each other's piece. They rival each other in finding ever more rhymes on -*are*, in their love of the musical nitty-gritty and in their basic irreverence. The 'flight' of Buclarus is indeed a singable one, a 'fugue': 'precor hanc fugam cantare'. Egardus is more resourceful and adds a whole long story about Buclarus's experience on the shores of the Black Sea, where he finds nicer parishioners than here at home, where the people just want the clergy to sing for them to elicit God's grace, without spending liberally for it – a direct pun on meagre endowments and hard work 'here at home'.

According to Egardus's text, frater Buclarus has left 'Furnos', which cannot mean 'the hearths' as Buclarus is not the type of person who sits before the fire all the time. It is the town of Furnes (Flemish: Veurne; Latin: Furni) in West Flanders. Even if Buclarus walked on the water, his pilgrimage to the Holy Land, or crusade to Bulgaria against the Turks like the unsuccessful one of John the Fearless in 1396, could well end on the shores of the Black Sea, having started in the port of Gravelines near Veurne. Buclarus (perhaps a version of the Flemish name Bouclers) could have been a musician in the collegiate church of St Walburga in Veurne. But I suggest that he did not exist, and that the musical correspondence is entirely between Egardus, the master, and Thomas Fabri, the pupil. Magister Egardus must have been Johannes Ecghaerd, the succentor of St Donatian's in 1370/71 who also held a chaplaincy in Dixmuide near Veurne.[33] Perhaps the correspondence happened at a time when both musicians were abroad – Fabri in Austria, Egardus in the papal chapel in Italy, or in Padua, where his isorhythmic Gloria of *Uu 37*[1] (see above) was transcribed. The exchange may equally well have taken place in Bruges itself.

Chansonniers and tenor parts

Of the early fifteenth-century chansonniers which contain something like a 'Burgundian court' repertory, and which were definitely not written abroad, only one survives complete, the 'Escorial' chansonnier (*EscA*). A recent study proposes Bruges as a likely place for its origin.[34] Of the two main copyists, the first may have been a native Fleming, as he wrote out the songs *Ope es in minnen* and *Al eerbaerheit* without any striking mis-spellings. He drew the staves parallel to the spine, not across, which is exceptional; the second scribe continued this arrangement. What he did not continue was the six-line staves drawn by the first scribe, who had even added up to two more stave-lines for *contratenores* of wide range. The six-line stave is a well-known characteristic of Italian manuscripts at that time – *c.*1430 – and earlier, and may be accounted for by Italian influence on musicians in Bruges, where Italian copyists of literary manuscripts also worked. The repertory of *EscA* centres in the 1420s – many of the pieces copied by scribe 1, including the Flemish songs, are composed in *prolatio maior* ($^6_8$). Binchois is by far the best represented author, but none of his songs is attributed by the original scribes, which suggests that the repertory – planned to be ordered alphabetically – was compiled in Binchois's immediate surroundings. The same may be said of a fragment in Munich which contains only songs by Binchois, this time with attributions.[35] That it comes from the Low Countries is suggested by its original binding – part of a grammar treatise of *c*.1350 in East Flemish(?) calligraphy. Curiously enough, this chansonnier, together with the old binding, was used as binding material for (German?) sixteenth-century music partbooks.

As suggested above, part of the material in the Reina codex (*Pn 6771*) may have been collected by an Italian in Bruges. If this is true, then we ought to have a fresh look at some Italian chansonniers of the time, in which modern French music predominates, or is added to a traditional native repertory. A cluster of such manuscripts comes from Venice. Codex *Ox 213*, the largest secular collection of the period,[36] was written in Venice *c*.1429–36 and contains among many works from the Burgundian court the only surviving piece by Coutreman (see p. 21), and one piece which recurs in the Fabri fragment *HEI*.[37] *Ox 213* is partly based on two other extant chansonniers,[38] *Pn 4917* and *Pn 4379 II*, which are written by northern, Italian-influenced hands; they contain many 'jour de l'an' pieces. Another similar collection forms the last part of *Pn 6771* itself. Although the codex must have long been in Italy by then, the copyist of this section was surely French or Flemish, and the chansons from Burgundian circles. There are biographically significant works by Dufay: in *Ce moys de may* the composer mentions himself by name, as well as (apparently) the Burgundian musician Pierre Fontaine; and in *Je vueil chanter* he pays homage, by means of an acrostic, to Jehan de Dinant, a minstrel of Philip the Bold(!). This comparatively esoteric Burgundian material was transcribed in *Pn 6771* around 1430, when Dufay actually lived in Italy; but it may be suggested that it was collected in Venice in collaboration between northern musicians who arrived there, and Venetian merchants who also had connections in Flanders.

Around 1430, the Italian scribe of *Ox 213* also wrote a smaller manuscript in which he entered only the tenor parts of songs in his possession. Hans Schoop, in his excellent study of *Ox 213*, calls this a 'tenor part-book'.[39] It must be doubted whether the performer of the tenor in a chanson needed separate music – iconographic evidence is not on Schoop's side. It seems that the extracted tenors served a different purpose: the monophonic performance of an instrument, for entertainment or for dancing.

A recent study[40] has revealed, in fact, that a Venetian trumpet-player who travelled on a galley, Zorzi Trombetta (!), possessed a manuscript in which he entered the tenors of French chansons for professional purposes. He played for weddings and probably other festivities in the ports along the Adriatic coast, and was also on the ship when it carried goods to Sandwich in Kent, which would have involved, according to the usual itineraries of the Venetian galleys, at least one visit to Sluis, the port of Bruges. This was in 1447/48. Trombetta's manuscript also contains an older musical section, written by a hand closely resembling that of the above-mentioned chansonnier *Pn 4917*. The contents of the little collection are striking, to say the least. Firstly, all the music is written, although by different hands, in a notation which splits all longer note values into equal semibreves or minims – as does the so-called 'stroke notation' found in the Gruuthuse manuscript and other sources from the Low Countries and England.[41] This kind of notation served an instrumentalist or singer who was not familiar with the rules of mensural notation. Secondly, however, the whole repertory transmitted here is Flemish-Burgundian. The series starts with *Jour à jour la vie*, includes a very early Binchois song (*Je me recommande*) and a *ballatina franceise* – tenor only – which closely resembles his *Je loe amours*; there are a few anonymous songs from the Burgundian repertory, and the chanson *Puisque m'amour* by Dunstable (?) which inspired Trombetta so much that he added several new contratenors, probably of his own and certainly not on the artistic level of the original. Moreover, there is the old (?) chanson *Une fois avant que mourir*, which is also known as a Burgundian *basse danse*, and a tune with the incipit *Gie se far danser le dames* which speaks for itself. An interesting analogy to Trombetta's manuscript is to be found in an English source, a page (fol. 131v) in MS Digby 167 of the Bodleian Library. There are three monophonic tunes, all in stroke notation, the first of which is labelled 'Quene note', i.e. bagpipe tune; the second has been identified as the chanson tenor *Au ce bon jour de la bone estren*.[42] Whether or not these are *basse danse* tunes in the true sense, the second certainly derives from a 'Jour de l'an' chanson, which makes it almost certain that a musician picked it up in some Burgundian festivity. One wonders whether he also heard the elaborate polyphonic version of it which is preserved in codex Trent 87 (*Tr 87*) – a textless piece for three voices, whose tenor proceeds in *tempus imperfectum cum prolatione maiori* (₵). The other voices are called 'trebulus per diminutionem' and 'contratenor per diminutionem', respectively. The diminution is necessary because they are written in the more modern notational style of *tempus perfectum cum prolatione minori* (O), but with doubled note values.[43] This is exactly the mensural relationship between the tenor and the outer parts in much English and early Franco-Flemish church music – the apparently primitive notational practice of the minstrel who plays for dancing, and the mensural usage of Leonel Power, Dunstable, Ockeghem and Busnois are interconnected. How is this possible, and how can the typically English denomination 'trebulus' be given to the setting of a Burgundian tune in a South German source?

Bruges is the only place in Europe where *all* these components come together: Burgundian courtly balls, Flemish and English minstrels, Venetian galleys and their crew, French and Flemish church composers, 'stroke notation', South German merchants, and, last but not least, the girls of the town who danced to these tunes. It was for them that Binchois wrote *Filles à marier*, using a text which is also the name of a *basse danse*, and a tenor which is the popular song *Se tu t'en marias*.

The development of the courtly *basse danse* itself cannot be described here. The largest fifteenth-century source of this genre is a Burgundian court manuscript (*Br 9085*) which was apparently copied at the end of the century.[44] The splendid illumination and the use of dark-stained parchment are strongly reminiscent of a prayerbook which the Bruges bookseller Marc le Bongeteur produced for Charles the Bold in 1468. But there is stronger evidence that the dance manuscript actually reflects the repertory of the ballrooms in Bruges.

The *basse danse* melodies usually have names, many of which point to some town, region or nation: *Avignon, Barcelonne, Flourentine, La navaroise, La Spagna, Venise*, and so on (Bruges is not among them). It has often been assumed, hesitantly perhaps, that these nicknames designate the origin of the tune. This theory is squarely contradicted by the case of the tune called *La portingaloise*, which closely resembles a tenor called *Portugal[er]* in some polyphonic sources.[45] There, it functions as the tenor of a ballade *Or me veult Esperance mentir* which may well be by an English composer. In fact, the tenor is a 'square' found in English sources as well – a melody which was set against the tenor in polyphonic compositions, but then extracted and used for other purposes. The names *Portugal* and *La portingaloise* cannot mean, therefore, that the tune itself originated in Portugal. One is tempted to connect it with the duchess, Isabella of Portugal. *La portingaloise* has some melodic similarity[46] with another *basse danse*, labelled *La Basine* – which may refer to the musicians Adrien or Pierre Basin. The former was actually employed by Isabella of Portugal in 1457.[47] Although the name *La Basine* may thus denote the compositional origin of the tune (which is doubtful), and although there are also *basse danse* tunes whose titles are the texts of the chansons from which they came, the same arguments cannot be used for *La portingaloise*.

The clue is provided by the chanson *Jour à jour la vie*, the tenor of

which was labelled 'comitis de flandorum jorlavie': the name comes
from the *patron* who liked the tune and for whom it was often played.[48]
La portingaloise – and perhaps *Portugaler* – would thus be Isabella's
favourite tunes, played for her at courtly balls. (The tenor of the ballade
may have received the name only because of an apparent similarity, or
one of the two tunes may be consciously derived from the other.)
Unlike the dance names of other kinds, the 'geographical' nicknames,
and those referring to persons of rank, must have been introduced to
pay homage to prominent guests at a ball or other ceremony by playing
'their' tunes. This practice presupposes large gatherings at which
people from different countries were present – not only princes, but also
merchants and diplomats, from Florence and Venice, for example. The
minstrels on the balcony would greet them with 'their' national tune
when they entered the room, or when one of them led the dance with
his lady. The distinction of the tunes by names made sense only where
many such guests had to be welcomed, and where the audience met
regularly. The recurrent festivals of Bruges, where the foreigners were
present year by year, as many of them lived there permanently, fulfill
this condition. Here, the nomenclature could become established. Not
surprisingly, the practice of nicknaming instrumental pieces, often with
reference to a patron or patroness, found a particular development in
Italian music of the sixteenth century: Italian merchants and diplomats
had long frequented the ballrooms of Bruges.

Sacred music under English influence

Several large collections of sacred music were compiled around 1440–
1445 in South Germany and Austria, which contain hundreds of compositions of local and foreign origin (*Em, Ao, Tr 87, Tr 92*). Researchers
have often concentrated their efforts on the works of important composers in this repertory (Dufay, Binchois, Brassart) and on those of
presumed English origin. Music which could have come from the Low
Countries has less often been sought in these collections; names of composers who worked in the cathedrals and collegiate churches of this
area – apart from Brassart and Binchois – were hardly known to the
copyists themselves. Nevertheless, they did transcribe a few identifiable
works from the Bruges repertory; many more are likely to be hidden in
anonymity.

The codices in question contain, between them, about two thirds of
the sacred works by Binchois that are known today.[49] Many of them
were composed for the Burgundian court, of course; some probably for
St Waudru in Mons, where Binchois was educated and later held a
prebend; and it would be surprising if St Donatian's had not possessed
a few works by Binchois in its repertory after 1430. Binchois served

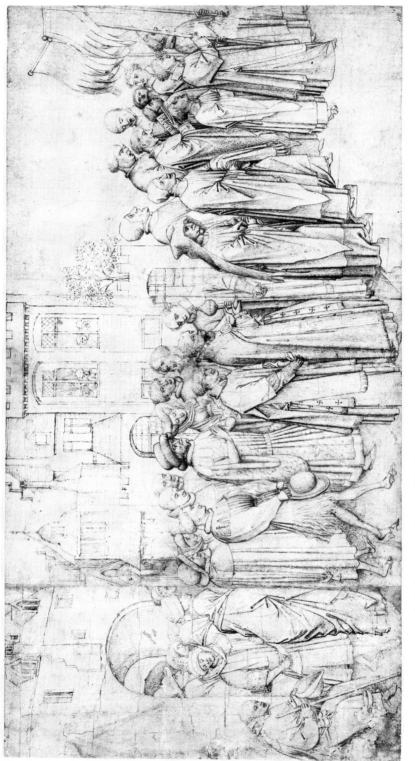

1. Religious procession in a Flemish town. School of Rogier van der Weyden, mid – fifteenth century.

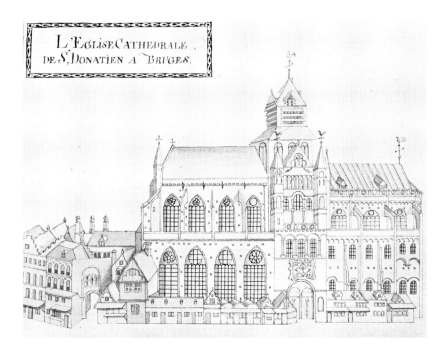

L'EGLISE CATHEDRALE DE S. DONATIEN A BRUGES.

2. The Collegiate Church of St Donatian. (*Above*) Front view and (*right*) plan, with cloister and 'burg' square. Eighteenth-century drawing.

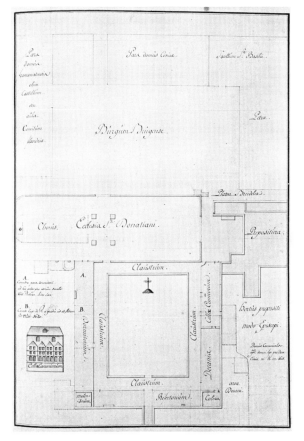

3. May in Bruges: Calendar page from a Flemish Book of Hours, *c.*1500.

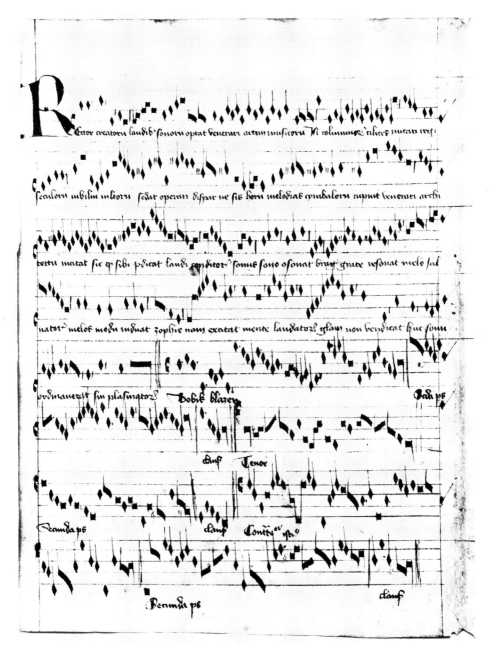

4. Ceremonial motet for Count Louis de Male (see music ex. 1) in an Austrian manuscript of
c.1400.

5. Chansonnier with works of the Bruges succentor Thomas Fabri (see music exs. 2 and 3); early fifteenth century.

6. The Lucca Choirbook (fol. 25v): Gloria of the anonymous English *Missa Te gloriosus*.

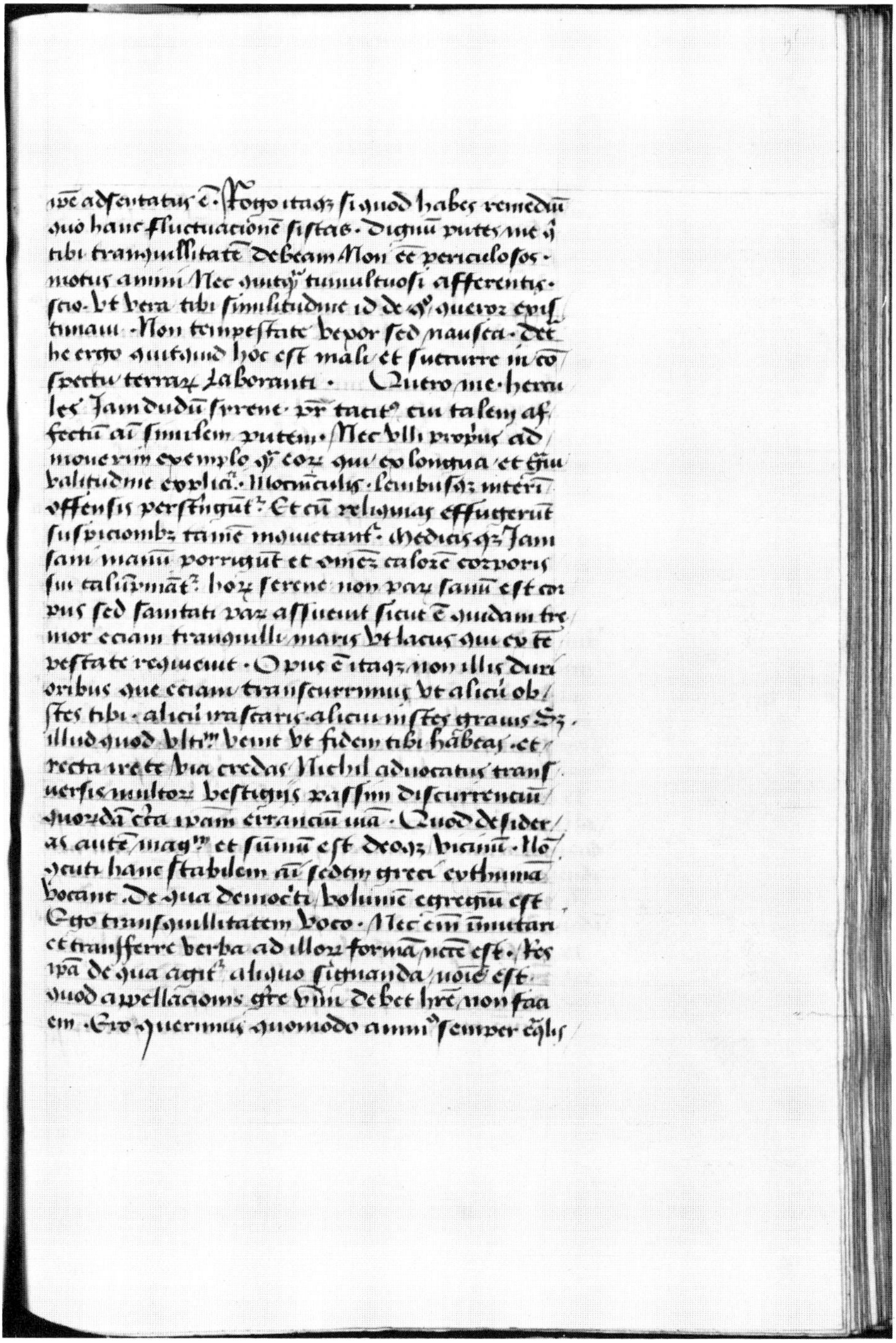

7. Works of Seneca, University Library of Leiden, MS BPL 43A, fol. 196r. Probably copied in the same scriptorium as the Lucca Choirbook (Bruges *c.*1470).

8. The Lucca Choirbook (fol. 38v): Gloria of the anonymous *Missa Hec dies* (see music ex. 8), with an additional voice written in Italy.

English patrons in France in the 1420s as a layman, and he did not take holy orders until 1437; apart from the motet *Domitor Hectoris* (see p. 95) and a Sanctus (*Ao*, fol. 147r) in an older style, most of his sacred works must be dated relatively late, although their predominantly simple, declamatory style and the use of *fauxbourdon* may be interpreted as a lingering English influence which may well have been kept alive through the composer's contacts with Bruges. His four-part Agnus Dei was certainly known there (see below).

To the copyist of *Tr 87*, the composer of a Credo (fol. 162v) was known as 'Georgius a Brugis'.[50] He must have been Georgius Martini, who became a canon of St Donatian's in 1431, when he was a singer in the chapel of Pope Eugene IV together with Dufay, Malbeque, Poignare and Arnold de Lantins; from 7 June 1432 until his death in 1438, Martini lived in Bruges. The Credo in *Tr 87*, however, must stem from an earlier part of Martini's career, perhaps 1427–1431 when he resided at the cathedral of Treviso, where his Flemish origin was in fact known.[51] The work in question shows Martini to be a more conservative composer than the other northerners whom he met in Italy. It could almost be taken for a late work of Johannes Ciconia, who lived in Padua in the first decade of the century. One is reminded of Ciconia by the balance of two texted voices of equal range which are supported by a lower, untexted voice; the short snatches of imitation, or rather alternation, between the voices in lively motives; the freely roaming melodic style with the occasional awkward leap; the chromaticism; and many other traits. It is a very interesting work, not least for its cleverly contrived duets, and would have been suitable for Sunday masses at St Donatian's if Martini made it known there.

Jacobus de Clibano, who was succentor at St Donatian's when Martini arrived there and who stayed in Bruges permanently until 1449, is a less inspired but much more modern composer. We know that he was in touch with Dufay, on whose behalf he received twenty ducats from Ferrara in a Bruges bank in 1443;[52] but he is even more intimately connected with Binchois. A section of *Ao*[53] (the fourteenth gathering) contains an interlocked series of works by Clibano and Binchois; a Gloria by Clibano, paired with an anonymous Credo, is attributed in *Tr 92* to Binchois himself.[54] This Gloria recalls Binchois's purest chanson style, but its repetitiveness and short melodic breath betray the second-rank composer. The same is true of the Credo; both these movements could have been performed at St Donatian's under the terms of an endowment like that of Symon Coene, which called for the Gloria and Credo in discant on the feast-day of SS. Simon and Jude (28 October) from 1439.[55] There is also a Sanctus with the rare trope *Gustasti necis pocula* (for Easter?), which is attributed in one of the sources (*Em*) to a certain 'Sweitzl', but is more likely to be by Clibano.

His fourth surviving work, an Agnus using chant XVII (Vatican edition), is so modest in scope that it cannot fail (music ex. 5). Its superius is but a series of five charming little tunes, to be sung by choirboys in the range d'-f''; the tenor carries the chant but is rhythmicised like a dance melody. The changes of metre and the separation of the monophonic but rhythmicised intonation split the piece into the smallest units. The almost jubilant triplets on the word 'peccata' (!), bars 28–36, add just enough spice to the piece to make it interesting to sing – perhaps in the daily *Missa de Salve* as a last song before going to school. This composition is almost a variant version, 'ad usum delphini', of Binchois's four-part Agnus[56] on chant XVII, which is a longer and highly original work. But it is in the same overall form, has similar changes of metre, and, especially, the same jubilant triplets near the end. A feature which Clibano did not imitate is the technique of using structural fourths between the cantus firmus and superius – a technique almost unknown to continental composers of the time, but frequent in the so-called 'English discant' repertory. It seems no coincidence, however, that the first section of Clibano's Agnus is combined, in *Tr 93* (fol. 361), with the second section of yet another Agnus by Binchois on chant XVII.

The motet *O sanctissime presul Christi Donatiane* (music ex. 6) belongs to a different world. Strangely enough, this world had an outpost in Bruges as well. The work is transmitted in only one source, codex *Tr 92* (fol. 141v),[57] although its text cannot have been of much use to the German musicians, as it reflects the local usage of St Donatian's in Bruges. The text of the two upper voices (which is surely the original text) is the eighth responsory on the feast of St Donatian (14 October) or its octave; the cantus firmus in the tenor is the Magnificat antiphon *O Christi pietas* for second vespers on the same feast.[58] Compositions on this popular antiphon existed in Bruges in the fourteenth and fifteenth centuries (see p. 16); of the many discant singers who were sometimes required for the ceremonies, some would have performed the usual vespers motet, probably with the organ. This would normally have been sung in the vespers procession, but not as a substitute for the vespers antiphon itself, and not as a responsory at matins, for which the form of the setting is unsuitable.

If the work had not been provided with text in the source, all specialists would guess that it was English.[59] It is great music, which combines the freedom of expansive melismatic lines with the precision of an almost pure counterpoint. Dissonances on longer notes are avoided; as a consequence, the intervals between the upper voices and the tenor are often the third, sixth and tenth. There are many full triads, even at resting points, and the triadic style pervades the melodic lines as well. The length and shape of the phrases is unpredictable, almost irrational. There is a constant rhythmic ebb and flow, an irregular slowing down and quickening of the pace, with many syncopations, proceeding from more spacious gestures to fidgeting diminutions before cadences. The cadence formulas are carefully differentiated, although there is a certain preference for the fall of a third into the penultimate note (bars 32, 96, 106) and for the so-called 'English figure' which uses a triplet (bars 52–53 and 57–58). The juxtaposition of *b* and b^b in the top voice and some more or less hidden tritone intervals produce a sound reminiscent of English music; this can also be said of the passage in bars 109–110, which may be intended as word-painting ('suspirancia'). The words are set with almost no regard for spoken word-accents (which in Latin are hypothetical anyway); most syllables are extended melismatically, and in different ways in the two top voices. Despite the amazing variety of detail, the large-scale structure is worked out with arithmetic precision. On the condition that the last chord (containing the last note of the cantus firmus) is excluded from the calculation, the work is built upon the proportion 80:81. This is the ratio of the syntonic comma, the difference between the Pythagorean and the pure major third. Of the three sections (**a**, **b** and **c**), **b** and **c** stand in the relation 80:81 in length, **a** and **b** in the relation 27:16 (the Pythagorean major sixth) and, consequently, **a** and **c** in the relation 5:3 (the pure major sixth). The addition of a single semibreve at the end of the middle section, which would increase its length from 80 to 81, would make section **a** relate to **b+c** in the ratio 5:6 (the minor third). Passages with and without the tenor are almost equal: they stand in the relation 150:149 if all final chords are counted, or 48:49 if all are excluded. If two-part passages are compared with three-part passages, disregarding which voices are employed, they relate exactly like the sections themselves:

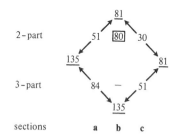

Simple arithmetic proportions are a characteristic of English music of the fifteenth century, and have been shown by Brian Trowell[60] to exist in many of Dunstable's motets. *O sanctissime presul*, however, has a melodic and rhythmic surface which recalls the free, even fanciful, style of Leonel Power. The work resembles, in particular, Power's motets

Alma redemptoris mater (B) and *Regina celi letare* (C);[61] the latter follows immediately on *O sanctissime presul* in the source, *Tr 92*, and the preceding motet is by Power as well. No known motet by Power has a cantus firmus in the tenor, though. John Forest wrote two cantus firmus motets, also in a very similar style,[62] whereas Power used cantus firmi in mass movements, and for his cyclic mass *Alma redemptoris mater* (*c.*1430?).[63]

Power seems to have been on the continent for some time between 1421 and 1438, when he served Duke Humphrey of Gloucester or Cardinal Henry Beaufort of Winchester. This cardinal visited Bruges several times around 1430; he was also a special patron of John Forest.[64] *O sanctissime presul* may have been composed by either Forest or Power during a visit to Bruges; if not, then it is an imitation of their style by somebody who knew both their mass music and their motets thoroughly.

The Lucca choirbook

In the second half of the fifteenth century, a rich store of European sacred music was assembled in the books of the singers of St Donatian's. Much of this repertory found its way from Bruges to other countries, especially to the Mediterranean area. In Italy, the nascent court and cathedral chapels demanded more and more music, and singers, from the North. There is tangible evidence for this musical export in a fragmentary codex which once belonged to the cathedral of Lucca. Today, the fragment survives in the form of 31 bifolia and one single folio of parchment (size of folio *c.*465 × 335 mm) which were used as binding covers for archival volumes as early as 1609–1612. All except one bifolio are in the State archive of Lucca, where I discovered most of them in 1967; the remaining bifolio came to my attention (also in 1967) in the Biblioteca Maffi in Pisa.[65] Three of the sheets were recovered, by Agostino Ziino and myself, in 1978. It is not impossible that more material is still extant in Tuscan archives.

The fragment (*Las 238*) contains 17 masses, 9 motets and 2 Magnificats, none of them complete (see the catalogue, Appendix B). The leaves have suffered much damage from their use as binding covers, and most of the multi-coloured initials were cut out when the codex was disassembled. There is no original foliation, but the original order of the contents can be reconstructed approximately, and it can be established that the codex once had at least 250–300 folios. Most of it was copied by one scribe, probably the same for text and music, who signed his name three times in the codex: 'Waghes' on fol. 7r and 15r; 'Waghe' on fol. 49v. This is a Flemish word, meaning 'scales' or 'weighbridge'; as a proper name, it has been frequent in Bruges since the fifteenth century. At least four citizens with this name lived in Bruges in the 1470s.[66] The copyist wrote a beautiful and somewhat unusual '*lettre bourgognonne*'. After many comparisons, I found a strikingly similar calligraphy in a Seneca codex of the University Library of Leiden (see plate 7). This manuscript belonged, in the sixteenth century, to a member of the family Perez de Malvenda, who were Spanish immigrants in Bruges.[67] The musical notation of *Las 238* is similar to that of a Neapolitan codex with six *L'homme armé* masses, which seems to have belonged to Charles the Bold.[68] There are no downward stems, which did not begin to appear in Italian manuscripts until about 1480. Little is left of the decorated initials. On fol. 1v, there was an L-shaped decorated border of which a little corner has been spared by the scissors: this shows Flemish work in a style *preceding* that of the so-called Ghent/Bruges school which arose in the 1480s. A surviving multi-coloured initial on fol. 17v (see frontispiece) has been identified as Flemish work by Professor Otto Pächt. Specialists of palaeography agree that the calligraphy is a Flemish type of the later fifteenth century.[69]

The codex was a very beautiful and expensive book. Its size and splendour foreshadow the famous 'Chigi Codex' of *c*.1498 and the later choirbooks of the so-called 'Netherlands court' group (see n. 178). The particular parchment size of *c*.465 × 335 mm is not frequent in the fifteenth century. I know of only four examples of the same size: the city accounts of Bruges of the 1470s; leaves from a codex[70] recovered in the State Archive of Bruges; and two graduals, for the two sides of the choir, which can be identified with two graduals copied for St Donatian's in 1468/9, mentioned in the account books. The graduals also have very similar decorated initials.[71] In 1479/80, a 'liber missarum et motetarum' was copied for St Donatian's, which probably contained 280 folios (see p. 30) – but this codex was even more richly illuminated than *Las 238*.

Several later additions have been made to the codex, and it can be shown that they were all written in Italy. The scribe of the mass by Cornelius Heyns (no. 13) probably worked in the 1470s; the later scribe of a mass each by Johannes Martini and Heinrich Isaac (nos. 14 and 9 respectively), had a similar hand to the one found in two Florentine chansonniers of *c*.1480–85;[72] he may have been connected with the Servite friary of SS. Annunziata in Florence, where both Isaac and Martini may have sung in the mid-1480s.[73] Italian (humanist) hands also added or substituted text on many pages, and corrected errors of the original scribe. In one case at least, the error must have been detected by singing the piece, because the original notation is correct as such, but the page could not be turned for all voices at the same moment (fol. 27v/28v). One scribe also added a newly-composed voice to two passages of a Gloria (no. 10). An even later addition (c.1500?) is the last work in the codex, a Magnificat (no. 25).

It can be established that the place where these Italian musicians had access to the choirbook was the cathedral of Lucca. On the first page, originally left blank, there are two notices, dated 1549, which refer to the deaths of Pope Paul III and of Bartolomeo Guidiccioni, bishop of Lucca, who both died in that year. An inventory of the items kept in the sacristy of Lucca cathedral, drawn up in 1492, mentions the choirbook.[74] Among dozens of other codices, there is but one with polyphonic music: 'Uno libro di canto figurato alla moderna chiamato il libro de cantori'. Another hand has added: 'Lo quale donò messer Io. Arnorfini [sic] alla sacrestia'. What must have been the same codex is mentioned again in the cathedral's inventories of 1540 and 1566.

Of the four people named Giovanni Arnolfini who lived in the fifteenth century, only one was of the right age to have made such a substantial gift to the cathedral before c.1480: the famous banker and courtier who had been portrayed by Jan van Eyck and who died in Bruges on 11 September 1472. In his will, he made a rich endowment to Lucca Cathedral for the erection of the chapel of the Holy Cross, which contained Lucca's most venerated object, the *Volto Santo*. The choirbook is not mentioned in the will, and must have come to Lucca during Arnolfini's lifetime. Under bishop Stefano Trenta (1448–1477), a polyphonic choir was founded in the cathedral. It was endowed, according to a charter of 23 February 1467, by the nobleman Nicolao da Noceto, in memory of his father Pietro (†1467). A choirmaster and chaplain was appointed who had to teach plainchant and *cantus figuratus* to the clergy: this man was the English Carmelite John Hothby who held the post from 1467 until 1486, when he returned to England.[75]

Bishop Trenta, Pietro da Noceto and Giovanni Arnolfini knew each other from 1454 at the latest, when Noceto, a noted humanist and papal secretary, was asked by Trenta to intercede with the pope for Arnolfini concerning a palace which the latter owned in Lucca and which had been occupied by some monks. Although Arnolfini did not return to Lucca, as had then been hoped, he met Stefano Trenta, a member of a banking dynasty like himself, in 1467 in Bruges. The bishop had been sent as a papal legate to Flanders and England to negotiate the exports of the papal alum to these countries, and to look after the papal collections. Trenta was in Bruges before October 1467; he spent the following 6–8 months in London, where he signed, on 17 May 1468, the papal bull of dispensation for the marriage of Margaret of York with Charles the Bold.[76] This gesture of the pope must have played a role in the intended alum deal with Burgundy which was, in fact, ratified around that time.[77] These events were beneficial to the interests of Italian merchants in Bruges, above all

Tommaso Portinari, who exported the papal alum on behalf of the Medici bank, and who supplied all the silk worn by Margaret of York and her retinue at the wedding. Arnolfini had his own reasons for being grateful to bishop Trenta. I interpret the Lucca choirbook as Arnolfini's gift to the newly-founded chapel in Lucca. He must have commissioned it between 1467 and 1472, probably in the earlier part of that period.

As the chapel also needed trained discant singers, it is possible that some were hired in Bruges, perhaps by John Hothby himself who may have accompanied the bishop and also supervised the copying of the choirbook. There is evidence that he had musical contacts with Bruges, particularly with the Carmelite convent. He must have used the choir-book in Lucca as a matter of course. One of the hands who added texts may actually be his. In his *Dialogus de arte musica*, written well before 1482, he quotes the otherwise unknown *Missa 'Te gloriosus'*, no. 6 in the choirbook.[78] The treatise also gives a list of notable composers, including all but one of the identified authors represented in the choir-book: Dufay, Walter Frye, John Plummer, John Stone and a certain 'Fich'. The last-named is to be identified with 'Henricus Tik', composer of the mass no. 1, whose name appears twice, in the spelling 'Henricus Thik', in a Spanish treatise of 1480.[79] 'Fich' is just an Italian trans-literation of the correct pronunciation of this English name, which the copyist of the treatise must have heard from Hothby himself. It is pos-sible that Henricus Thick (as we may then call him) lived in Bruges for some time; the Jacobus Tyck who was succentor of St James's in 1463 was perhaps a relative.

Waghes, the main copyist of *Las 238*, carried out his work in two stages, which are distinguishable by the shape of his *custos* (see Plates 6 and 8). In the first stage, he copied the masses nos. 1–8; in the second, the masses nos. 10–12, all the motets and the Magnificat no. 24. This repertory, which was collected in Bruges, is almost an anthology of English music of the period from *c*.1440 to 1470, especially the first-stage masses and the motets.

Mass no. 1, by Henricus Tik, is a *Missa de Beata Virgine*[80] which uses the beginning of the Marian Kyrie chant (Vatican edition no. IX) as its head-motive and in the tenor of several movements, although there is no cantus firmus as such. The Credo exhibits the English device of 'telescoping' the text underlay – two voices sing different verses of the text simultaneously – which was not accepted by the Lucca musicians who tried to redistribute and complete the underlay. The style and mensural usage of this three-part work point to a date of composition around 1450. That it was given such a prominent place in the codex – and the only decorated border – suggests that it was sung regularly in Bruges, perhaps as the Lady-mass of the confraternity of the Dry Tree.

The *Missa 'Spiritus almus'* by Petrus de Domarto (no. 2) is widely distributed in sources after *c.* 1460. Tinctoris knew it as an older, influential work: the use of *prolatio maior* in the tenor, calling for augmentation, is criticised by him as the 'error Anglorum' which was also taken over by continental composers such as Guillaume Le Rouge, Pullois, Regis, Caron, Boubert (succentor of St Donatian's 1454–61), Faugues, Courbet and even Ockeghem and Busnois.[81] Another mass by Domarto, which must have existed before 1458,[82] is preserved in the choirbook of St Peter's, Rome (*SP*); two of his chansons survive as well. He was in all likelihood the Burgundian chaplain Pierre Maillart 'dict Petrus', a canon of St Gudule's in Brussels (from 1432) and of St Donatian's (1440–48), who was a friend of Dufay.[83] In 1418, he had been a clerk of Notre-Dame in Paris; Domart, a little town near Amiens, may have been his home. The *Missa 'Spiritus almus'* is an outstanding work. The cantus firmus is notated in the same graphic shape for all statements, and rhythmically varied only by attaching different mensural signs to it – a 'mensuration canon' of the type also used by Dufay, Busnois and Ockeghem. Domarto's recurring head-motive recalls the ancient trope *Spiritus almus adest* for the introit of the Mass of the Holy Ghost, *Spiritus domini*.[84] The cantus firmus is drawn from the final melisma of the responsory *Stirps Jesse* for Marian feasts, especially the Nativity. It alludes to the popular image of the 'Tree of Jesse' (i.e. Mary's genealogy) which could be seen in pageants of Bruges at least in 1440 and 1462/3, and in many illuminated manuscripts of the time.[85] *Stirps Jesse* was also sung in the processions of the Holy Blood in Bruges. Its theological significance is related to that of the 'Dry Tree'. Busnois used the chant as the cantus firmus for his motet *Anima mea liquefacta est.* Domarto's work is, in its contrapuntal technique, a virtual twin of the English *Missa 'Caput'*; both works must predate the middle of the century.

The *Missa 'Caput'* itself follows immediately in the manuscript (no. 3). It is anonymous here (see frontispiece); this adds to the evidence that it is not by Dufay, as formerly believed, but an English work. The scribe was apparently not familiar with the liturgical provenance of the cantus firmus, the *Mandatum* ceremony, although this was known in churches of Bruges. The scribe labelled the tenor 'Caput drachonis', obviously confusing it with the antiphon of that name; the mistake seems to persist in the Chigi codex in connection with Ockeghem's *Missa 'Caput'*.[86] Waghes copied the English *Missa 'Caput'*, however, in strict adherence to the original text, which incorporates the Kyrie prosula *Deus creator omnium*, and to the bipartite form of the Kyrie.[87] On the other hand, he omitted the text in the lower voices which is found in English sources of the work. The singing of masses with organ accompaniment was normal practice in Bruges.

Mass no. 4 (of which only the superius of the Kyrie survives) is

attributed to 'Walterus ffrie', i.e. Walter Frye. In an ingenious reconstruction, Brian Trowell has shown[88] that this was a three-part work,
the tenor of which was exactly the same as that of Frye's ballade *So ys
emprentid*, while the other voices paraphrase their respective counter-
parts. The superius of the Kyrie even changes from triple to duple time
and back, although the tenor goes on in triple time as in the ballade.
This kind of 'derivative composition' seems to be a unique experiment,
related to both the strict, 'isorhythmic', cantus firmus treatment and
the incipient 'parody' techniques. It is quite unlike the 'isomelic' technique as used by Guillaume Le Rouge in his mass setting on *So ys
emprentid*, and Frye's own setting (certainly a full cycle) may have been
the earlier of the two.[89] The Kyrie includes two Christe sections and
must be performed *alternatim* – the invocations 2, 4, 6 and 8 are sung in
polyphony, the others in plainsong. The audience therefore heard a
Kyrie chant in alternation with a well-known secular tune. Although
Frye's three other masses[90] – all based on chant – survive only in the
Burgundian choirbook *Br 5557*, there is no documentary evidence that
he was ever on the continent. He may have had connections with
Bruges, where his *Ave regina celorum* was also known, through the
London branch of the Merchant Adventurers.

Mass no. 5 is an English work as well: it uses the Kyrie prosula
Omnipotens pater, known also from a Kyrie by Dunstable and a mass in
Br 5557 which is perhaps by John Plummer. (It is noteworthy, however,
that St Donatian's had a chapel called 'Omnipotens pater', founded in
1359 by Bishop Philip de Arbosio.) The Kyrie of no. 5 is in three
sections, corresponding not to 3+3+3 invocations but to 4+4+1; this
layout recurs in the present mass no. 8, in Frye's mass *Nobilis et pulchra*
and was the intended form of Plummer's(?) mass in *Br 5557*, although
the scribe shortened the text there and obscured the form. The scribe of
Las 238 did not.

What is left of the masses nos. 5a and 5b is contained in the same
bifolio. The anonymous mass *Quem malignus spiritus* (5a) is built on a
chant for St John of Bridlington;[91] the anonymous *Missa 'O rosa bella'*
(I) on Dunstable's(?) famous chanson. One wonders why these particular works were put together here. I have argued above that the pair
of masses *O rosa bella* (I) and (II) could be works by Gilles Joye, from
the time when he sang at St Donatian's and had a mistress called
'Rosabelle' around 1454. Joye was in charge of the choirbooks of St
Donatian's in 1467–69 – just at the time when Waghes had to collect
material for his codex. The two *O rosa bella* masses do exhibit some
English traits. The *tour de force* of using only one mensuration for a
whole cycle is also encountered in Frye's *Missa 'Summe trinitati'*, and the
contradiction between the metres of cantus firmus and mass setting has
just been discussed with regard to Frye's *So ys emprentid*. On the other

hand, the *O rosa bella* masses employ Le Rouge's 'isomelic' technique of varying the rhythm of the cantus firmus from statement to statement while preserving the pitches. A similar combination of styles can be found in the *Missa 'Quem malignus spiritus'*. An English copy of this mass carries the superscription 'longue joy bref langour' ('longue' and 'bref' being expressed as mensural notes); although this kind of motto is not entirely unknown elsewhere, it could in this instance be a pun on Gilles Joye. We know that he loved puns.

Joye's five attributed works are all chansons: three with French texts, one textless and one with an Italian text.[92] The last-named is preserved in a manuscript (*Porto 714*) which contains several songs by English composers with French and Italian substitute texts or text incipits.[93] Had the original words of Joye's song been French, there would have been no reason to replace them by the Italian ballata *Poy che crudel fortuna* which does not entirely fit the music. I suggest that the original text of the song was English – perhaps addressing 'Fortune' like other Anglo/Italian songs of the time. It has been believed for a long time that Dufay composed a mass for the English rite; Gilles Joye had much better opportunities in Bruges to serve English patrons.

The masses no. 6 and 7 are both of English origin; they are also the only genuine five-part mass cycles datable before about 1470. No. 6, the *Missa 'Te gloriosus'*, was mentioned by Hothby for its use of the g-clef and the pitch g''; the additional fifth voice, however, is inserted between the ranges of the tenor and the 'tenor secundus' (i.e. bassus) and is labelled 'medius' according to the English tradition. The Kyrie includes the prosula *Conditor Kyrie*; the cantus firmus is an antiphon for All Saints which, in turn, quotes the Te Deum. No. 7 has a cantus firmus derived from a setting of the processional or votive antiphon *Sancta Maria virgo intercede* which was often sung polyphonically in England.[94] The cantus firmus is not identical with this chant, because its notes constitute a voice lifted out of a setting of the antiphon where the chant migrated between tenor and contratenor; this voice is therefore identical with the chant in some passages, and a counterpoint to it in others. This method of deriving a cantus firmus, which has not yet been found elsewhere, is related to but not identical with the practice of English 'squares'. The mass is composed on a grand scale, with two cantus firmus statements in each movement, the first in triple metre, the second in duple, just like the *Missa 'Caput'*.

Mass no. 7a, a very fine work for four voices, is also known from the Cappella Sistina choirbook *CS 14*,[95] where it has a decorated initial showing St Andrew. The unidentified cantus firmus may be related to the verse *Gratulare ergo tanto patre Achaja* of the sequence for St Andrew in the Parisian and Sarum rites, *Sacrosancta hodierne*. St Andrew was the patron saint of the House of Valois, and polyphonic masses were performed for him at the Burgundian court. The mass is neither by Dunstable nor by Dufay, as has been assumed;[96] it seems to predate *c.*1460, and its cantus firmus technique and bipartite layout of the movements again resemble the *Missa 'Caput'*.

No. 8 is an English *Missa 'Alma redemptoris mater'* for four voices (music ex. 7). Unlike earlier English mass settings on this antiphon, the work paraphrases the cantus firmus very freely; the tenor often moves in duos or trios with the upper voices. The tripartite form of the movements corresponds to the main sections of the antiphon,[97] whose melody is present in the following bars of the example: 17–38 'Alma . . . mater'; 39–48 'quae . . . manes'; 67–81 'et stella . . . cadenti'; 82–107 'surgere . . . genitorem'. There are also some hidden imitations between the chant-carrying tenor and the upper voices (bars 31–36, 41–45, 71–72); elsewhere in the mass (not in the example), the superius quotes passages from the chant previously heard in the tenor. The composer avoids, however, all strict repetition or sequential patterns; while all the material appears as if it had grown from the mother-antiphon, it is also continuously transformed. The bassus has, at times, a rather instrumental character (bars 52–8, 110–114), although it might be performed by one good singer alone. This work stands just about half-way between Dunstable, on the one hand, and the music of the Eton choirbook, on the other.

In contrast to the masses of the first stage of Waghes's work, those of the second stage (nos. 10–12) are all Franco-Flemish, and generally a little younger as well. No. 10, the *Missa 'Hec dies'* (music ex. 8) was not written by a great composer, although it has a learned, even didactic, flavour. This composer uses imitation more often, but with less skill than the author of no. 8. He disguises simple musical invention with proportional complications which exist only on paper, including the unusual notation of the lower voices in augmented, rather than diminished note values. The work seems to be of the 'isomelic' variety; the cantus firmus is the gradual for Easter week, and its text, which is underlaid to the tenor, is intended to be sung. The composer makes great efforts to bypass the irregular mode of this chant, the choice of which may not have been his. The pretty duets, playful imitations and sequential passages in the upper voices suggest performance with choirboys; the bassus requires a singer who can, on occasion, produce a sound like a kettledrum (bars 52–58, 110–114). The tenor requires two strong *tenoristae* and perhaps a small organ. This is 'succentor's music', more suitable for a merry convivial feast than for High Mass on Easter Sunday, when the whole parish attends the service. Such a feast was the *beianenfeest* on Easter Monday at St Donatian's, held in honour of the newcomers to the choir. From 1488, it is recorded that the succentor had to compose a new mass each year for this ceremony (see

p. 35). The custom may have been older, with at least some polyphonic contributions to the feast long before 1488. The present work was probably written by one of the succentors of St Donatian's in the 1460s – Cornelius Heyns, Perchevaldus de Polinchove or Pierre Basin.

Mass no. 11 (music ex. 9) is based on the rondeau *Nos amis* by Adrien Basin, which we have characterised above as belonging to a group of chansons from the court of Charles of Charolais.[98] Johannes Tinctoris also wrote a mass on *Nos amis* (not Basin's rondeau but a similar one with the same text) around 1465. In the Agnus, he appears to quote all the voices of his model, thus taking the last step towards the so-called 'parody'-mass. The mass no. 11 does the same in the last sections of the Gloria and Credo, which can be partly reconstructed because of this adherence to the model, and because of the strict cantus firmus technique. The tenor, which is identical to that of the rondeau, is notated in the same graphic shape for all its statements (complete or incomplete), but is rhythmically transformed by applying duple or triple proportions. The last statement of each movement is complete and is performed 'ut jacet', i.e. as written, so that the original rondeau comes to the fore in the final sections, where the other voices are also borrowed from it. Proportional transformations of a cantus firmus are also found in Dufay's masses *Se la face ay pale* and *L'homme armé*, but without quotations from upper voices (which was impossible in the latter work because it is not based on a polyphonic model; see below). 'Ut jacet' sections which also quote from upper voices of the model occur, however, in Busnois's *Missa 'L'homme armé'*,[99] in the *Missa 'Pour quelque paine'* by Cornelius Heyns (see mass no. 13 below) and in an anonymous *Missa 'Quand ce viendra'* based on Busnois's chanson.[100] In this work, the layout of the movements is exactly the same as in the present *Missa 'Nos amis'*. We have, therefore, a closely-knit group of works connected with both the court of Charles of Charolais (Busnois, A. Basin) and with Bruges (A. Basin, Heyns). In the present *Missa 'Nos amis'*, the rhythmic and melodic detail seems artistically inferior to that of the *Missa 'Quand ce viendra'*; either mass could be by the composer of its respective chanson model.

Music examples 10 and 11 present the only other two chansons that are attributed to 'Basin' in sources of the time. Both attributions are disputed: that of *Vien avante* (ex. 10) conflicts with an attribution to Robert Morton, and that of *Madame faites-moy* (music ex. 11) with another composer whose name has been erased.[101] Almost all sources for these songs are Italian; the Italian (substitute?) text *Vien avante* betrays Neapolitan spelling. The two chansons are more similar in style to *Nos amis* than to the songs of Robert Morton; it is also unlikely that the little-known name of Basin was added to Italian copies of works that were not his. In any case, they seem to have reached Italy via

Naples. *Nos amis* occurs in the 'Mellon chansonnier'[102] with the fuller ascription 'A. Basin', and is the last piece in the codex before the concluding motet by Tinctoris, *Virgo dei throno digna*. The chansonnier was copied under Tinctoris' own supervision around 1475; its somewhat self-contained last section – ending with *Nos amis* – includes several English songs by Frye and Bedingham; it begins with *So ys emprentid*. All this suggests that this last section, whose repertory is older than that in the rest of the manuscript, came from Bruges, perhaps through the hands of Aragonese merchants.[103] We still do not know who wrote *Vien avante* and *Madame faites-moy*: Adrien Basin himself, his brother Pierre, or even his other brother Jean, who was dean of the music-loving guild of the barbers in Bruges.

No. 12 in the Lucca choirbook is Dufay's *Missa 'L'homme armé'*.[104] Together with Ockeghem's mass on the same tune, it is thought to be one of the oldest members of this famous 'family' of masses whose last descendant is a work by Palestrina.[105] The origins of the cantus firmus are still disputed. It has been claimed that it was originally a folksong, or that it was the tenor of a lost chanson. Attempts have also been made to find a definition somewhere between these two concepts,[106] which are both unrealistic. The cantus firmus, with its text, is written down, monophonically, in the Neapolitan codex *Nn VI E 40* with six anonymous interrelated *L'homme armé* masses.[107] The *L'homme armé* song, as we shall call this melody, has the specific function in the codex of showing how the composer derived the mass settings from it. The codex must have originally belonged to Charles the Bold and was later presented to Beatrice of Aragon. Although the six masses have much material in common, they do not seem to be 'parodies' of a common polyphonic model such as a chanson; if that were the case, then the compiler of the codex would have positively misled the first user, Charles the Bold, into believing that there was no such model. No: the 'Neapolitan' masses are certainly based upon the *L'homme armé* song only. The same is true for other early *L'homme armé* masses, including Dufay's. Only one composer, Busnois, may have used a polyphonic model for one section of his setting: the 'Tu solus dominus' in his mass is strikingly similar to a chanson by Robert Morton, and it is, moreover, an 'ut jacet' section of the kind described above. Morton's song – which survives in a three-part and a later four-part version – combines the text and melody of the *L'homme armé* song with a free top voice and a new second text which makes a personal pun on the Burgundian chaplain Symon le Breton.[108] This new text is a four-line rondeau (*Il sera pour vous combattu*) whose form is superimposed onto the very different structure of the *L'homme armé* song, which has seven lines and the form **a b a**. It is even possible that Morton derived his song from Busnois's mass section rather than vice-versa.[109] But as both of them are cast in the form of a four-line rondeau, neither of them can be the context in which the *L'homme armé* melody first appeared – they are derivative settings. Moreover, neither of them can be based, in voices other than the tenor, on a presumed polyphonic *L'homme armé* chanson – the tenor alone seems to generate the texture – and the same is true for Dufay's setting and the 'Neapolitan' masses, which also seem to come from the circle of Charles the Bold. In that circle at least, a polyphonic setting of the *L'homme armé* text alone, which could be regarded as the lost source of the melody, simply did not exist.

The conclusion is that the *L'homme armé* song as known to these composers, was monophonic. It would be equally wrong, however, to call it a 'folksong'. It is, as it stands in the Neapolitan codex, a composed, mensural song – a work of art. The author of the song, an ingenious poet and composer, describes in a semi-dramatic, semi-narrative form what he heard in a late medieval town: the warning sound of the watchman's horn from the tower, as a hostile army is approaching across the plains – 'L'homme armé!'[110] The words that match the agreed warning signal of the falling fifth are at once shouted round the whole town: 'On a fait partout crier, que chascun se viegne armer d'un aubregon de fer' – i.e. according to an order given by the magistrate, everyone arm himself with an iron hauberk. Such a call would be totally ineffective in the countryside, but it would not fit the military organisation at a court, either. The poet records the soundscape, the hectic activity of a town in a state of alarm, spinning his song round the vital three-note-signal. He follows well-established rhetorical traditions of poetry which reports events: for example the *pastourelle*, a more narrative type, and the *alba*, a more dramatic dialogue type. The *Tagelieder* of the Monk of Salzburg and Oswald von Wolkenstein also integrate the call of the *wachterhorn* which sounds only fourths and fifths or triads.[111] Trumpet-calls, bird-song and the sound of hunting horns are familiar to the western European tradition as well; they are the most loved elements of the late medieval soundscape which found their way into music. It is in this tradition that our song belongs: *L'homme armé* is, at the same time, a horn-signal and a street-cry.

The vitality of the song has seduced scholars into believing that it originated among the common people. But it is clearly an artistic reflection and stylization of reality. It was probably composed by a *rhétoriqueur* for an audience, at a time in the late fourteenth or early fifteenth century when its metre (*prolatio maior*, $\frac{6}{8}$) was so usual. The signal must come from a French-speaking area (no Flemish equivalent of 'men at arms!' would fit the rhythm); the song may be the work of a Northern French or French-Flemish *rhétoriqueur*. Later, Charles of Charolais may have become fond of the song, as it depicted a situation which was his daily bread. He appears to have encouraged his musicians to compose chansons and masses on it, perhaps dreaming himself into the role of the fearful enemy. But this was a secondary stage: like so many other elements of the 'Burgundian' civilisation, the *L'homme armé* song comes from one of the great cities of the North.

All this may well reflect on Dufay's own setting, its date and purpose, or rather its early distribution. The Lucca choirbook of *c.*1470 happens to be the earliest source of Dufay's mass (just as the Bruges entry of 1467/68 happens to be the earliest date for Ockeghem's mass: see p. 30). Dufay's work is also preserved in a Scottish choirbook of *c.*1500. At least this odd phenomenon of transmission finds an easy explanation from the Bruges angle: the Bonkil family or other members of the confraternity of St Ninian carried the work from Bruges to Scotland.

The *Missa 'Pour quelque paine'* by Cornelius Heyns (no. 13) was once thought to be by Ockeghem,[112] because a nineteenth-century hand altered the attribution – so it seems to me – in another source (*Br 5557*) from 'c.heyns' to 'ockegan'. Heyns, who lived in Bruges more or less continuously from about 1447 until his death in 1485, seems only to have left this single work, in which he uses strict transformation of the cantus firmus as well as parody, the latter in the 'ut jacet' section at the very end, where for the first time the top voice of the rondeau is also heard. The fact that Heyns's mass was added to *Las 238* in Italy indicates the continuing contact between Lucca and Bruges; perhaps the work had not been composed by the time the codex left Bruges. In *Br 5557*, it is copied on the same paper as Dufay's *Missa 'Ave regina celorum'* (*c.*1472).[113]

The masses no. 14 and no. 9 were composed by the Flemings Johannes Martini and Heinrich Isaac in Italy.[114] The evidence of *Las 238* suggests that Isaac's *Missa 'Chargé de deuil'* was written shortly after his arrival in Florence (1484). It would be worth investigating from what other works he had learned his developed technique of parody and, especially, imitation. The *Missa 'Nos amis'* could have been among his models.

The motets nos. 15–23 and the Magnificat no. 24 were all copied during the second stage of the scribe's work. Nevertheless, they must have belonged to the original plan of the choirbook, which envisaged such a section at the end. In fact, the motet section has in common with the masses of the first stage that it is like an anthology of English music covering more than two decades, interspersed with one or two Flemish works. It is not possible to determine the original order of the motets in the choirbook.

Only the motet no. 15 cannot be liturgically placed with certainty; as only the contratenors of this four-part work are preserved, there may be gaps in the surviving text, which reads as follows:

A cordibus fidelium | des corda iam concordie | caput infidelium | partis divini auxilium | detur toto secordie | horumque in opprobrium | ac tue laudis gaudium | et post cursum terrestium (sic) | nobis vitam celestium.

The help of God, or of the Virgin, is invoked against the infidels; the diction recalls the Magnificat: 'dispersit superbos mente cordis sui'. The piece could be a Magnificat antiphon setting, with the chant in the (lost) tenor. The contratenor altus has the high range of c'-e'', for choir-boys; the superius must have reached g''. The motet may be by one of those composers who, according to John Hothby, used the g-clef in their *cantilene* – perhaps John Stone.

The motets nos. 16 and 19 are *Deo gratias* substitutes (see p. 29), presumably sung at the end of mass. This widely distributed genre is found in the fourteenth-century repertories of England and Avignon; there are straight settings of the words *Deo gratias* as well as large motets with rhymed paraphrases of the words in the upper voices. The work *Deo gratias papales* | *Deo gratias fidelis* of *c.*1400 may be of Bruges origin (see p. 104 f.). The text of John Stone's motet (no. 16) is very similar: '*Deo gratias agamus* | *sue matrique dicamus* | *laudes et preconia* | *voce cordis intima* | . . .'. This work was in four parts, with long introductory duets for both(?) of the two sections; the first one started in imitation. Stone may have written the motet for the conclusion of a Lady-mass in the chapel of King Edward IV, to which he belonged in 1465/6.[115] In Bruges, there is more evidence for the singing of *Deo gratias* motets at the end of the greater hours. The endowment of Pierre Basin for St Donatian's in 1489 provides, at the end of vespers, 'post collectam motetum deo dicamus more solito' – but the scribe himself later altered this to read 'post collectam motetum et post motetum deo dicamus more solito', which would make the motet an insertion, not a substitute of the *Deo gratias*.[116] In any case, the practice must be distinguished from the so-called 'mass-motet cycle', ending(?) with a motet which is not a *Deo gratias* but which is musically related to the mass;[117] the endowment of Philip the Good for Our Lady's (1451) may be an example for this practice in Bruges. The motet no. 19 is a much shorter work than no. 16, but may also be English; it was for three voices. The complete text reads:

Agimus tibi gratias | omnipotens deus noster | qui nos de bonis satias | agimus tibi gratias | domine tua voluntas | sit hic et ubique semper | agimus tibi gratias | omnipotens deus noster.

It follows precisely the formal scheme of the rondeau, and seems to refer to a *Missa 'Omnipotens pater'*.

Nos. 17, 20, 21, 22 and 23 are all Marian motets. *Ave mater gloriosa, virga iesse generosa* (no. 17) is probably an English work, and dates from before *c.*1450. The tenor, in long notes like a cantus firmus, resembles the *Alma redemptoris mater*. The work is in three parts, but has a fourth, optional voice, called 'contratenor concordans cum omnibus'. With its reference to the 'Tree of Jesse', the motet would be suitable for Marian vespers, especially for the Nativity of the Virgin. We have only the second half of the lower voices of no. 20; the surviving fragment of text permits an identification with the ancient motet text *Ave gloriosa mater salvatoris* – a composition of the thirteenth century. One of its many sources is the well-known 'Summer canon' manuscript (British Library, Harley 978). The present composition, for four voices, is an English work in an advanced style, with a concluding section in (correctly written) triple proportion. No. 21, *Tota pulchra es*, is a well-known work by John Plummer, one of the most progressive English composers of the mid-fifteenth century; the motet dates from before *c.*1450, but makes systematic use of declamatory imitation.[118] The chant, a responsory from the Song of Songs, is ornamented in the top voice. All three voices are eminently singable; emphatic pauses or simultaneous rests and chordal declamation, interrupted by imitative duets, make the delivery of the text appear spontaneous. The term 'song-motet' (*Liedmotette*), which is often applied to pieces of this type, would sound much too unsophisticated for Plummer's work, which interprets the text as highly rhetorical prose. For the fifteenth century, a 'song' – in whatever language – is a *patterned* piece with repetitions and some kind of metrical scheme. 'Song-motet', or even '*lauda*-motet', is therefore not a good term for works like no. 21. The same applies to no. 22, *O pulcherrima mulierum*, in which we find no formal scheme, but only the unity of the expressive flow. The emphatic simultaneous pauses, the sudden changes of texture and declamation, the imitations 'across the barline' are, despite the consciously simple style, the means of a rhetorical strategy which carves out every word: imitation between the voices becomes '*imitatio naturae*'. All the voices should be sung with text, although the tenor omits some phrases and is not texted in the sources. The transcription (music ex. 12) is taken from the earliest source, *Tr 93* (*c.*1455). I have no doubt that the composer is the same as that of *Tota pulchra*: John Plummer. The motet shared the success of the even more popular *Ave regina celorum* by Walter Frye; one or the other of these works (sometimes both) is regularly found in chansonniers of the time, often at the beginning or end of a collection.[119]

No. 23, *Vidi speciosam*, is based on a responsory for the Assumption, whose text also comes from the Song of Songs. The chant (in the Phrygian mode) is used imitatively in all four voices. The work is preserved complete in the Cappella Sistina choirbook *CS 15* (of *c.* 1490) and may have come, like other motets in that collection, from the Burgundian orbit. Gaspar van Weerbeke used the chant as a cantus firmus for his *Stabat mater*. The present work may have been sung in

Bruges in the ceremonies of 15 August. The rhythmic-melodic style recalls liturgical motets by Antoine Busnois, but even so the smooth integration of the chant into a thoroughly imitative texture is strikingly progressive for the time around 1470.

It would be most interesting to know where and when *O rex gentium* (no. 18) originated. It was an extraordinary work. The surviving voices are a tenor with the range *A-b*[b], which carries the chant in ornamented form, and a contratenor with the range *F-d'*; but the counterpoint requires an even lower second contratenor which must descend to *D*. The reason is that the antiphon is kept in its original range of the second mode, but treated as if it were transposed an octave higher, into an ornamented top voice. Together with the two lower voices, it often seems to proceed in 'faburden'-like parallel sixths. The application of the English 'sight'- technique – extemporised transposition a fifth higher – would bring the voices into a normal range. There must, however, also have been a superius with a written range of perhaps *f-a'*, and the work is far removed from the simple chant-settings in *faburden* known from English sources of the time. The chant is one of the solemn 'O-antiphons' sung in Advent. In several churches of Bruges, there were special endowments for the singing of these antiphons, some of which may have included discant.[120] The chant begins with the melodic variant *d-f-e* as opposed to the Roman version *c-f-e*. This important variant can be found in the Sarum rite, as well as in those of Cambrai and Tournai, and Obrecht used it in his *Missa de Sancto Donatiano*. The third, untexted section of the motet is labelled 'Pneuma' – this refers to the special melisma which was attached to antiphons on high feasts;[121] it is found here in the tenor. The 'Pneuma' is composed in *prolatio maior*. The final chord contains the third, *f*, written into the contratenor as an additional (fifth) note.

The Magnificat no. 24 could be sung together with *O rex gentium* as its Magnificat-antiphon, since both works are in the second mode. They are of different origin, however. An approximate reconstruction of the whole Magnificat can be achieved – and it reveals a composition of amazing sophistication and balance.

Magnificat settings of the fifteenth century,[122] which normally use one of the eight Magnificat tones (corresponding to the eight psalm tones) as cantus firmus, either provide polyphony for alternate verses only (the others being sung in plainchant), or have polyphony for all twelve verses, but repeat some of the music according to a patterned scheme. Although the verses are of different length, two or more of them could be sung to the same music by using declamatory passages on the 'reciting' pitches, which could accommodate more or less syllables, as in the chant. One of the most frequent patterns of repetition provides different musical sections for the first three verses, but repeats them for the verses 4–6, 7–9 and 10–12, as in a strophic song with three sections. A technique traditionally applied to Magnificat settings is that of *fauxbourdon* in its stricter or freer forms, which is, however, not normally used for all verses. Since the mensuration, the number of voices and the cantus firmus technique are also often varied from section to section, the Magnificat could unite a variety of styles within a closely circumscribed, symmetrical form. The first word was often sung as a plainsong intonation, leaving only three words 'anima mea dominum', for the first verse.

No. 24 of the Lucca choirbook consists of four recurring musical sections, plus the half-verse 'anima mea dominum' at the beginning, which is the only one in triple metre and which does not recur. The remainder is constructed around verse 7 as a centrepiece, but in a two-layered symmetry:

$$2 \quad 3 \quad 4 \quad 5 \quad 6 \quad 7 \quad 8 \quad 9 \quad 10 \quad 11 \quad 12$$

The musical characteristics of the verses are carefully varied. Verse 2=6=11 is a duo with the chant in the superius, mostly in long notes, over a fast-moving contratenor. Verse 3=8=12 is a four-part setting with the chant slightly ornamented in the tenor. Verse 4=7=10 is a three-part setting with the chant in the superius, over a fast-moving duet of tenor and contratenor. Verse 5=9 is a duo in fauxbourdon-like parallels with the chant in the superius, written in *sesquialtera* proportion. The other sections alternate between 'C' and '₵' but there are also internal passages in proportion. The scheme is as follows (chant-carrying voice in bold type):

voices	mensuration	verse numbers		
S, T, Ct 1	O	1		
S, Ct 1	₵	2	6	11
S, **T**, Ct 1, Ct 2	₵	3	8	12
S, T, Ct 1	C	4	7	10
S, T	₵3	5	9	

The corresponding verses are not exactly identical. Besides the varying number of syllables, the music also takes account of the meaning of the text. For example, a melismatic expansion on the word 'spiritus' in verse 2 becomes a stormy flight on 'dispersit' (*sc.* superbos) in verse 6 – the same passage moves more quietly, but is notated in triple proportion at 'et filio' in verse 11, commemorating the Trinity. As far as we can see from the fragments, the overall impression of the piece must have been one of astounding variety, as well as great melodic and rhythmic energy. The whole work is arithmetically balanced: verses 1–6 and 7–12 total 307 semibreves each; the odd-numbered verses total 308 semibreves, and the even-numbered verses 306.

Three other Magnificats of this period are remarkably similar in style and form. One of them, in *Br 5557* (fol. 70v), is attributed to Busnois. The second, also in *Br 5557* (fol. 62v) is anonymous – it shares with the present work the rare feature of the untransposed second tone (starting on *c*). The third is anonymously preserved in *SP* and other sources. Both the second and third Magnificats have been tentatively ascribed to Busnois because of their similarity with the first.[123] If the criteria for these ascriptions are at all valid, then no. 24 of the Lucca choirbook must also be regarded as a work by Antoine Busnois.

Music from Bruges in late fifteenth-century sources

After the Lucca choirbook, no other extant source written before the end of the century can definitely be shown to have originated in Bruges. We shall, however, try to trace some of the works in the surviving sources to that city by exploiting all the clues provided by composers' names, texts, patterns of transmission, codicological and historical considerations.

Secular music, and singers, from the Low Countries, were much in demand at Italian courts, especially those of Ferrara, Naples and Florence. The role of Ferrara has been investigated by Lewis Lockwood, whose archival sources mention Bruges from time to time. In 1479–80, the singer Vittore Tarquinio 'de Bruges' served Duke Ercole I d'Este;[124] in 1487, the singers Cornelius Laurentii and Jean Cordier were sent by Ercole I on the well-known mission to St Donatian's to bring back Obrecht, who then spent about half a year in Ferrara. Jean Cordier was from Bruges himself, of course, and must have acted as an important agent for music distribution, as he shuttled between the courts of Ferrara, Florence, Milan, Naples and the Habsburg and papal chapels, often returning home. Cornelius Laurentii worked mainly for Lorenzo de'Medici and Ercole I d'Este; in Florence, he sang in the Servite friary of SS. Annunziata as well.[125] One wonders whether he was the 'zot' Cornelius f. Laurents who was rewarded by the city of Bruges on 15 March 1483 for having entertained, together with a certain Jan Bonelle, the French ambassadors.[126] In 1474–77, he had been in Milanese service, together with a certain 'Vittore de Bruges' – i.e. Vittore Tarquinio or Victor Brunijnc (see Appendix A)? Both may have been hired by the chapelmaster, Gaspar van Weerbeke, on his travels to Flanders in 1472–74. There are too few chansonniers from Milan or Ferrara at this time to substantiate a direct influence of Bruges on the secular repertory of these courts. However, if Lockwood is right in suggesting that the chansonnier *Porto 714* originated in Ferrara as early as 1449 or 1450,[127] then the inclusion of Gilles Joye's *Poy che crudel fortuna* (see p. 126) points to a specific connection: in 1449, Joye was 23 or 24 years old and not yet in the Burgundian service; he held the modest position of clerk at St Donatian's. The Ferrarese chansonnier of the 1480s, *Cas 2856*, does contain two works by 'Basin' (see p. 128), but seems to draw on Neapolitan sources.

Naples was a major centre for the reception of music from Bruges. The political and cultural links between the Aragonese kingdom and Burgundy were, however, really established only in 1471; they found their expression in the activities of Johannes Tinctoris, in the transfer of the *L'homme armé* codex *Nn VI E 40* from the court of Charles the Bold to Naples, and in the itineraries of artists. One of these was again Jean Cordier – he is said to have been in Naples as early as 1475. There is an amusing entry referring to him in the chapter acts of St Donatian's: on 13 December 1484, Johannes de Vuilles, 'cantor in capella regis Neapolitani', and Magister Petrus du Croquet alias le Picart, tailor of the king, tried to recover debts which Cordier had left behind in Naples. It is tempting to think that de Vuilles made the long journey to collect music as well as Cordier's money. A certain 'Johannes de Bruges' was a copyist in the scriptorium of King Ferrante between 1474 and 1486, along with a number of other northern scribes, any of whom could have been involved in the copying of the text of the Mellon chansonnier.[128] This manuscript, as has been stated, has a final section which suggests specific links with Bruges – but the remainder of the manuscript also includes all the three chansons by Gilles Joye that survive with French texts.

The cultural exchanges between Naples and Bruges were, however, much older than this. They rested mainly on the Aragonese merchants who had their establishment in the Carmelite convent of Bruges from the fourteenth century. King Alfonso V (1416–1458) of Aragon employed Flemish singers, and acquired at least two paintings by Jan van Eyck – one in 1444, in which St George was depicted with four shawm-players.[129] The other had formerly belonged to the Bruges/ Genoese merchant Giovanni Battista Lomellini. A work by Jan van Eyck even gave rise to a Neapolitan song, and then to a mass: the *Missa 'Ayo visto la mapa mundi'*, written by the Neapolitan court musician Johannes Cornago before *c*.1465, is based on a song which must refer to the lost map of the world which van Eyck painted for Philip the Good.[130] This was an item which would have interested the merchants in particular. The chansonnier *EscB*, written about 1470, contains Adrien Basin's *Nos amis* and Petrus de Domarto's *Je vis toujours*. It also contains the apparently Flemish song *So lanc so meer*, attributed to 'W. Braxatoris' (de Brauwere?) here, and to Johannes Pullois in *Tr 90*; whichever of the two the composer was, neither served the Burgundian court. Songs by Bedingham, Dunstable(?) and Frye in *EscB* also suggest that Flemish, not necessarily courtly 'Burgundian', sources were used.[131] Another Neapolitan chansonnier, the codex Seville (*Sev*) of *c*.1480, contains the Flemish songs *Myn hert lyt smert, Ten is niet leden* and *O Venus bant*.[132] Gaspar van Weerbeke composed a mass over this last tune; two masses *O Venus banden* were copied into a choirbook of St Donatian's in 1475/6. We have mentioned that the almost unknown composer Henricus Thick, an Englishman who may have worked in Bruges, was known to the author of the Spanish treatise in El Escorial c.III.23, copied in Seville in 1480 under Tinctoris's influence. The Carmelite convent in Bruges was the obvious point of contact for such English-Neapolitan-Spanish lines of transmission.

In the later fifteenth century, a lot of secular music must have travelled back and forth between Naples and Florence – a process which is testified by the contents of several chansonniers of this period.[133] Musicians and other artists shuttled between these centres as well; among them were Jean Cordier and the Neapolitan composer Vincenet. It has not yet been pointed out that this connection is, in many respects, a triangular one – the third corner was Bruges. This pattern becomes clear when one reads the interesting letters of Alessandra Macinghi negli Strozzi,[134] the wife of a Florentine banker who, like many prominent opponents of the Medici, was exiled in the 1450s; the business went on, however, and the sons of Alessandra were sent to the Strozzi offices in Naples and Bruges as apprentices. From there, they had to supply the mother in Florence with all kinds of luxury goods and even works of art. A member of the Strozzi family did business with the English Merchant Adventurers in Bruges (see p. 64). The Medici family and their allies, the families Tani, Portinari, Ricasoli, Cavalcanti and Altoviti (including leading members of the confraternity of the 'Dry Tree'), were, of course, even more involved with the musical imports from Bruges. Like the Venetian merchants in the earlier part of the century, these educated men must have collected secular music in Flanders, and may even have had their own musicians. It is known that Piero de' Medici was in touch with Dufay; a little chansonnier which belonged to him in the 1460s (*RU*) contains the song *'O rosa bella'*, here attributed to Bedingham. The head of the Medici bank in Bruges, Angelo Tani, helped Cosimo de'Medici in 1448 to find singers in Flanders, and the pattern is repeated in 1467 with his successor Tommaso Portinari who hired Cordier, among others.[135] Tani and Portinari were, of course, also patrons of Memling and van der Goes.[136] From the personal affiliation between Heinrich Isaac and the Florentine church of S. Maria Nuova, whose patrons included the Portinari family[137] – Hugo van der Goes's 'Portinari altar' was erected there in 1483 – it may be concluded that Isaac came to Florence in 1484 on the initiative of Tommaso Portinari, and possibly from Bruges.

Lorenzo de'Medici seems to have visited Bruges in 1466.[138] The Florentine chansonniers *Fn 176* of *c.*1480 and *Ric 2356*, copied a little later, which share a scribal hand, contain not only many 'Burgundian' pieces (including some by Joye, Domarto and Basin), but also some relatively obscure English songs. The copyist who worked on both manuscripts (see p. 121) may have been associated with the Servite friary of SS. Annunziata, as was the student of Hothby in Lucca, Matheus Francisci de Testadraconibus, who later became prior of the convent.[139] The group of discant singers at San Giovanni, which counted several Flemings among its members, was organised almost exactly like the singers of St Donatian's in Bruges. A contract of 1482 stipulates that the singers of San Giovanni had to sing polyphony in the Servite convent together with some of the monks (one of the latter was a certain 'Andrea di Giovanni da Fiandra') – just as the 'Dry Tree' had drawn its musical personnel from both the clerks of St Donatian's and the Friars Minor as early as 1414. In 1484, when the chapel at SS. Annunziata counted seven Servites among its eighteen members, one of their regular obligations was the 'messa de canto figurato' every Saturday in San Giovanni[140] – just like the weekly Lady-mass of the 'Dry Tree'. Moreover, the music in the churches of Florence was supported and even controlled precisely by those trade guilds whose business kept them in touch with Flanders all the time: the 'Arte della Lana' and the 'Arte di Calimala' (cloth merchants and processors). Their patronage of music was shared with that of the Medici in a way similar to that in which the 'Dry Tree' and other confraternities of Bruges collaborated with the dukes and the local nobility. The analogies are so close because Florence, like Bruges, was a centre of trade as well as of the fine arts and music – a similar culture arose from similar social patterns. Florentine convents also housed special confraternities for foreign merchants and craftsmen. Two of these were the confraternities of St Barbara and St Catherine,[141] which at some stage had formed a single entity; but by about the middle of the century, the members of St Barbara had become established in the Servite convent, those of St Catherine with the Carmelites. Both groups consisted mainly of foreigners from Flanders and Germany, weavers and cloth-makers, as well as musicians: trumpeters and pipers from Switzerland, Augsburg, Basel, Maestricht and Damme. The provost of the St Barbara group around 1450 was a certain 'Cornelius Gualteri de Brugia'.

St Catherine and St Barbara are the two saints represented on the wings of the famous triptych of Polizzi Generosa, on which Walter Frye's *Ave regina celorum* is depicted in a performance by musician angels.[142] Three paintings are known today which contain such an *Ave regina* motet, and all three originated in Bruges around 1480–1490.[143]

The Polizzi triptych is, therefore, not a result of special English-Italian contacts in music, or even of a sojourn of Frye in Italy, as previous scholars have thought: the simple truth is that it was painted in Bruges for Italian merchants who knew, and wanted to imitate, the particular decoration of a Bruges confraternity chapel. At least one confraternity of St Catherine and St Barbara existed there (at St Saviour's), but the altar-pieces could have served any of the confraternities dedicated to either saint, or to the Virgin, since the subject of the three panels is, after all, the 'Queen of Heaven'. It is to her that Walter Frye's famous motet is dedicated, as is also the almost equally well-known motet *O pulcherrima mulierum* (by Plummer?) in the Lucca choirbook. The pictures and the motets typify Marian devotion in Bruges; their very wide distribution, particularly in Italian chansonniers, reflects the analogous attitudes of confraternities and guilds in several European countries. There is a legend concerning the history of the Polizzi Generosa triptych which rings true: the Genoese captain Luca Giardini was shipwrecked in the Mediterranean in 1496, carrying the panels on board, which he then donated, after his rescue, to the Sicilian church. The destination of the picture would, therefore, not have been Sicily, but rather Genoa or, equally likely, Naples or Florence. In all three places, the motet was already well-known (in Genoa, it was copied *c*.1460 into the manuscript *Fn 112bis*, together with other *Ave reginas*[144]). All three towns had a flourishing trade with Bruges. Italian merchants must have introduced the music in the first place, or have been patrons of the Flemish musicians who brought it to Italy.

The picture of the distribution of liturgical music from Bruges is at least as diffuse as in the case of chansons and devotional motets. It is impossible to trace the ways in which certain English and Flemish works which survive in the middle and late codices of Trent (*Tr 93, 90, 88, 89* and *91*) were transmitted. A note about some of the early mass cycles may be in order, however. The codices *Tr 93, 90, 88* and *89* are the earliest extant sources for the masses nos. 1, 2, 3, 5a and 5b in the Lucca choirbook, and *Tr 90* is the only extant source for the *Missa 'O rosa bella'*(II) which must be by the same composer as *O rosa bella*(I) – possibly Gilles Joye. I have argued elsewhere[145] that the copy of the Kyrie and Agnus of the *Missa 'Caput'* in *Tr 88* goes back to the same source, presumably an English one, as that in the Lucca fragment; and Margaret Bent has shown that the copy of the *Missa 'Quem malignus spiritus'* in *Tr 93* presupposes a model written in the English notational manner.[146] One wonders whether these copies came from Bruges, although Cambrai is also possible. Johannes Wiser of Trent copied the masses *Spiritus almus* (no. 2), *O rosa bella*(I) and (II) and the motet *O pulcherrima* (no. 22) at about the same time (around 1460). The version of the last-named work in *Tr 88* (no. 239) is followed, albeit in a different hand, by a motet *Salve virgo mater* which has been edited as a work by Walter Frye, and which may well be the missing Kyrie of his *Missa 'Summe Trinitati'* with a substitute text. The next major work in the source is an anonymous mass-cycle on Binchois's dance-song *Filles a marier*. This particular conglomerate points very much to a Flemish model source.

The relationship between Bruges and the Burgundian choirbook *Br 5557*[147] is also difficult to assess. The first, rather self-contained section of this manuscript, consists of five English masses (including the three by Walter Frye that survive more or less complete) and is almost complementary to the repertory found in the Lucca choirbook. The composer of a fourth mass, Riquardus Cockx, is definitely not traceable in Bruges, while the fifth mass, *Omnipotens pater*, which is perhaps by Plummer, is 'replaced' in *Las 238* by a similar *Omnipotens pater* mass (no. 5). Perhaps the dukes of Burgundy inherited this mass collection from some English establishment on the continent other than Bruges (Calais?); the English Kyries are partly suppressed or altered, quite unlike *Las 238*. The remainder of *Br 5557* has only one work in common with *Las 238*, Cornelius Heyns's *Missa 'Pour quelque paine'* (no. 13) – but this was copied into *Las 238* after *c.* 1470 in Lucca (see p. 131). Among the nine motets in *Las 238*, there seems to be no work by Busnois, who had several of his motets copied into *Br 5557* at about the same time or a little later; if the Magnificat no. 24 is by him, then it is striking that *Br 5557* contains two different Magnificats, presumably both by Busnois. Of the three late masses by Dufay, one is preserved in Lucca, the other two in Brussels. It is as if the compilers of the two manuscripts had tried to avoid duplication while drawing on closely related sources. This presupposes some kind of contact, however, between the compilers or their advisors.

The oldest layer of the choirbook of St Peter's, Rome (*SP*) was transcribed, according to Christopher Reynolds,[148] from an earlier Roman choirbook, dating from 1458. The collection starts with six masses not found elsewhere, only one of which is attributed – to Petrus de Domarto. The sixth mass, which is the only one for four voices, is dedicated to St Thomas of Canterbury; the first mass is stylistically similar to the fragmentary mass by Frye in *Las 238* (no. 4). It is also strange that the Domarto mass originally lacked the Kyrie, which was composed later by the singer Egidius Cervelli; likewise, a mass on fol. 61v–70v in the later layer (1463) has an arranged Kyrie (two seemingly complete settings); comparison with other sources shows that the original Kyrie was bipartite in the English manner, a problem which is solved differently in the three sources (*SP, Tr 88, Verona 759* fol. 20v). This mass is very probably English: its Gloria is identified in *Tr 90* as 'anglicum'. Singers from Bruges may have been involved in taking this repertory, including the Domarto mass, to Rome (see Appendix A: Fraxinis, Maes, Raes, Rosa).

The Cappella Sistina choirbooks 14 and 51 clearly draw on music from Bruges. In the case of Domarto's *Spiritus almus* which is preserved in *CS 14*, a filiation of the four sources based on the variant readings suggests that the papal copy itself depends directly or indirectly on *Las 238*. *CS 14* is also the codex which contains the only extant mass composition by Johannes de Wreede (a Marian Kyrie and Gloria), who is, furthermore, described as '*brugen[sis]*' in the manuscript. This would hardly have been known to the scribe had the work arrived from Spain where Wreede worked from *c.*1476. Of the four extant manuscripts of Dufay's *Missa 'L'homme armé'*, the versions in *CS 14* and *Las 238* seem most closely related. *CS 14* also has the 'St Andrew' mass of Lucca (no. 7a). In *CS 51*, written at about the same time as *CS 14* (*c.*1485), we find two works which were certainly part of the Bruges repertory: the mass by Heyns and Weerbeke's *Missa 'O Venus bant'*[149] (assuming that the latter is one of the two masses 'de O Venus banden' copied at St Donatian's in 1475/6); Flemish connections can also be put forward for *Vinnus Vinna*[150] and Busnois's *O crux lignum*.[151] It is just possible that Jeronimus (or Nicasius) de Clibano's *Missa 'Et super nivem dealbabor'*, known only from *CS 51*, was part of the repertory of Bruges around 1485 as well – Jeronimus was not engaged as succentor of St Donatian's until 1492, but he came from s'Hertogenbosch with which place music had been exchanged for a long time. I suggest that some of the masses in *CS 14* and *CS 51* were taken to Rome by Jean Cordier, Guillelmus Rosa or other singers from Bruges. A later group of Cappella Sistina manuscripts – *CS 15, 26, 35, 41* and *63* – has a few more works which also existed in the Bruges repertory. It is strange that of the six mass compositions by Ockeghem that are preserved in these choirbooks,[152] four were also copied at St Donatian's, where almost no other composer's name is mentioned in the account books. They are the Credo *sine nomine* (*CS 26*, identified by Dragan Plamenac as the Credo *de Village* by Ockeghem, copied by Martinus Colins in 1475/6); the *Missa 'Mimi'* (*CS 41* and *63*; copied by Colins in 1475/6); the *Missa Cuiusvis toni* (*CS 35*; copied by Colins in 1476/7); and the *Missa 'L'homme armé'* (*CS 35*; copied by Johannes Smout in 1467/8). In *CS 15*, a motet codex, we find the motet *Vidi speciosam* of the Lucca choirbook (no. 23) which is not known from other sources. Like the Ockeghem works, it was probably not composed in Bruges. Several works by Obrecht, however, which were or seem to have been written in Bruges, are contained in the papal choirbooks: the *Missa de Sancto Donatiano* (*CS 35*: *c.*1490?); the *Missa 'Ave regina celorum'* (*CS 160*, of 1518–19) and the *Missa 'Salve diva parens'* (*CS 51*, but added later by the copyist of *CS 35*).

The Castilian choirbook of the cathedral of Segovia (*Seg*), discovered by Higinio Anglés in 1922,[153] contains, on its first 207 folios, a homogeneous collection of Franco-Flemish music of the last quarter of the century. The selection of composers does not seem to tally with the personnel of any known chapel at the time; the absence of works by Pierre de la Rue seems to rule out a connection with the chapel of Philip the Fair, who went to Spain in 1501. Obrecht's works are most prominent; other important authors are Tinctoris, Agricola, Compère and Brumel. The provenance of some of the music is distinctly Italian (Milan and Naples); other works point strongly to the Low Countries (s'Hertogenbosch: Matheus Pipelare; Bergen-op-Zoom or Bruges: Obrecht). Two works could have come directly from Bruges: the motet *Salve sancta facies* (no. 69), the hymn to St Veronica which is prominent in almost all Books of Hours from Bruges at the time, because it was associated with the wool- and cloth-merchants; and the chanson *J'ay bien nori* by a certain 'Johannes Joye' which also exists in different versions attributed to Johannes Japart and Josquin, but could be by Gilles Joye. A clue is provided by a piece with the strange attribution(?) 'Ferdinandus et frater ejus' and the even stranger text incipit 'Cecus non judicat de coloribus' ('The blind man does not judge about colours'). This work is transmitted in many other sources with different texts, often attributed to Alexander Agricola.[154] I suggest, however, that it came into the present source from the repertory of the blind brothers Johannes and Carolus Fernandes, who astonished Tinctoris in Bruges in 1482 (see p. 88) with their instrumental duos. Could it be that this whole repertory was collected by Tinctoris, partly on his travels in the North which he reports in his latest work (*c*.1482–83), *De inventione et usu musicae*? In this treatise[155] he also narrates that he heard his fellow-countryman Gherardus of Brabant sing the chanson '*Tout a par moy*' by Walter Frye in two parts on his own (this was in Chartres); there is, indeed, a two-part arrangement of the song in this source, attributed to Tinctoris – a transcription of what he heard from Gherardus? The manuscript contains no fewer than 35 Flemish songs, which is very unusual for a Spanish source, but again, Tinctoris would have been in a position to transmit the text incipits accurately. Among other *unica*, there are many arrangements or elaborations of famous chansons like '*Comme femme*', '*De tous biens pleine*', '*Le souvenir*' and many pieces starting with the word '*Helas*' – often for two voices only, and showing an instrumental and even didactic experimentalism. These pieces are mostly attributed to Tinctoris, Agricola and Compère; the last-named was Tinctoris' colleague at Cambrai cathedral in the 1460s, where he mentioned him among other musicians in his motet '*Omnium bonorum plena*', based on Heyne's '*De tous biens pleine*'. Agricola may have met Tinctoris at the Aragonese court of Naples, where Compère also worked for some time. Brumel was one of Tinctoris's successors at Chartres cathedral (1483–86); perhaps Tinctoris' own service in Chartres, not otherwise datable, falls into the time of his travels in the North in 1482–83.

Obrecht's works for Bruges

Of the 31 secular works by Obrecht that are known today,[156] no fewer than 16 are preserved in the Segovia choirbook. All their text incipits are Flemish. Although the absence of a full text in sources of the time does not necessarily preclude vocal performance, many of these pieces[157] appear to be instrumental fantasias over popular monophonic tunes, rather than polyphonic songs. A chanson of the time would always reflect, in some way, the structure of the poem; but these pieces often have long, contrapuntal duets, many internal repetitions or contrasting sections, especially those in triple metre at the end, or are rhythmically unsuitable for a clear delivery of the text. *T'Andernaken* (Wolf no. 3), for example, is a cantus firmus setting of the well-known tune, which appears in the tenor in very long notes, while the other two voices spin an elaborate counterpoint around it. The technique often resembles that of certain sections in 'parody' masses of the time. As in these, the composer refers to a popular melody, but imposes a different form on it. It may be suggested that the bulk of this *Spielmusik* in the Segovia codex was written for public serenades and concerts of urban wind bands, i.e. for the city minstrels of towns such as Bruges and Bergen-op-Zoom.[158] We have seen that the repertory of the city minstrels of Bruges in the 1480s included polyphonic 'motets' by Nicasius de Brauwere; Obrecht must have enriched this repertory with his own compositions. Pieces like *Mijn morken gaf*, a quodlibet on popular songs, fit particularly well into the atmosphere of a public serenade in the market square or *Burg*.

These minstrels' concerts were held in honour of the Virgin, and one has to assume that the minstrels played sacred works as well, especially the *Salve regina* and other Marian pieces, or sections from masses that were suitable for instrumental performance. From 1483, the Bruges minstrels gave their *Salve* or *Lof* in the church of St Donatian itself – this practice may be connected with the curious genre of *Salve regina*s which employ secular tunes as cantus firmi and are known from early sixteenth-century sources.[159] The vocal *Salve* concerts which were performed by the choirboys under the succentors Aliamus de Groote, Obrecht and their successors, may also have included sacred works over secular tunes, together with cantus firmus settings of well-known plainsongs such as the *Ave regina celorum*, *Alma redemptoris mater*, and so on. This was 'audience-directed' music; people had to be able to recognise the underlying tune or plainsong, and a combination of several

known tunes or a genuine quodlibet would have had a highly entertaining effect. The aesthetic principle is the same as that of Obrecht's
(and Isaac's) *Missae Carminum*. The cantus firmus technique was an
obvious vehicle for communication.

The *Salve* concerts seem to have existed in Antwerp and Bergen-op-
Zoom as well as in Bruges. For chronological and other reasons, however, we may suggest that the following motets[160] by Obrecht were
composed specifically for the Bruges concerts: *Alma redemptoris mater*
(Wolf no. 17); *Ave maris stella (Seg)*; *Ave regina celorum* (Wolf no. 6) –
based on the motet by Walter Frye which was so well-known in Bruges;
Beata es Maria (Wolf no. 7) – based on at least two cantus firmi, one
from the Marian litany and the other from the *Ave Maria*; perhaps the
Regina coeli (Seg); and at least one of the *Salve reginas* – that for three
voices, which resembles the instrumental song arrangements (Wolf
no. 16).

Four other motets by Obrecht belong to Bruges for more specifically
liturgical reasons. *O beate Basili / O beate pater* is based on two vespers
antiphons (with the same chant) for one of the most venerated saints
of the town whose chapel stood in the *Burg*, St Basil. The texts are
printed in the breviary of the church of St Donatian (1520).[161] *O
preciosissime sanguis* must have been written for a service in the Holy
Blood chapel in St Basil's, or for the great Holy Blood procession on
3 May. Another 'triple feast' of Bruges, that of the Exaltation of the
Cross (14 September), may be represented in the motet *Salve crux arbor
vite / O crux lignum*. This wonderful work combines three texts for the
Holy Cross, but gives prominence to the melody and text of the verse *O
crux lignum triumphale* from the sequence *Laudes crucis attollamus*. This
verse alone was sung in Bruges on 14 September, whereas the whole
sequence belonged to the liturgy of 3 May. In the motet *Homo quidam /
Salve sancta facies*, Obrecht's combination of liturgical material is most
peculiar. *Homo quidam fecit cenam magnam*, a responsory for Corpus
Christi, tells the story of the dinner for the poor given by a rich man; it
was part of many endowed services of Bruges, especially when these
also provided for a 'table of the poor'. The main text, however, is the St
Veronica hymn *Salve sancta facies* on the Holy Face or *Volto Santo*, a
popular prayer text in Books of Hours, especially, as already mentioned, with cloth-merchants, as the venerated object is the *sudarium* of
St Veronica (see above). The connection between this hymn and
charity must be explained thus: the motet was written for an endowment of a cloth- or silk merchant of Bruges which included a 'table of
the poor'. A painting by Petrus Christus seems to show such a merchant, possibly a Venetian, with a prayer-book and with a poster on the
wall which contains the *Volto Santo* and the full text of the hymn.[162]

The only mass by Obrecht which has traditionally been connected with Bruges, for obvious reasons, is the *Missa de Sancto Donatiano*. It has been identified with the mass which the composer sent to Bruges in 1491, after his departure, and which may be the one that was copied into a choirbook of St Donatian's in 1491/2.[163] In neither case, however, is the mass named; that it was the *Missa de Sancto Donatiano* is mere speculation. If Obrecht composed the work for a service at St Donatian's, it seems strange that he should have done so only after his departure. We have shown above (p. 41 f.) that the *Missa de Sancto Martino* was written for the collegiate church. The Donatian mass, however, was not. First of all, it must be remembered that St Donatian was the patron saint of Bruges and not only of one church; his feast-day (14 October) was celebrated in all the major churches of the town. Obrecht's cantus firmi in this mass do not suggest the use of the collegiate church in particular. The main cantus firmus of the work, the antiphon *O beate pater Donatiane*, was sung only on the sixth and seventh days of the octave; its melody was identical with that of *O beate pater Basili* (see above), and more commonly known in connection with the latter saint and his feast-day (14 June). As a plainsong for multiple use, it was widely known outside the collegiate church. Two subordinate cantus firmi are derived from the first and eighth responsories, respectively, of 14 October (*Confessor domini Donatianus* and *O sanctissime presul*; for an earlier use of this, see p. 118). Second, there are two more cantus firmi in Obrecht's mass which do not fit the St Donatian liturgy at all, and whose presence must be the clue to the destination of the work: the 'O-antiphon' *O clavis David*, usually sung on 20 December, and the Flemish song (or text only?) *Geeft den armen gefangen umb got, dat u got helpe mari ut aller not*, which seems otherwise unknown.

O clavis David was used not only as an antiphon for Advent but also as a prayer for the dead. It occurs as such in a Netherlandish prayer-book of the sixteenth century,[164] and very probably in other sources. The passage '. . . veni, et educ vinctum de domo carceris' could be adjusted to read 'vinctam' if the deceased person was a woman; Obrecht's text has 'vinctum'. This prayer is interlocked with the Credo text in such a way that the two texts complete each other's meaning. While the antiphon speaks of the captivity of death, from which the human soul wishes to be delivered by God, the 'key of David', the Credo text describes the passion and resurrection of Christ, after three days of captivity in hell, and his return 'to judge the living and the dead'. At the same time, the intercession of St Donatian is invoked in another voice, with the words of the eighth responsory – all these texts have to be sung in Obrecht's mass, together with the mass text itself.[165] What happens is that the human soul, 'sitting in the shadow of death', prays to be delivered through the resurrection of its saviour, like a prisoner from his cell. This analogy, in turn, is somehow linked to the

Flemish song in the Kyrie II, which asks for alms to be given to the 'poor prisoners'. This wonderful and complex imagery was 'composed' by Jacob Obrecht for a citizen of Bruges, Donaes de Moor.

De Moor was a rich furrier, for a long time dean of his guild, and a known well-doer. With his wife Adriaene de Vos, he endowed the church of St James, where his confraternity was established, with chaplaincies, a panel for the high altar, and a number of liturgical services. But the couple also founded an almshouse in the parish (see p. 57); it is documented that one of their endowments included alms to the inmates of the city prison, the *donckercamere*, as did that of Johannes de Hagha (see p. 18). After Donaes's death in 1483, his widow extended the endowments to include one polyphonic mass each on the days of their respective patron saints, Donatian and Adrian. The masses were to be sung in St James's, 'in discant with six musicians of the church, a priest, deacon and sub-deacon and the great organ, at seven o'clock in the evening or thereabouts. One has to ring with the great peal of bells throughout the mass.' The document is dated 14 March 1487.[166] Besides the precious references to the environment of the performances, we are reminded of the other works by Obrecht whose combinations of cantus firmi reflect the complex conditions of private endowments, often linked with charity and centred on anniversaries or requiems. The polyphonic mass endowed by Adriaene de Vos for herself – a *Missa de Sancto Adriano* – may have been composed by Obrecht as well, but seems to be lost.

A chronology of Obrecht's style has not yet been worked out, but we may be able to move a step closer to it when examining other masses which he could have written in Bruges. First, it would be logical to assume that he composed the *Missa 'Ave regina celorum'* in the same place and time as the motet of that name, i.e. in Bruges around 1485–1490; the mass is even closer to Frye's model in some respects than is the motet. The effect of both 'parodies' would not have been lost on a Bruges audience. The 'parody' technique of the mass, which quotes the tenor of the model literally for very long stretches, but only occasionally borrows material from other voices, is similar to those in the masses *L'homme armé* and *Caput*. Both these works have already been connected with Bruges: the former because it is based on Busnois's mass, and Busnois held a position in the town at this time; the latter because of its models (the English *Caput* mass, definitely known in Bruges, and Ockeghem's work) and because it requires the organ for the performance of the cantus firmus throughout, which at least rules out Cambrai as the place of composition.[167] It seems to me that several other parody masses by Obrecht are earlier, predating 1485, although largely contained in a Ferrarese choirbook of *c.*1505 (*ModD*),[168] such as *Plurimorum carminum II (Scoen lief)* or *Rosa playsant; De tous biens pleine* and *Fors* *seulement* have always been regarded as the earliest works. It might have been in Bruges where Obrecht first transferred the technique of using more than one model from the chanson masses to those on plainsong, for example in the Donatian and Martin masses. At the same time he appears to have developed and differentiated this technique, as is shown in the (more advanced) *Missa Plurimorum carminum I (Adieu mes amours)*. This work uses, among other tunes, the chanson *Madame faites-moy savoir* by Adrien(?) Basin: could this be the work which Obrecht sent from Antwerp to his colleagues at St Donatian's in 1491, paying homage to their favourite chansons? Also the *Missa 'Je ne demande'* is based on a model with Bruges connections, a chanson by Busnois, and it has actually been dated before *c.*1491.[169] Its parody technique is, again, more advanced than that of *Caput* or *L'homme armé*, which suggests a date rather close to 1490, if the other two are really as late as the Bruges period. Among the plainsong masses, the general style of the *Missa 'Beata viscera'*, datable before *c.*1493, is strikingly similar to the Donatian and Martin masses; it could have been used as a Lady-mass in the chapel of the confraternity of the 'Dry Tree'.

Obrecht's most widely distributed work, the *Missa 'Salve diva parens'*, has a title which is meant to recall the introit of the *Missa de Salve*. Although such *Salve* masses must have existed also outside Bruges, for example in Antwerp, there is documentary evidence that St Donatian's had a whole collection of such works by 1499. Obrecht himself collaborated (by drawing staves!) in the production of a codex 'missarum de Salve sancta parens et aliis' in 1499/1500 at St Donatian's.[170] Within a collection of works with the same function as in this case, there would be every reason to vary the reference to the Marian introit in an interesting way. If this work was composed for Bruges (in 1485–1490?), then its peculiar cantus firmus should also have something to do with the town. The text is remarkable for its allusions to classical antiquity; the melody seems similar to the cantus firmus of Antoine de Févin's *Missa 'O quam glorifica'*. It turns out that the poem *Salve diva parens* has exactly the same metre as the Marian hymn *O quam glorifica luce coruscas*. This hymn is thought to have been composed by the great Flemish musician of the ninth century, Hucbald of Saint-Amand. *Salve diva parens* could be a newly-composed stanza for the ancient hymn, which was sung to more than one melody.[171] The humanist flavour of the stanza could well have been within the reach of a Bruges poet such as Aliamus de Groote.

With some of these suggestions, we are still in the realm of speculation – but speculation can be a science, too. Obrecht is a prime example of a 'speculative' composer in this sense of the word. He was a curious mediator between Hucbald and humanism.

EPILOGUE

There is no obvious break in the musical traditions of Bruges in the decades preceding the religious struggles and the political rebellions which marked the second half of the sixteenth century. Despite the economic and political decline of the town, the cultural climate was still a favourable one. Notable composers continued to work in Bruges: Antonius Divitis, Benedictus Appenzeller, Lupus Hellinck, Jan Richafort and even Clemens non Papa. Some of their works are preserved, together with those of their great predecessors, in musical manuscripts which were actually copied in Bruges: the London chansonnier Add. 35087 (c.1510),[172] the Brussels-Tournai partbooks of 1511,[173] the Cambrai partbooks 125–128 which belonged to Zegher van Male in 1542.[174] In 1559, the copyists of St Donatian's were able to compile six codices with a total of 400 motets.[175] Bruges seems to have been the musical background for Adrian Willaert, as well as for his deputy in Venice, Jacques Buus. While some musical institutions of Bruges were disrupted by religious controversies (the confraternity of the 'Dry Tree' as early as 1518), at others music received a fresh impetus; St Saviour's, in particular, had the resources to rebuild its church music, and was helped therein by important benefactors such as Michiel van Hille and the confraternity of Our Lady of the Seven Sorrows (see p. 55 f.). A choirbook which contains music for their particular devotion, the Brussels MS 215–216, has been connected with Bruges.[176] Although the codex was probably copied in Malines during the later life of its first owner, Charles de Clerc, it is significant that his first wife had been Eleonora Lem, daughter of the exiled burgomaster Martin Lem and one of the richest heirs of Bruges. Their wedding had taken place in St Donatian's in 1499. One might speculate that de Clerc had connections with the confraternity of the Seven Sorrows.[177] But the codex itself has as little to do with Bruges as have any of the other choirbooks of the so-called 'Netherlands court group' – even if they contained music that was copied from Bruges sources (such as, possibly, some works in the Chigi codex), the initiative for their compilation did not come from the Flemish town.[178]

In the first decades of the sixteenth century, Bruges lost its wealth (as it had lost many of its merchant colonies) to other centres in the Low Countries: Antwerp, Brussels, Malines. This transition is a social and political as well as an economic one. The new choirbooks like Brussels 215–216 were written for the Habsburg court or other European dynasties, and for the nobility which was affiliated to these courts. The days were gone when the patronage of music had been so successfully shared between the clergy, the self-confident urban middle class with its foreign merchant guests, and a Burgundian court which mixed freely with this balanced urban culture. The cultural strength of Bruges had relied on the *continuity* of communication and exchange between all these elements. The continuity had been broken, politically, by Charles the Bold's imperialist ambition and by his downfall in 1477, after which political hegemony started to shuttle between the major European powers as in a ball-game – and the medieval cities were the first to be left behind. Bruges had somehow succeeded in defending its ancient privileges against the nobility and the claims of the rulers within the framework of the Burgundian state; but the citizens lost out against the territorial grip of Maximilian of Habsburg and his armies who used fire-arms against the guilds of archers and crossbowmen – and they were to lose out even more against the Spanish kings who paid their mercenaries with American gold.

The increasing control of the courts over the culture of their territories (including the churches) did allow some major cities to maintain an important secondary role – but only those which had the commercial muscle to conquer such a position, like Antwerp or Augsburg. Bruges, once the banking centre of Western Europe, was found penniless after the extortions of the Valois dukes and after the departure of its richest merchants to the better-situated port of Antwerp, which also commanded the increasingly important trade routes to Central Europe. Antwerp did not, however, simply take over the cultural role of Bruges: it was to become the place where music was printed rather than composed. The musical initiative, which had once been in the hands of the minstrels, *rederijkers, socii de musica,* friars and canons of Bruges, passed over almost completely to the musicians employed by one or another major European court. The leading works of the sixteenth century, and most of the secondary ones, were not produced for urban communities, but for the pope, the kings, and the dukes.

It is for this reason that the music of late medieval Bruges is not lost forever – it has only been pushed aside. The courtly and absolutist culture of early modern Europe has now also passed away; just before it did so, the works of Johann Sebastian Bach recalled the profound tension and balance between technique and message which Obrecht had displayed in another European city. Such images cannot be blurred; they are hidden but precise. Even today, the musical experience of Bruges can be rediscovered because it has never lost its authenticity.

NOTES

Preface

1. My thoughts on this subject have been greatly influenced by the writings of Johan Huizinga. See, in particular, his *Herfstij der Middeleeuwen* (Haarlem, 1919), Engl. transl. as *The Waning of the Middle Ages* (Penguin books, 1955); and his 'Das Problem der Renaissance', in J. H., *Parerga*, ed. W. Kaegi (Basel, 1945), pp. 87–146.

Chapter One

1. For interpretations of this and other paintings showing angels' performances, see Reinhold Hammerstein, *Die Musik der Engel* (Munich, 1962); Emanuel Winternitz, article 'Engelskonzert' in *Die Musik in Geschichte und Gegenwart*, Supplement (Kassel etc., 1976); *idem, Musical Instruments and their Symbolism in Western Art* (London, 1967); *idem*, 'Secular musical practice in sacred art', *Early Music* 3 (1975), pp. 221–226; Carapezza, *Regina angelorum* (see bibliography); A. P. de Mirimonde, 'Les anges musiciens chez Memlinc', *Jaarboek van het Koninklijk Museum voor Schone Kunsten* (Antwerpen, 1962–63), pp. 5–55.

2. For a broad and instructive survey of musical life and soundscape in late medieval towns, see Walter Salmen, 'Vom Musizieren in der spätmittelalterlichen Stadt', in *Das Leben in der Stadt des Spätmittelalters*, Internat. Kongress Krems/Donau 1976 (Vienna, 1977) (Österreichische Akademie der Wissenschaften, Phil. -hist. Klasse, Sitzungsber., 325), pp. 77–87.

3. See Walther Boer, *Het Anthonius-Motet van Anthonius Busnois* (Amsterdam, 1940); Willem Elders, 'Zur Aufführungspraxis der altniederländischen Musik', in *Renaissance-Muziek 1400–1600. Donum Natalicium René Bernard Lenaerts*, ed. J. Robijns, (Louvain, 1969), p. 89 ff.

4. Louis Gilliodts-Van Severen, *Le carillon de Bruges* (Bruges, 1912) (Essais d'archéologie Brugeoise 1).

5. See chapter IV n. 8.

6. These observations correspond to the statements in Johan Huizinga, *The Waning of the Middle Ages* (see preface n. 1), Chapter 20: 'The Aesthetic Sentiment'.

7. See Leo van Puyvelde, *Schilderkunst en Toneelvertoningen op het einde van de Middeleeuwen* (Ghent, 1912).

8. Edmund A. Bowles, 'Musical Instruments in Civic Processions during the Middle Ages', *Acta Mus* 33 (1961), pp. 150–161; *idem*, 'Musical Instruments in the Medieval Corpus Christi Procession', *JAMS* 17 (1964), pp. 251–260; *idem*, '*Haut* and *Bas*: The Grouping of Musical Instruments in the Middle Ages', *MD* 8 (1954), pp. 115–140; *idem*, 'The Role of Musical Instruments in Medieval Sacred Drama', *MQ* 45 (1959), pp. 67–84.

Chapter Two

1. See Moreau, *Histoire*.
2. Van Houtte, p. 13ff.; Letts, p. 2; B. Janssens de Bisthoven, 'Het Kapittel van Sint-Donatiaan te Brugge', in *Sint-Donaas*, pp. 51–60.
3. Luc Devliegher, 'Het Koor van de Romaanse Sint-Donaaskerk te Brugge', in *Sint-Donaas*, pp. 32–46; Frederik Suys, 'Dood van een Katedraal', ibid. pp. 47–50.
4. An (incomplete) list of the beneficiaries of St Donatian's is given in Foppens.
5. Dewitte, *SD* p. 133 ff.
6. Acta *SD*, 5 October 1360; 13 August 1365; De Schrevel, p. 149 (23 June 1366, 28 April 1367).
7. De Schrevel, vol. II, p. I, n. 1.
8. Dewitte, *Boek*, pp. 72–76.
9. Acta *SD*, 30 September 1415, fol. 17r–v.
10. Acta *SD*, 1417, fol. 27v.
11. Acta *SD*, 16 August 1417, fol. 38v–39v.
12. Accounts *SD*, 1385/6, fol. 6r.
13. Adolphe Duclos, 'Saint Maclou', *ASEB* 28 (1876–77), pp. 355–384.
14. They received 3s each. Accounts *SD*, 1401/02, fol. 7v (referring to both years).
15. Accounts *SD*, 1381/2, fol. 8r.
16. Dewitte, *Boek*, p. 93.
17. Dewitte, *SD*, p. 134; Accounts *SD*, 1375/6, fol. 4v; 1400/01, fol. 8r; 1401/02, fol. 7r, etc.
18. Acta *SD*, 14 February 1385. From now on, all dated notices about St Donatian's are drawn from the Acta *SD* unless otherwise indicated.
19. Gilliodts, *Inventaire* II, p. 338 ff.
20. Planarius *SD*, 14 September; Acta *SD*, 30 September 1415; see also n. 9 above.
21. Acta *SD* 26 April 1384.
22. Accounts *SD*, 1383/4, fol. 6v.
23. Acta *SD*, 9 March 1388.
24. Wright, *Burgundy*, p. 56 ff.
25. Wright, *Burgundy*, *passim*.
26. Acta *SD*, 16 August 1370.
27. Bisschoppelijk Archief Brugge, Ser. N. 26: will of J. Ondanch, dated 1425; his prebend (no. XXIII) was given in 1426 to Radulphus Majoris (Foppens).
28. E. Pognon, 'Ballades mythologiques de Jean de le Mote, Philippe Vitry, Jean Campion', *Humanisme et Renaissance* 5 (1938), pp. 402–406, 411; Gilbert Reaney, 'A Postscript to the Codex Chantilly', *MD* 10 (1956), p. 57ff. 'Bergibus' (i.e. Berges), a place mentioned by de le Mote as being famous for its music school, is not Bruges, as Reaney suggests, but rather Bergues-Saint-Winnoc in French Flanders.
29. R. de Keyzer, 'Individueel en collectief boekenbezit bij de Kannunijken van het Sint-Donaaskapittel de Brugge tijdens de late Middeleeuwen

(1350–1450)', *Archives et Bibliothèques de Belgique* 42 (1971), pp. 347–378; 43 (1972) pp. 141–175 and 493–516; Albert Derolez, *Corpus*, p. 33ff.

30. Günther, *Biographie*, p. 190.
31. Wright, *Burgundy*, p. 63.
32. E. van Steenberghe, 'Gerson à Bruges', *Revue d'histoire ecclésiastique* 31 (1935), p. 35ff.; Joyce L. Irwin, 'The Mystical Music of Jean Gerson', *EMH* 1 (1981), pp. 187–201.
33. Acta *SD*, 30 December 1411.
34. Acta *SD*, 27 October 1410: Jacobus Vide, *clericus tornacensis diocesis* received as canon on the basis of '*littere pape moderni*'. He was not in holy orders then. See also Foppens, p. 136.
35. Schuler, *Martin V*, p. 41.
36. Schuler, *Konstanz*, p. 158.
37. Dewitte, *Boek*, p. 84ff., nos. 91, 102, 104, 110.
38. De Schrevel, p. 152ff.
39. Edited by Gilbert Reaney in *Early Fifteenth-Century Music*, 2 (1959).
40. See article 'Clibano, Jacobus de' in *New Grove* (David Fallows); Acta *SD* 3 June 1449: Clibano resigns the *custodia* of the chapel of St John, a major benefice in Bruges.
41. Full text in De Schrevel, p. 31ff.
42. An endowment of *c*.1400 by the canon Petrus de Lobus (Planarius *SD*, fol. 101v) specifies that the *Missa de Salve* was sung every Saturday except in Lent and on the three 'Nativities', i.e. Christ, Mary and St John the Baptist.
43. He was Jacobus Berout, who lived with the canon Georgius Potshooft; admitted 19 February 1420 (Acta *SD*).
44. Dewitte, *Boek*, p. 84.
45. Edited by Margaret Bent in *Four anonymous masses*.
46. Planarius *SD*.
47. See also Acta *SD*, 18 August 1434; Dewitte, *SD*, p. 145.
48. Herman Vander Linden, *Itinéraires de Philippe le Bon, duc de Bourgogne (1419–1467), et de Charles, comte de Charolais (1433–1467)* (Bruxelles, 1940).
49. The election on 7 January 1438 led to an interesting incident concerning Binchois. He arrived late at the meeting and was not admitted at once, because he could not produce written evidence that he was in holy orders. After having been told that only canons in holy orders had a vote, he asserted that he had taken orders, and the canon Pierre Godefroy, another ducal singer, confirmed this by taking an oath. Binchois was then admitted, having to promise to send his letter of promotion by 2 February. It arrived in Bruges on 16 January, confirming that Binchois had been promoted to the rank of sub-deacon by the general vicar of the bishop of Cambrai on Saturday of the Ember days in June 1437.
50. Acta *SD*, 23 June and 30 June 1440; see also Wright, *Dufay*, p. 169ff.
51. The prebend was refused for 1440/1 and 1445/6. Dufay was present in Bruges to ask for the payment on 24 January 1442, 24 September 1442, probably 4 October 1443, and on 4 April 1446.
52. Wright, *Dufay*, doc. 24.
53. Wright, *Dufay*, p. 173.

54. For all of these, see also Marix, *Histoire*.

55. Acta *SD*, 19 March to 2 April 1449.

56. Acta *SD*, 7 June 1452.

57. Acta *SD*, 12 April 1458.

58. Tayaert's specialism seems to have been medicine. A medical glossary, copied by him, is preserved in Stadsbibl. Bruges, MS 473: 'Liber pandecte scriptus per me Jacobum Tayaert, artium magistrum, [7 July 1473]' (fol. 243r).

59. Joye was fond of rhetoric. On 27 September 1451 he was admonished for a verbal exchange with the schoolmaster whom he had told 'confabulando . . . ut iret in locum suum'.

60. A version of the song with newly-composed voices in *Tr 90* fol. 444v– 445v is attributed to one 'Hert'. A priest named Bartholomaeus Hert received a chaplaincy at St Donatian's on 9 February 1453; also a citizen Johannes Hert lived in the town at the same time.

61. Acta *SD*, 24 February 1443.

62. Frans van Molle, *Identification d'un portrait de Gilles Joye attribué à Memlinc* (Bruxelles, 1960) (Les Primitifs Flamands III); article 'Joye, Gilles' in *New Grove* (David Fallows); Nino Pirrotta, 'Music and Cultural Tendencies in Fifteenth-Century Italy', *JAMS* 19 (1966), p. 131 (all with reproductions of the portrait). Van Molle and Fallows reject Foppens's statement that Joye was a theologian and poet (p. 136ff.), on insufficient grounds. Foppens did not, as van Molle seems to believe, draw his information from the tombstone alone, where this notice did not, in fact, occur, but also from the commemorative board near the tomb, which is documented thus: '. . . concessum est assem reputationis sue in pictura appendi iuxta eius sepulturam' (Acta *SD*, 2 December 1485). The chapter acts also confirm Foppens's statement that Joye received a *parva prebenda* as a canon as early as 1459 (16 September), although it does not seem to have been the prebend no. XX as Foppens indicates.

63. The two masses, together with a third *O rosa bella* mass which is perhaps by Johannes Martini, have been edited in *Sechs Trienter Codices, 2. Auswahl*, ed. G. Adler and O. Koller (Vienna, 1904; repr. Graz, 1959) (DTÖ XI/1 vol. 22), pp. 1–69.

64. There were, of course, also endowed requiems for the duke (Acta *SD*, 23 June 1467 and 18 July 1467).

65. Not in Dewitte, *Boek*, but see Acta *SD*, 26 May 1460.

66. The following list is extracted from Dewitte, *Boek*, p. 89ff.; the notice about the *Patrem trium regum*, overlooked by Dewitte, comes from Accounts *SD*, 1467/8, dated entry 5 January 1468.

67. In 1472/3, a *Liber de arte speculativa musicali* was bound: Dewitte, *Boek*, p. 92.

68. See the list above. It is, of course, possible that the composer was Rolandus's son, Johannes de Wreede. On him, see p. 43.

69. There is more documentary than iconographic evidence for this practice at the time; for the latter, see James McKinnon, 'Representations of the Mass in Medieval and Renaissance Art', *JAMS* 31 (1978), pp. 21–52; Bowles, *Musikleben*, pp. 106–120; Frank d'Accone, 'The performance of

Sacred Music in Italy during Josquin's Time', in Lowinsky, *Josquin Des Prez*, pp. 601–618. The question has been discussed also in Edmund A. Bowles, 'Were Musical Instruments used in the Liturgical Service during the Middle Ages?', *Galpin Soc. Journal* 10 (1957), pp. 40–56.

70. Dewitte, *SD*, p. 135ff.
71. Dewitte, *SD*, p. 141ff.
72. Acta *SD*, 18 December 1482.
73. See also Dewitte, *SD*, p. 138 and 144. Material for comparison is provided in Edmund Bowles, 'Musical Instruments in Civic Processions during the Middle Ages', *ActaMus* 33 (1961), pp. 150–161.
74. The following notices are largely drawn from Dewitte, *SD*, p. 136ff. and 145ff.
75. De Schrevel, p. 46 (following a manuscript of 1546).
76. Acta *SD*, 26 December 1483 and 30 December 1483.
77. An explicit text of an endowment for the *Missus* ceremony has been edited by M. van Dromme, 'Gulden Mis of Missus-Mis', *ASEB* 58 (1908), pp. 389–396.
78. Description of parts of the custom in De Schrevel, pp. 27–29; Luc Danhieux, 'Uit het handboek van de roedragher van de Sint-Donaaskerk te Brugge', *Biekorf* 74 (1974), pp. 243–254 (including several other ceremonies).
79. Accounts *SD*, 1407/08 (Weale: *Accounts SD*); Gilliodts, *Inventaire*, 6, p. 400 and *Glossaire flamand*, p. 816.
80. See Gilliodts, *Inventaire*, 3, pp. 302–304.
81. M. English, 'Brugge en de eeredienst van Onze-Lieve-Vrauwe van Aardenburg', *ASEB* 69 (1926), pp. 167–202.
82. Dewitte, *Boek*, 92ff.; Dewitte, *SD*, p. 149.
83. Dewitte, *Boek*, p. 89 and 93.
84. Acta *SD*, 3 November 1480 and 11 December 1480.
85. Dewitte, *Scholen*, p. 164ff. Motet settings of lines from the *Aeneid* exist by some of the greatest composers of the age, including Josquin and Willaert; several of them use the last words of Dido. They have repeatedly been discussed. Rather than courtly humanism, which is normally suggested as a background for this genre, one may put forward the school-plays of the cathedrals and collegiate churches.
86. Jean Maréchal, 'Le départ de Bruges des marchands étrangers', *ASEB* 88 (1951), pp. 26–74.
87. De Schrevel, p. 34ff.
88. The following notices about endowments are drawn from the Planarius *SD*.
89. Raphael de Mercatellis seems to me to be the donor of a panel (perhaps by the Master of the St Ursula Legend) in Detroit: the Nativity with Archangel Raphael. The Salviati and Visch panels by Gerard David are well known. On the Pardo panel, see Dirk de Vos, *Stedelijke Musea Brugge. Catalogus Schilderijen 15de en 16de eeuw* (Brugge, 1979), p. 37ff.
90. On his life, see Jeremy Noble, 'New Light on Josquin's Benefices', in Lowinsky, *Josquin Des Prez*, p. 82ff.
91. Haberl, *Schola*, p. 232, n. 1; Accounts *SD*, 1472/3 (Weale: *Accounts SD*).

92. Acta *SD*. Foppens, who makes him a canon from 1480, is in error.
93. He was installed as a clerk, in spite of being a priest, on 23 July 1460 (Acta *SD*).
94. Arnald Grunzweig, 'Notes sur la musique des Pays-Bas au XVe siècle', *Bulletin de l'Institut Historique Belge de Rome*, fasc. 18 (1937), pp. 73–88.
95. Further on his biography, see De Schrevel, p. 167ff.; Doorslaer, p. 30ff.; Luigi Parigi, *Laurentiana. Lorenzo de'Medici cultore della musica* (Florence, 1954) (Historiae Musicae Cultores, Biblioteca III), p. 103, n. 6.
96. Acta *SD*; see also De Schrevel, p. 160ff.
97. City Accounts, 1480/1, fol. 174v (and later); Gilliodts, *Inventaire* 6, p. 470ff.
98. Acta *SD*, 26 January, 30 January, 28 August and 10 November 1486; 17 August and 16 December 1489; Planarius *SD*, fol. 122r–123v.
99. Obrecht, *Werken*, vol. 2, pp. 117–164.

Chapter Three

1. Jean de Vincennes, *The Church of Our Lady, Bruges* (Gidsenbond, 1960); Patrice Beaucourt de Noortvelde, *Description Historique de l'Église Collégiale et Paroissiale de Notre-Dame à Bruges* (Bruges, 1773); Joseph Gailliard, *Inscriptions funéraires et monumentales de la Flandre Occidentale* 2 (Bruges, 1856) (with edition of an *Obituaire* of the church pp. 435–524).
2. But see Dewitte, *OL*.
3. Dr Nolte, 'Manuscrit du XIe siècle, ayant appartenu à l'église de Notre-Dame, à Bruges', *La Flandre* 4 (1872–73), p. 232.
4. See Confraternity *OL*. The endowment for the Lady-mass: Charter Onze-Lieve-Vrouw, Rijksarchief Brugge, prov. no. 995 (31 December 1428).
5. Acta *SD*, 30 August 1451; Cartulary *OL*. For the musical personnel, see also Appendix A.
6. See Meersseman.
7. *Cathalogus prepositorum OL*.
8. Gailliard, *Inscriptions* (see n. 1), p. 211; Accounts OL, 1 January to 1 July 1474.
9. Acta *OL*, 15 March 1491; 3 September 1495.
10. Accounts *OL*.
11. Cartulary *OL*: 'capellania Jacobus Bodekin retro chorum'.
12. Charter Onze-Lieve-Vrouw, Rijksarchief Brugge, prov. no. 1364 (2 November 1464).
13. Planarius *OL*, 14 October and 15 August (*c*.1420); 21 and 17 March (*c*.1450, *c*.1459).
14. Charters Onze-Lieve-Vrouw, Rijksarchief Brugge, prov. no. 1120 and 1385 (foundation of the chapel of the Holy Sacrament, 12 February 1473); 1386 (endowment of £14 annually, 25 March 1473); charter R.21, Rijksarchief Brugge. See also Gailliard, *Inscriptions* (n. 1), p. 34ff. n. 2 (will of Louis de Gruuthuse, dated 18 August 1474).
15. Acta *OL*, fol. 48r (1491).
16. Planarius *OL*, 6 January. See also Dewitte, *Scholen*, p. 174ff.

17. Planarius *OL*, appendix fol.(y) recto: 'Franciscus Lootghietere legavit 10s 5d . . .'.
18. Accounts *OL*, 1445, fol. '1'.
19. Dewitte, *Scholen*, p. 175.
20. The following endowments are all recorded in Planarius *OL*. See also Gailliard, *Inscriptions*, with the edition of another Planarius of 1474. For most of the endowments, charters exist in the Fonds Onze-Lieve-Vrouw, Rijksarchief Brugge.
21. See *Primitifs Flamands Anonymes. Exposition Bruges, Groeningemuseum 1969*, 2nd edn. (Bruges, 1969), no. 15.
22. All the notices concerning the confraternity are drawn from: Rekenboek 1468 à 1499, Onze-Lieve-Vrouw van der Sne, Rijksarchief Brugge. R. 498.
23. See also Derolez, *Corpus*, p. 18ff.
24. Charters Onze-Lieve-Vrouw, Rijksarchief Brugge, prov. no. 999 (4 April 1470) and 1241 (18 April 1477).
25. Gailliard, *Inscriptions*, p. 456.
26. The endowments of Mary of Burgundy, Philip the Fair and Maximilian of Habsburg are recorded in the charters Onze-Lieve-Vrouw, Rijksarchief Brugge, prov. no. 1330 (27 October 1483), 1022 (4 January 1495), 1020 (8 June 1496) and others. Edition of charter 1022 in Gilliodts, *Inventaire* 6, p. 404ff.; Gailliard, *Inscriptions*, p. 23ff.
27. A transcript of his will is charter Onze-Lieve-Vrouw, prov. no. 1273 (22 March 1488); ed. in Gailliard, *Inscriptions*.
28. Charters Onze-Lieve-Vrouw, prov. no. 1396 (3 November 1488); Acta *OL*, 22 September 1488.
29. Acta *OL*, 27 July 1489; the choirboy with the *vox angelica* had defected from St Donatian's to Our Lady's on 29 October 1499.
30. The fundamental study is Karel Verschelde, *De katedrale van Sint-Salvators te Brugge. Geschiedkundige beschrijving* (Brugge, 1863).
31. On the artistic heritage of the church, see Luc Devliegher, *De Sint-Salvatorskatedraal te Brugge. Inventaris* (Tielt, 1979) (Kunstpatrimonium van West-Vlaanderen 8).
32. Important references are contained, however, in Alfons Dewitte, 'De kapittelschool van de collegiale Sint-Salvator te Brugge (1515–1594)', *ASEB* 104 (1967), pp. 5–65.
33. Verschelde (n. 30 above), p. 205; Confraternity *SS*.
34. Dewitte, *Scholen*, p. 151.
35. Liber Planarius, Rijksarchief Brugge, Fonds Découvertes 104 (henceforth 'First Planarius'). This manuscript, whose oldest layer goes back to the early fourteenth century, has not been studied previously. It is the most ancient manuscript of its kind that survives of a church in Bruges.
36. Liber Planarius Sint-Salvator, Bisschoppelijk Archief Brugge, Reeks S. no. 47 (*olim 39*) (henceforth 'Second Planarius'). It dates from the mid-sixteenth century and has been used by Verschelde.
37. Devliegher (n. 31 above), p. 108f.
38. Devliegher, p. 112.
39. First Planarius, 14 December.

40. First Planarius, fol. 4r: endowment by the *magister fabrice* Jooris Munter; for his funeral monument, see Devliegher, p., 109f. The following texts of *Missus* ceremonies of other churches of Bruges have been edited: St Donatian's, 1380 (see Chapter II, n. 77); St James's, 1519 (William H. J. Weale, 'Drame liturgique: Le Missus', *Le Beffroi* 1 (1863), pp. 165−178; the date is erroneously given as 1545, but see van Dromme − Ch. II, n. 77 here − p. 392, n. 2); St Giles's, 1459 (L. Lavaert, 'De Missus − of Gulden-Mis in de St Gilliskerk te Brugge', *Biekorf* 81 (1981), pp. 293−297). The ceremony at St James's in 1519 included a polyphonic mass; prominent chants were *Ne timeas Maria* and *Ecce ancilla domini*. I suggest that the cantus firmus masses by Dufay, Ockeghem, Regis and others, which are based on these chants, originally belonged to *Missus* ceremonies. The same may well be true for motets with the text *Missus est Gabriel angelus* (there are two settings by Josquin), which is the main gospel text of the ceremony itself.

41. On the St Hippolytus altar, see Devliegher (n. 31 above), pp. 169−172.

42. Many ceremonies for Corpus Christi, supported by endowments, are described in the Second Planarius, fol. 37r and 44−45.

43. First Planarius, last (unnumbered) folio.

44. First and Second Planarius; Cartulary *SS*.

45. Accounts *SS*; Verschelde p. 269ff.

46. The endowment of Greffijnc is recorded in several sources, including First Planarius, fol. 6r. See also Verschelde, p. 260.

47. Van de Casteele, *Maîtres de chant*, p. 143f.

48. All the information about music books is drawn from the Accounts *SS*.

49. Confraternity *SS*. The date of the manuscript can be deduced from the time of death of the chaplain Walterus de Raedt (13 May 1510).

50. Confraternity *SS*, fol. 22r.

51. Van de Casteele, *Maîtres de chant*, p. 142: 'Item eadem die' (6 November 1492) 'concluserunt domini quod per obitum cantoris Anthonii Busnois, dominus Walterus susciperat onus regendi cantoriam, donec provideretur ad utilitatem ipsius ecclesie de habili viro'. The chapter minutes of 1490−1516, used by Van de Casteele, (Bischoppelijk Archief Brugge, Reeks S. no. 205bis), have apparently been missing for many years. I have been able to consult some extracts, transcribed at the beginning of this century by Canon Adolphe Duclos (Duclos: *Acta SS*).

52. Accounts *SS*.

53. Duclos: *Acta SS*.

54. Doorslaer, pp. 28 and 30.

55. Devliegher, pp. 114−116.

56. Adolphe Duclos, *De eerste eeuw van het Broederschap der zeven weedommen van Maria in Sint-Salvators, te Brugge* (Bruges, 1922) (Société d'Émulation, Melanges 9); Jozef Robijns, 'Eine Musikhandschrift des frühen 16.Jahrhunderts im Zeichen der Verehrung unserer lieben Frau der sieben Schmerzen (Brüssel Kgl. Bibliothek, Hs. 215−216)', *Kirchenmusikalisches Jahrbuch* 44 (1960), pp. 28−43.

57. Second Planarius, fol. 60v−61r.

58. Albert Schouteet, 'Het ambacht van de oudkleerkopers te Brugge',

ASEB 107 (1970), pp. 45–87; see also Duclos (n. 56 above), p. 63ff.

59. Second Planarius.

60. 'Desen bouck dede maken donaes de moer int Jaer (1470)': Wiltwerkers-boek, Stadsarchief Brugge no. 345, Peltiers, liasse 45.

61. Weale: *Accounts SD*, vol. 32 (St James's), fol. 166. Several references in the Accounts *SJ* concerning wills and burials show the connection between the Arnolfinis (Giovanni d'Arrigo and Giovanni di Niccolò) and the church: Accounts 1461/2, fol. 42v; 1465/6, fol. 52v and 55v (G. d'Arrigo); 1449/50, fol. 14v (Elena, wife of G. di Niccolò).

62. Stadsarchief Brugge, no. 450, St Jacob: *Registrum sepulturarum novum*, fol. 3r–v; Rijksarchief Brugge, charter blauw no. 8128.

63. Weale: *Accounts SD*, vol. 32 (St James's), fol. 140r–v (3 November 1454).

64. The information in this paragraph is drawn from the Accounts *SJ*. See also Dewitte, *SJ*.

65. See n. 40 above.

66. A Hodüm, 'Oorsprong van de broederschap van Onze-Lieve-Vrouw Presentatie in de Sint-Jacobskerk te Brugge', *ASEB* 91 (1954), pp. 97–116.

67. Paul Declerck, 'Commuun en zeven getijden in de Brugse parochiekerken', *ASEB* 108 (1971), pp. 117–173 – a study which contains ample documentation of the liturgy of St Giles's.

68. Dewitte, *SG* p. 93.

69. Jan de Cantere is not identical with the priest Jan Wilhoudt, as Dewitte, *SG* assumed: see Resolutieboek 1486ff., Rijksarchief Brugge, Fonds S. Gillis, no. 4, fol. 11r–v.

70. See Lavaert (n. 40 above).

71. Resolutieboek (n. 69 above), fol. 115v; charter S. Gillis no. 204, Rijksarchief Brugge.

72. Declerck (n. 67 above) p. 137ff.

73. Charter no. 578, Kerkfabriek S. Walburga, Rijksarchief Brugge.

74. Information about these services is drawn from the church accounts, nos. 226–232, Kerkfabriek S. Walburga, Rijksarchief Brugge.

75. *Sint-Janshospitaal Brugge 1188–1976 (Exhibition Catalogue)* (Bruges, 1976). (Contains contributions by J. Mertens and A. Vandewalle on the archives, and by J. Geldhof on the community); Emmanuel vander Elst, *L'Hôpital Saint-Jean de Bruges (de 1188 à 1500)* (Bruges, 1975).

76. Rekeningen Sint-Janshospitaal, Stadsarchief Brugge, no. 429, folder XII, 187.

77. Jozef Penninck, *Het Memling Museum en het Sint-Janshospitaal Brugge* (Bruges, 1980), p. 30ff.

78. Désiré Van de Casteele, 'Un clavecin en 1404 à Bruges', *La Plume* no. 68 (31 Dec. 1871) and *ASEB* 23 (1871), p. 208ff.; see the correction by the same author in *ASEB* 23 (1871), p. 321.

79. *Officium de S. Judoco*, MS 20611, Bibl. Royale, Bruxelles.

80. Museum Potteriehospitaal Brugge, no. O.P. 36 I.

81. Memlingmuseum Brugge (Sint-Janshospitaal). See also Alfons Dewitte, *Muziek rond Memling – Het Orgel* (Exhibition Catalogue) (Bruges, 1979), p. 19.

Chapter Four

1. [Arnoldus Goethals], *Chronica monasterii Sancti Andreae iuxta Brugas, Benedictini Ordinis* (Ghent, 1844) (Société d'Émulation, Recueil de chroniques, sér. 1), p. 137.
2. Edmond de Coussemaker, ed., *Scriptorum de musica nova series*, 3 (1869; repr. 1963), 264–73.
3. N. N. Huyghebaert, 'De bibliotheken van de abdijen van De Duinen en Ter Doest', in *Vlaamse kunst*, pp. 61–71; Derolez, *Corpus.*
4. Obituaire de l'abbaye de Ter Doest, MS 395, Stadsbibliotheek Brugge, fol. 3r (21 February) records the obit of one 'Hugo succentor'. The same entry also mentions one 'Cornelius Heyns monachus', probably the same who copied part of a Seneca manuscript for the abbey in 1477 (Leiden, Univ. Bibl., MS BPL 45 A; see *Vlaamse kunst*, no. 60); but he was not identical with the composer Cornelius Heyns.
5. William H. J. Weale, 'Documents inédits sur les enlumieurs de Bruges', *Le Beffroi* 4 (1872–73), pp. 238–337.
6. Gilliodts, *Inventaire* 2, p. 229f. and 4, p. 340.
7. Gilliodts, *Inventaire*, especially 6, p. 106ff.
8. One of the manuscripts is still in the possession of the Confraternity of the Holy Blood in Bruges; the other is MS IV 210, Bibl. Royale, Bruxelles.
9. W. H. J. Weale, 'Le couvent des soeurs de Notre-Dame dit de Sion à Bruges', *Le Beffroi* 3 (1866), p. 322ff.
10. See *Tentoonstelling van miniaturen en boekbanden* (Exhibition Catalogue) (Bruges, 1927) 1, p. 92; Dewitte, *Muziek rond Memling* (see Chapter III, n. 81). p. 19.
11. Ambroise Keelhoff O.S.A., *Histoire de l'ancien couvent des Ermites de Saint Augustin à Bruges* (Bruges, 1869) (Société d'Émulation, Publications).
12. Several charters relating to this endowment survive; see *Archief Augustijnen, Ghent, Klooster Brugge* (typescript inventory), nos. 48, 55, 59, 60, 61, 62, 67, 69. See also Gilliodts, *Inventaire* 5, pp. 462–466.
13. Charter (frag.) of 1490: Rijksarchief Brugge, charters blauw no. 5118.
14. *Archief Augustijnen* (see n. 12), no. 84; Keelhoff (n. 11), p. 285f.
15. Keelhoff (n. 11), p. 190ff.; Joseph Maréchal, 'De betrekkingen tussen Karmelieten en Hanzeaten te Brugge van 1347 tot 1523', *ASEB* 100 (1963), p. 206f.
16. Charter, dated 30 November 1488, Rijksarchief Brugge, charters blauw no. 5719.
17. *William Caxton. An Exhibition to Commemorate the Quincentenary of the Introduction of Printing into England* (British Library Reference Division, 1977 Exhibition Catalogue), (British Museum Publications, 1977). See also Edmund Childs, *William Caxton: A Portrait in a Background* (London, 1976), p. 81ff.; N. F. Blake, *Caxton and His World* (London, 1969).
18. W. E. Lingelbach, *The Merchant Adventurers of England* (1902; repr. New York 1971); Eleanora Carus-Wilson, 'The Origins and Early Development of the Merchant Adventurers', *Economic History Review* 4 (1932–34), pp. 147–176; Laetitia Lyell and Frank D. Watney, *Acts of Court of the*

Mercer's Company 1453–1527 (Cambridge, 1936); De Smedt; Thielemans; Letts, pp. 110–113.

19. Cartulary *CC*, fol. 18v-19r. These documents, overlooked by all the writers on the Merchant Adventurers, have been published in Joseph Maréchal, 'De Kapel van de Engelsen te Brugge 1344–1563', *Archives et Bibliothèques de Belgique* 34 (1963), no. 1, pp. 48–59. The documents confirm the later claim of the Merchant Adventurers that they had descended from a brotherhood of St Thomas, and they solve the riddle of the association's origin itself: the Merchant Adventurers of the later Middle Ages *were* the confraternity of St Thomas Becket, which was founded in 1344 from a colony of English merchants under the mayor of the English staple in Bruges, Thomas Melchebourne. They are referred to as 'confraternitas nationis Anglie existentis seu frequentantis mercantias in eadem villa Brugensi'. See also B. Vermaseren, 'De Carmel van Brugge en de Buitenlandse Kooplieden', *Carmel* 3 (1950–51), pp. 19–31.

20. Cartulary *CC*, fol. 101r (Kyvir). See also Weale, *Obituaire*; Maréchal (n. 19 above), doc. II.

21. Richard Hakluyt, *The Principal Navigations, Voyages, Traffiques and Discoveries of the English Nation*, 3 vols. (London, 1599–1600), 1, pp. 208–210.

22. De Smedt, 1, p. 64ff.

23. Gilliodts, *Estaple*, 2, p. 48 (20 December 1456).

24. Letts, p. 51 and 53; see also Laborde, 2, p. 310ff.

25. Maréchal, 'De betrekkingen' (n. 15 above), pp. 206–227; Cartulary *CC*; Weale, *Obituaire*.

26. Joseph Maréchal, 'De devotie te Brugge tot Sint-Niniaan, Bisschop van Whithorn in Schotland, 1366–1548', *ASEB* 99 (1962), pp. 187–202.

27. Comte de Limburg-Stirum, 'Anselme Adornes, ou un voyageur du XVe siècle', *Messager des sciences historiques* (Ghent, 1881), pp. 1–43.

28. Cartulary *CC*, fol. 162v.

29. Florence Edler de Roover, 'A Prize of War: A Painting of Fifteenth-Century Merchants', *Bulletin of the Business Historical Society* 19, no. 1 (1945), pp. 3–11; W. P. Blockmans, ed., *Handelingen van de leden en van de staten van Vlaanderen (1467–1477)* (Commission Royale d'Histoire, Académie Royale de Belgique) (Bruxelles, 1971), p. 203ff.

30. Andre Vanhoutryve, *De Brugse Kruisboggilde van Sint-Joris* (Handzame, 1968), p. 84.

31. Colin Thompson and Lorne Campbell, *Hugo van der Goes and the Trinity Panels in Edinburgh* (National Gallery of Scotland, 1974). My suggestion that the panels originated in Bruges rests on the links between the Carmelite convent, Adornes, and the Scotsmen Robert Bonkil (*c.*1420) and Alexander Bonkil (*c.*1470). See also David McRoberts, 'Notes on Scoto-Flemish Artistic Contacts', *The Innes Review* 10 (1959), p. 91ff.

32. 'Littere pro subsidio capelle': Cartulary *CC*, fol. 87r–v.

33. Or 'Illeia' (Ely?). *Series Priorum Carmeli Brugensis*, MS E.III.3.3, Archief Klooster van de Ongeschoeide Karmelieten, Brugge, p. 9.

34. Thomas Reynas (Reynham?), †1484, and Johannes Persons, †1515. *Series Priorum* (see preceding note), p. 21.

35. Craig Wright, 'A Fragmentary Manuscript of Early Fifteenth-Century Music in Dijon', *JAMS* 27 (1974), p. 306–315; for the codex Faenza, Bibl. Comunale, MS 117, see *RISM* BIV³, pp. 898–920.

36. *Series Priorum* (see n. 33 above), p. 20: R. Nicasius Wyts †December 1459. The date is not the only error of this kind in the list (Weyts died in 1492).

37. See F. Stein, *Geschichte des Musikwesens in Heidelberg* (Heidelberg, 1921), p. 14.

38. All documents quoted in this paragraph have been found in Cartulary *CC*.

39. Cartulary *CC*, fol. 162v.

40. Cartulary *CC*, fol. 153r–v (11 April 1452); charter A.31, Archief Klooster van de Ongeschoeide Karmelieten.

41. William H. J. Weale, 'La procession et les confréries de Notre-Dame de Roosebeke', *La Flandre* 3 (1869–70), pp. 154–187.

42. This has already been recognised by Adolphe Duclos, *Bruges*, p. 425ff. On the *rederijkers*, see Henri Liebrecht, *Les chambres de rhétorique*, (Notre Passé V, 2) (Brussels, 1948).

43. A. Viaene in *Biekorf* 61 (1960), pp. 325–330 and 62 (1961), pp. 11–13; Gilliodts, *Inventaire* 4, p. 469; 5, p. 480 and 520f.; introduction, p. 517ff.

44. Peter Cockshaw, 'Mentions d'auteurs, de copistes, d'enlumineurs et de libraires dans les comptes généraux de l'État bourguoignon (1384–1419)', *Scriptorium* 23 (1969), p. 131, n. 35.

45. Heeroma, *Liederen*, p. 58ff. on Jan van Hulst; p. 211 on musical practice.

46. Gilliodts, *Inventaire* 4, p. 81f.

47. Annalenboek no. 1, Stadsarchief Brugge, no. 389. Although copied *c.* 1800, this manuscript seems to draw on earlier sources independent from Sanderus, who also mentions the custom.

48. Gilliodts, *Inventaire* (see n. 43 above). .

49. See *Vlaamse kunst*, no. 99.

50. Cartulary *CC*, fol. 99r (1426); charter A.22, Archief Karmelieten, ed. in Weale, *Obituaire*, p. 248–250 (1428); see also Karel Verschelde in *ASEB* 23 (1871), p. 120; and Weale, *Obituaire*, p. 184.

51. Cartulary *CC*, fol. 183v–184v; charter A.55, Archief Karmelieten (15 May 1485).

52. See L. Gilliodts-Van Severen in *La Flandre* 15 (1884), p. 399–401; Annalenboek (n. 47 above).

53. Gilliodts, *Inventaire*, introduction, p. 96; Duclos, *Bruges*, p. 571f.

54. Gilliodts, *Inventaire* 5, p. 315; 4, p. 455f. (archers); Rijksarchief Brugge, charter blauw no. 1300 (carpenter's chapel in 1369).

55. H. Nelis, 'Philippe le Bon et les Frères Mineurs de Bruges', *Franciscana* 7 (Izeghem 1924), pp. 115–117.

56. Charter (22 August 1472) Rijksarchief Brugge, charter blauw no. 5685.

57. Louis Gilliodts-Van Severen, *Cartulaire de l'ancien Consulat d'Espagne à Bruges* (Recueil de chroniques, sér. 3) (Bruges, 1901), p. 19ff.; Gilliodts,

Inventaire 4, p. 322f.; R. de Roover, *Money, Banking and Credit in Medieval Bruges* (Cambridge, [Mass.], 1948).

58. The fundamental study is Alphonse de Schodt, 'Confrérie de Notre-Dame de l'Arbre Sec', *ASEB* 28 (1876–77), pp. 141–187; see also Archangelus Houbaert O.F.M., 'De eeredienst van Onze-Lieve-Vrouw bij de Minderbroeders in Belgie', *Franciscana: Archief der Paters Minderbroeders* 12–13 (Sint-Truiden, 1958), pp. 5–45.

59. Charter without number, Stadsarchief Brugge, no. 505, Gilde Droghenboom, reg. IV, 6bis; Schodt (see preceding note), p. 144f.

60. See n. 46 above.

61. Stadsarchief Brugge, no. 505, reg. IV, 4. For Christus's panel, see Schabacker, cat. no. 14.

62. Charter without number (20 June 1469), Stadsarchief Brugge, no. 505, reg. IV, 6bis. The remaining eight signatories were: Zegher de Baenst, Pieter van Bouchoute, Jan van Huerne, Jan Tsolle, Colaert Dault, Jan van Ravescote, Anthuenis Damast and Staessin de Milles.

63. Stadsarchief Brugge, no. 505, reg. IV, 2.

64. Duclos, *Bruges*, p. 542. Many surviving charters refer to the foundation, especially Rijksarchief Brugge, charters blauw nos. 7511–7530.

65. Schabacker, cat. no. 17.

66. See Erwin Panofsky, *Early Netherlandish Painting* (Icon edn., 1971), 1, p. 432 (note 192/1). Panofsky rejects the authenticity of the panels for internal reasons. He goes too far, however, in disqualifying the crucial passage in Adornes's will of 1470 – where the panels are mentioned – as a later insertion. The wording of this passage, 'van meester Jans hand van Heyck' is not, as Panofsky believes, grammatically 'impossible', but a very common construction in Flemish texts of the time. Any doubts arising are met if one assumes the surviving panels to be copies by Petrus Christus of the 1460s, and the lost original to have been in Adornes's possession in 1470, together with a faithful copy: he would not have wanted to disclose in his will that one of his daughters was to receive a copy.

Chapter Five

1. A fundamental study is Walter Salmen, *Der fahrende Musiker im europäischen Mittelalter* (Kassel, 1960).

2. Gilliodts, *Ménéstrels*. Notices in this chapter which involve the city administration are drawn from Gilliodts. *Ménéstrels*, and Gilliodts, *Inventaire*, unless otherwise indicated.

3. See also L. Gilliodts-Van Severen, 'Ce que nous apprennent nos comptes sur la procession du Saint-Sang à Bruges', *La Flandre* 9 (1878), pp. 149–166.

4. Van der Straeten, *Musique*, 4, p. 107ff.

5. On minstrels on ships, see also Wright, *Burgundy*, p. 50; C. E. C. Burch, *Minstrels and Players in Southampton 1428–1635* (Southampton, 1969); Leech-Wilkinson, *Libro*; and p. 114 below.

6. Marix, *Histoire*, p. 56, n. 6.

7. Van der Straeten, *Ménéstrels*, p. 29.

8. Marix, *Histoire*, p. 123; Gilliodts, *Inventaire*, 5, p. 98ff.

9. See Salmen (n. 1 above), pp. 180–184; Gordon Greene, 'The Schools of Minstrelsy and the Choir-School Tradition', *Studies in Music from the University of Western Ontario* 2 (1977), pp. 31–40; Marix, *Histoire*, p. 96ff.

10. Gilliodts, *Ménéstrels*, p. 31: 'Den menestruelen die hier scole hilden buten Carmers inde vastene, jn hovescheden thueren coste, £16 4d.' (from City Accounts 1318/9).

11. Wright, *Burgundy*, docs. 10–13 and 17–19.

12. A 'Cardinal van Inghelant' visited Bruges in 1373/4 (City accounts, fol. 66v–67); the duke of Lancaster in 1375–6 and 1392; the bishop of London in 1387, 1425, 1434, 1435 and 1436; Cardinal Henry Beaufort, bishop of Winchester, in 1419, 1428, 1431 and 1433 (see Gilliodts, *Inventaire*, 4, p. 432, 5, p. 9f., 48, 443, 504; City accounts 1435/6, fol. 58v).

13. City Accounts 1431/2, fol. 71v.

14. It should be noted that, in 1413, the gift went to the minstrels of Count Philip of Charolais.

15. Van de Casteele, *Préludes*, p. 143f.; see also Van de Casteele in *ASEB* 23 (1871), p. 215f.

16. Wright, *Burgundy*, p. 40 and 44; Van der Straeten, *Ménéstrels*, p. 48.

17. Wright, *Burgundy*, p. 20.

18. Marix, *Histoire*, p. 76.

19. Gilliodts, *Inventaire*, 6, p. 402, n. 1.

20. *La tryumphante Entrée de Charles Prince des Espagnes en Bruges en 1515*, facs. edn. by Sydney Anglo (Amsterdam-New York, *c*.1978).

21. *Cronicke van Vlaenderen*, MS 436, *Stadsbibliotheek Brugge, fol. 208v–214v.*

22. Gilliodts, *Inventaire*, 5, p. 146 and 285.

23. *Kronyk van Vlaenderen 580–1467*, ed. by the Maatschappy der Vlaemsche Bibliophilen, ser. 1, no. 3, 2 vols. (Ghent, 1839–40), pp. 105–110.

24. City expenditures went mainly to the 'painters of the *Carmersstrate*': Gilliodts, *Inventaire*, 5, pp. 194–197.

25. Gilliodts, *Inventaire*, 5, pp. 532–534 and 565–571.

26. See especially Gilliodts, *Inventaire*, 2, p. 262ff. (for 1394); 4, p. 5f.; 9, p. 432.

27 Gilliodts, *Inventaire*, 6, p. 483, n. 8.

28. See Daniel Heartz, 'The Basse Danse: Its Evolution circa 1450–1550', *Annales Musicologiques* 6 (1958–63), pp. 287–340; Frederick Crane, *Materials for the Study of the Fifteenth-Century Basse Danse* (New York, 1968, Musicological Studies vol. 18).

29. The chanson is edited in Marix, *Musiciens*, p. 46; and in W. Rehm ed., *Die Chansons von Gilles Binchois (1400–1460)* (Mainz, 1957) (Musikalische Denkmäler vol. 2). The tenor is the popular song 'Se tu t'en marias, tu t'en repentiras': see Martin Picker, 'The cantus firmus in Binchois' *Files a marier*', *JAMS* 18 (1965), p. 236f.

30. Acta *SD*, 16 April 1483.

31. Van de Casteele, *Préludes*, p. 61; Van der Straeten, *Musique*, 4, p. 99.

32. On the music of the minstrels' bands, see especially Polk, *Wind Bands*.

33. *Het Boeck van al 't gene datter geschiet es binnen Brugge sichtent Jaer 1477, 14 Februarii, tot 1491*, ed. C. Carton (Maatschappy der Vlaemsche Bibliophilen, ser. 3, no. 2) (Ghent, 1859).

34. See Wright, *Burgundy*; Marix, *Histoire*.

35. Wright, *Burgundy*, p. 94, n. 53.

36. William H. J. Weale, 'La lotterie de Bruges', *La Flandre* 1 (1867–68), p. 182.

37. Van der Straeten, *Ménéstrels*, p. 47.

38. He writes in *De inventione et usu musicae* (Weinmann, p. 45): '. . . quod exiguo tempore lapso duos fratres Orbos natione Flamingos: viros quidem non minus litteris eruditos quam in cantibus expertos: quorum uni Carolus alteri Johannes nomina sunt, Brugis audiverim: illum supremam partem et hunc tenorem plurium cantilenarum tam perite tamque venuste hujusmodi viola consonantes'. In this context, 'orbos' means 'blind men'; in the same paragraph, Tinctoris mentions a certain 'orbus ille Germanus' as a player of polyphonic instruments – conceivably Conrad Paumann – and the organist Henricus Bredemersch.

39. César Egasse du Boulay, *Historia Universitatis Parisiensis*, 5 (Paris, 1670), p. 869f. and 923; H. Denifle, ed., *Auctarium Chartularii Universitatis Parisiensis* (Paris, 1894ff.), 3, pp. 387, 515, 590–593; 6, p. 587, n. 3, 601, 623–626; Reese, *Renaissance*, p. 148.

40. Marix, *Histoire, passim*; Albert Vander Linden, 'Les Aveugles de la Cour de Bourgogne', *RBdM* 4 (1950), pp. 74–76.

41. Van der Straeten, *Ménéstrels*, p. 30ff.

42. Gilliodts, *Inventaire*, introduction, p. 99; 5, p. 520.

43. Van der Straeten, *Musique*, 1, p. 96ff.; see also Kathi Meyer-Baer, 'Saints of Music', *MD* 9 (1955), p. 14ff.

44. Jean Gessler ed., *Le Livre des Mestiers de Bruges et ses dérivés* (Bruges, 1931). One of the derivatives is the French-English *Livre des Mestiers*, published by William Caxton in 1483.

45. On the evolution of the instrument see Janez Höfler, 'Der "Trompette des Ménéstrels" und sein Instrument', *TVNM* 29 (1979), pp. 92–132; Polk, *Wind Bands*.

46. Pierre François, 'Brugse Orgelmakers', *Biekorf* 49 (1948), pp. 121–126 and 155–162.

47. Wright, *Burgundy*, p. 118.

48. Wright, *Burgundy*, p. 46.

49. Wright, *Burgundy*, docs. 139 and 161; Marix, *Histoire*, p. 102ff.; Van der Straeten, *Musique*, 7, p. 38ff.

50. Marix, *Histoire*, p. 105, n. 2; Gilliodts, *Inventaire* 5, addenda (Willay); Van der Straeten, *Ménéstrels*, p. 51f. (Thierry); Van der Straeten, *Musique* 7, p. 380, n. 3 (Rakeman).

51. Marix, *Histoire*, p. 12.

52. Van der Straeten, *Ménéstrels*, p. 208f.

53. Gilliodts, *Estaple*, no. 1153.

54. Henry Leland Clarke, 'Musicians of the Northern Renaissance', in *Aspects of Medieval and Renaissance Music: A Birthday Offering to Gustave Reese*, ed. Jan LaRue (London, 1967), p. 71.

55. Marix, *Histoire*, p. 61. Jeanne Marix has already stated that the ducal chapel did not always have choirboys, but she did not investigate the reasons for their absence.

56. Marix *Histoire*, p. 162ff.

57. Edited in Marix, *Musiciens*, p. 212.

58. See Guillaume de Van, 'A Recently Discovered Source of Early Fifteenth Century Polyphonic Music', *MD* 2 (1948), pp. 5–74; edition of the motet pp. 66–69.

59. Marix, *Histoire*, p. 34.

60. John Hothby, *Tres tractatuli contra Bartholomeum Ramum*, ed. A. Seay (CSM 10) (American Institute of Musicology, 1964), p. 75.

61. Marix, *Histoire*, p. 33ff. The feasts of the Order in Lille in 1431, Bruges in 1432 and Brussels in 1436 were all held on the vigil and day of St Andrew.

62. Gilliodts, *Inventaire*, 4, p. 355; Acta *SD*, 13 December 1419.

63. Laborde, 1, p. 296ff.

64. Acta *SD*, 23 July 1449.

65. Marix, *Histoire*, pp. 85–87.

66. Marix, *Histoire*, p. 28; Gilliodts, *Inventaire*, 4, p. 515.

67. Marix, *Histoire*, p. 30f. (but the wedding took place in St Omer, not in Bruges).

68. *Chroniques de Jean Molinet*, ed. J.-A. Bouchon, Collection des Chroniques Nationales Françaises, tom. XLIV, vol. 2, p. 156–162.

69. Marix, *Histoire*, p. 37–43.

70. This initiative has recently been taken by Gilbert Reaney, 'Music in the late Medieval Entremets', *Annales Musicologiques* 7 (1964–77), pp. 51–65.

71. Gilliodts, *Inventaire*, 5, pp. 565–571; *Les Memoires de Messire Olivier de la Marche, premier Maistre d'Hostel de l'Archeduc Philippe d'Autriche. . .*, ed. Denis Sauvage (Chronique de Flandres pt. 2) (Lyon, 1562), p. 348–392; Luc Devliegher, 'De blijde inkomst van Karel de Stoute en Margaretha van York te Damme in 1468', *ASEB* 102 (1964), pp. 232–236; Cartellieri, p. 157–163.

72. Arthur Piaget, 'La Cour amoureuse de Charles VI', *Romania* 20 (1891), pp. 417–454; *idem*, 'Un manuscrit de la Cour amoureuse de Charles VI', *Romania* 31 (1902), pp. 597–603; Marix, *Histoire*, p. 98ff.

73. The following are a few polyphonic chansons for May:
anon., *Renouveler me feist* (Apel, *French Secular Compositions*, no. 272); anon., *Jollis joueulx; S'en mai est fai* (N. Wilkins, ed., *A Fifteenth-Century Repertory of the Codex Reina*, (CMM 37) (Amer. Inst. of Musicology, 1966), nos. 32 and 49); A. de Lantins, *Sans desplaisir*; J. Coutreman, *Vaylle que vaylle*; Gautier Libert, *Belle plaisant/Puisque je sui*; Raulin de Vaux, *Savés pour quoy* (Reaney, *Early Fifteenth Century Music* 2); Gilles Binchois, *Vostre alée; Se j'eusse un seul; Toutes mes joyes*; Guillaume Dufay, *Je vueil chanter; Ce moys de may; Lune tres belle; Ce jour le doibt; Resvelons nous*.

74. Strohm, 'Nos amis', p. 34–39.

75. Marix, *Histoire*, p. 53f.

76. There is also a chanson which specifically refers to St Valentine's day, i.e. the feast-day of the *Cour d'amour*: anon., *Il a long temps* (Wilkins, ed.,

Fifteenth-Century [see n. 73 above], no. 190). The following are some chansons for the New Year: Baude Cordier, *Belle, bonne et sage*; *Ce jour de l'an* (ed. G. Greene); anon., *Souviegne vous d'estriner*; *Au temps que je soloye amer*; *A mon poöir je garde*; *La grant beauté*; A. da Caserta, *Tres nouble dame* (Apel, *French Compositions*, nos. 280, 183, 181, 80, 273); anon., *Vostre servant* (*Pz*); *Belle vuillés*; *Donés confort a vostre ami*; *Ce premier jour que commanche l'année* (*PC II*); A. de Lantins, *Ce jour de l'an*; *Tout mon désir*; *Amours servir* (*PC III*); N. Grenon, *La plus belle et doulce*; G. Binchois, *La merchi*; *Marguerite fleur*; *Je cuidoye*; G. Dufay, *Estrinés moy*; *Se madame*; *Pourray-je avoir*; *Bon jour bon mois*; *Entre nous gentils*; *Belle veulliés*; *Je requier*; *Ce jour de l'an*; *Je donna*; *Mille bonjours*; *Le serviteur*.

Chapter Six

1. Charles van den Borren, ed., *Missa Tornacensis* (CMM 13) (American Institute of Musicology, 1957). See also *RISM* B IV², p. 48ff. Connections with Avignon are discussed in Hanna Stäblein-Harder, *Fourteenth-Century Mass Music in France* (MSD 7) (American Institute of Musicology, 1962), p. 97ff.

2. J. Warichez, *La Cathédrale de Tournai et son chapitre*, (Wetteren: De Meester, 1934), p. 63f.

3. Ursula Günther, ed., *Motets*, no. 5; pp. xxix–xxxiii.

4. Smijers, *'s-Hertogenbosch*, p. 46.

5. The work is transcribed here, with some adjustments of text readings and underlay, according to the only surviving source, *Nst 9*, fol. 1v–2r (see also below, n. 9). I am grateful to the Manuscript Department of the Stadtbibliothek Nürnberg for the kind permission to publish the work. Fol. 2r is given in facsimile as pl. 4. Another source was the lost codex *Sm 222* (fol. 28r–30r). See Reaney, *New Sources*, p. 65f., and *RISM* B IV³, p. 556 (no. 37). Fortunately, the copy in *Sm 222* has been transcribed by E. De Coussemaker before the destruction of the manuscript; his copy shows significant musical and textual variants, only some of which may be due to problems of decipherment. Part of the *triplum* text reads, according to Coussemaker: '. . . laudibus divinis tangens corda placet(?) est isto illis(?). Nam infra species toni ultra semitonium qui pros(?) soni penes testimonium volens hoc enucleare per experientiam. Nam sit cantui magis clare melos per tangentiam quolibet ostiblo(?) debet Dominus benedici . . .'. Although these more extended references to music theory may well be the original text, I have chosen not to conflate our version in *Nst 9* with Coussemaker's partly doubtful reading. See Albert Vander Linden ed., *Le Manuscrit Musical M 222 C 22 de la Bibliothèque de Strasbourg* (Brussels, Office International de Librairie s.d.) (Facsimile of Coussemaker's transcription.)

6. *Cronicke van Vlaenderen*, MS 436, Stadsbibl., Bruges, fol. 149v–150r.

7. Luc Danhieux, 'Uit het handboek van de roedrager van de Sint-Donaaskerk te Brugge', *Biekorf* 75 (1974), pp. 244 and 253. Reaney, *New Sources*, p. 66 suggested some kind of instrumental performance. See also Willem Elders' 'Zur Aufführungspraxis der altniederländischen Musik', in *Renaissance-Muziek* (see n. 31 below), p. 89ff.

8. Harrison, *Motets*, nos. 9 and 33.

9. Nuremberg, Stadtbibliothek, frag. lat. 9 and 9a (*Nst 9/9a*). See *RISM* B IV², p. 84f. (*Nst 25* should now read *Nst 9a*), and my note in *Census Catalogue* vol. 2, p. 258f. After publication of the *Census Catalogue*, I found that also two fragments discovered by J. Angerer in Melk, Stiftsbibl. cod. 749 (*Census Catalogue*, 2, p. 140), came most probably from the same choirbook, and that this was used at St Stephen's, Vienna. See R. Strohm, 'Einheimische und fremde Mehrstimmigkeit im spätmittelalterlichen Österreich', in *Tagungsbericht Neustift 1982*, ed. Ursula Günther (in preparation).

10. See Harrison, *Motets*, p. xv; Harrison, *Britain*, p. 226ff.

11. Tom R. Ward, 'A Central European Repertory in Munich, Bayerische Staatsbibliothek, Clm 14274', *EMH* 1 (1981), p. 330f.

12. Günther, *Motets*, no. 2; pp. xxi–xxiii. The text of the motetus is not an address to St Peter, but 'Petrus' (nominative, not vocative) is the composer's own name. The second line of the motetus should read: 'astrologici logici, quid agam Petrus? Miserere'. A possible composer could be Pierre des Moulins.

13. Reaney, *New Sources; RISM* B IV².

14. Metha-Machteld van Delft, 'Een Gloria-Fragment in de Universiteits-Bibliotheek te Utrecht', *TVNM* 19 (1960), p. 84f.

15. Edward Stam, 'Het Utrechts fragment van een Zeeuws-Vlaamse marktroepen-motetus', *TVNM* 21 (1968), pp. 25–37 (with facsimile).

16. It is the Gloria *Spiritus et alme*, fol. IAv. See *RISM* B IV², p. 318.

17. August Scheler, *Trouvères Belges du XIIe au XIVe siècle* (Brussels, 1876), p. 154ff.

18. See C. Lemaire, 'De bibliotheek van Lodewijk van Gruuthuse', in *Vlaamse kunst*, p. 225. The trouvère song is written by an Anglo-Norman hand on fol. 204 of MS B. N. fr. 19525. For *MachA*, see *RISM* B IV², pp. 174–78.

19. See, most recently, Gordon Greene, ed., *French Secular Music Manuscript Chantilly, Musée Condé 564* (Polyphonic Music of the Fourteenth Century 18) (Monaco: L'Oiseau-Lyre, 1981).

20. Willi Apel, ed., *French Secular Compositions*, 3, no. 256. A facsimile of the copy containing the tenor label is in Karl Dèzes, 'Der Mensuralkodex des Benediktinerklosters Sancti Emmerami zu Regensburg', *ZMW* 10 (1927/28), p. 100.

21. There is a survey of music on Flemish texts before 1500 in Lenaerts, *Nederlands polifonies lied*; see especially pp. 6–10.

22. See *RISM* B IV³, p. 550ff. (*Sm 222*) and pp. 255–262 (*Pr*)

23. On this piece, see also p. 115. The tenor *'Portugaler'* was identified as an English 'square' by John Caldwell, 'Keyboard Plainsong Settings in England', *MD* 19 (1965), p. 137f., n. 7. The identification with the ballade *Or me veult* in the Mellon chansonnier is due to Margaret Bent, 'The Transmission of English Music 1300–1500', in *Studien zur Tradition in der Musik. Kurt von Fischer zum 60. Geburtstag*, ed. H. H. Eggebrecht and M. Lütolf (Munich, 1973), p. 68.

24. *RISM* B IV³, p. 485ff.; Kurt von Fischer, 'The Manuscript Paris, Bibl.

Nat., nouv. acq. frç. 6771', *MD* 11 (1957), pp. 38–78; Nigel Wilkins, 'The Codex Reina: A Revised Description', *MD* 17 (1963), pp. 57–73, and von Fischer's reply in the same volume. I agree with Wilkins about the distinction of the scribal hands, but ,with von Fischer about the provenance (Venice). The two Flemish songs are in Nigel Wilkins ed., *A Fourteenth-Century Repertory from the Codex Reina* (CMM 36) American Institute of Musicology 1966, nos. 5 and 31.

25. Heeroma, *Liederen*. See also *Vlaamse Kunst*, no. 99.

26. See, most recently, Ewald Jammers, 'Die Melodien der Gruuthuse-Handschrift', *TVNM* 25/2 (1975), pp. 1–22.

27. Both works, which appear in codex *BL* in direct succession (fol. 47v–50r), are edited in Reaney, *Early Fifteenth-Century Music*, 1. Tapissier's Credo, however, appears already in the Avignon repertory (MS *Apt*, fol. 48v–50); shared composition of the pair would mean that Fabri's contact with Tapissier dates from the 1390s at the latest. For both composers, see most recently *New Grove*. The surname 'Fabri' occurs in documents of St Donatian's around 1400 very often; the first names are Eynardus, Johannes, Maiolus, Martinus (the last-named without date); there was also a ducal chaplain Henricus; see Günther, *Biographie*, p. 188f. I cannot attach much importance to the occurrences of this frequent surname.

28. *RISM* B IV³, p. 77ff. I am grateful to Prof. Craig Wright for providing me with photographs of the manuscript.

29. The Flemish texts have been reconstructed for me by Dr T. M. Guest, Bedford College, University of London; she managed to read some almost illegible lines, but insists that the readings cannot all be established beyond doubt. I owe Dr Guest my warmest thanks.

30. Charles W. Warren, 'Punctus Organi and Cantus Coronatus in the Music of Dufay', in Atlas, *Dufay Conference*, pp. 128–143.

31. Hélène Wagenaar-Nolthenius, 'De Leidse fragmenten: Nederlandse polifonie uit het einde der 14de eeuw', in *Renaissance-Muziek 1400–1600. Donum Natalicium René Bernard Lenaerts*, ed. Jozef Robijns (Louvain, 1969), pp. 303–315. See also *RISM* B IV² pp. 311–317.

32. Ursula Günther, 'Das Manuskript Modena, Biblioteca Estense, α.M.5, 24 (*olim* lat. 568 = *ModA*)', *MD* 24 (1970), pp. 17–67. The canon is completely edited in Apel, *French Secular Compositions*, 3, no. 295.

33. Acta *SD*, 26 March 1371.

34. Facsimile edition: *Codex Escorial. Chansonnier. Biblioteca del Monasterio El Escorial/Signatur: Ms.V.III.24*, ed. Wolfgang Rehm, (Documenta Musicologica, 2nd series, 2) (Kassel, etc.: Bärenreiter, 1958), Thomas J. McGary, *Codex Escorial Ms.V.III.24: An Historical-Analytical Evaluation and Transcription*, Ph.D diss., Univ. of Cincinnati, 1973 (University Microfilms, Ann Arbor 73–23, 846).

35. See Wolfgang Rehm, ed., *Die Chansons von Gilles Binchois (1400–1460)* (Musikalische Denkmäler vol. 2) (Mainz: Schott, 1957), p. 7* and *passim*.

36. Gilbert Reaney, 'The Manuscript Oxford, Bodleian Library, Canonici Misc. 213', *MD* 9 (1955), pp. 73–104.

37. The rondeau *Par un regart et un ris amoureux* (no. 221), edited by Gilbert

Reaney in *Early Fifteenth-Century Music*, 4 (1969), no. 8. Reaney overlooked the concordance with *HEI*.

38. Hans Schoop, *Entstehung und Verwendung der Handschrift Oxford Bodleian Library, Canonici Misc. 213* (Berne, 1971). See also Leech-Wilkinson, *Libro*, p. 19, n. 12.

39. Schoop, *Entstehung*, p. 85.

40. Leech-Wilkinson, *Libro*.

41. For a newly discovered manuscript in 'stroke notation' and further information on this notation, see Margaret Bent and Roger Bowers, 'The Saxilby Fragment', *EMH* 1 (1981), pp. 1–27.

42. Frederick Crane, 'The Derivation of some Fifteenth-Century Basse-Danse Tunes', *ActaMus* 37 (1965), pp. 179–188.

43. The piece is edited in Raymond Meylan, *L'énigme de la musique des basses danses du quinzieme siecle* (Berne, 1968), plates V–VI. See also Manfred Bukofzer, 'A Polyphonic Basse Danse of the Renaissance', in Bukofzer, *Studies*, pp. 190–216.

44. See Daniel Heartz, 'The Basse Danse: Its Evolutions circa 1450–1550', *Annales Musicologiques* 6 (1958–63), pp. 287–340. Facsimile and transcription of a page of *Br 9085* also in Heinrich Besseler and Peter Gülke, *Schriftbild der mehrstimmigen Musik* (Musikgeschichte in Bildern vol. III/5) (Leipzig, n.d), p. 96ff. The late date (*c*.1500) proposed by Heartz is entirely convincing, paleographically and historically.

45. See n. 23 above.

46. See Meylan (n. 43 above), p. 20.

47. Article 'Basin' in *New Grove* (David Fallows).

48. See also Strohm, 'Politics', p. 321ff.

49. See Arthur Parris, *The Sacred Works of Gilles Binchois*. Ph.D diss., Bryn Mawr College, 1965 (University Microfilms, Ann Arbor, UM 66–1536).

50. Rudolf Ficker ed., *Sieben Trienter Codices, V. Auswahl* (Vienna, 1924; repr. Graz, 1960) (DTÖ XXXI, vol. 61), no. XIII.

51. Giovanni d'Alessi, *Il tipografo fiammingo Gherardo de Lisa* (Treviso, 1925).

52. Lewis Lockwood, 'Dufay and Ferrara', in Atlas, *Dufay Conference*, p. 13, n. 1.

53. See the inventory of the manuscript by Guillaume de Van, 'A Recently Discovered Source of Early Fifteenth-Century Polyphonic Music', *MD* 2 (1948), pp. 5–74.

54. For Clibano and his works, see *New Grove* (David Fallows).

55. Planarius *SD*, 28 October.

56. Edited in Marix, *Musiciens*, pp. 185–187. The chant is in the lowest voice, where also the intonation should have been placed.

57. Previously edited in Rudolf Ficker, *Sieben Trienter Codices, VI. Auswahl* (Vienna 1933; repr. Graz, 1960) (DTÖ XL, vol. 76), p. 82.

58. See *Breviarium ad usum insignis ecclesie sancti Donatiani Brugensis Dyocesis Tornacensis, pars aestivalis* (Paris: Antonius Bonnemere, 1520), fol. Piii recto – [Pvii] verso.

59. This suggestion has, in fact, been made by Charles Hamm, 'A Catalogue of Anonymous English Music in Fifteenth-Century Continental Manuscripts', *MD* 22 (1968), p. 74.

60. Brian Trowell, 'Proportion in the Music of Dunstable', *PRMA* 105 (1978–79), pp. 100–141.

61. Leonel Power, *Complete Works*, ed. Charles Hamm (CMM 50) (American Institute of Musicology, 1969), 1: Motets.

62. See art. 'Forest, John' in *New Grove* (Margaret Bent). The motet *Ascendit Christus/Alma redemptoris mater* is printed as a work of Dunstable in John Dunstable, *Complete Works*, ed. Manfred Bukofzer, rev. edn. by Brian Trowell, Margaret Bent and Ian Bent (Musica Britannica 8) (London, 1969), no. 51.

63. Leonel Power, *Missa Alma Redemptoris Mater*, ed. Laurentius Feininger (Documenta Polyphoniae Liturgicae Sacrae Ecclesiae Romanae ser. I, no. 2). (Rome, 1949). See also Harrison, *Britain*, p. 251f.

64. Roger Bowers, 'Some Observations on the Life and Career of Lionel Power', *PRMA* 102 (1975/76), p. 110. As regards Forest's connection with Bruges, I hesitate to identify him with one John Forster, *'anglicus'*, who was a non-resident canon of St Donatian's from 1424 until about 1428.

65. Reinhard Strohm, 'Ein unbekanntes Chorbuch des 15.Jahrhunderts', *Mf* 21 (1968), pp. 40–42. In a forthcoming article, to be published in *RIdM* (1985), I shall discuss the Italian history of the codex in more detail.

66. Lauwereyns Waghe f. Jans, allegedly from Stralsund, bought his citizen- ship of Bruges on 28 November 1474: R. A. Parmentier, *Indices op de Brugsche Poorterboeken*, (Bruges, 1938), 2, p. 702. Jacop Waghe and Hendric Waghe were members of the guild of the archers of St George: André Vanhoutryve, *De Brugse Kruisboggilde van Sint-Joris* (Handzame, 1968), p. 204ff. Jacop and Hendric were probably both resident in Sijssele in the parish of the Holy Cross, where they had estates. Jacop Waghe and his wife Lijsbette made endowments for the church of St James, and for the abbey of the 'Rich Clares' (1481), whose benefactor was Giovanni Arnolfini. Jacop Waghe was a churchwarden of the Holy Cross and made his will in that parish; it was proved in 1495: Rijksarchief Br., ch. bl. 3540. He – or his death – is mentioned in accounts of St James in 1492: Dewitte, *SJ*, p. 343, n. 15. Hendric Waghe and his wife Lauwerette are mentioned several times in connection with endowments and rents for Our Lady's, for example on 12 December 1476: Rijksarchief Br., ch. Onze-Lieve-Vrouw, prov. no. 44. Cornelius Waghe is mentioned many times as dean of the barbers' guild in St James's and elsewhere, for example in a charter of the Austin friary of 14 December 1472: *Archief Augustijnen*, Ghent, charters of the Klooster Brugghe, typescript catalogue, no. 83. He was a witness to the contract in which the nephews of Tommaso Portinari (Folco and Benedetto Portinari) sold all their rights on the recovery of the vessel captured by the Hanseatics in 1473 – which had carried Memling's 'Last Judgment' – to the city; this contract of 27 November 1499 ended one of the most notorious political-commercial-cultural affairs of the period: Gilliodts, *Inventaire*, 6, p. 446ff.

The surnames 'Waghers' and 'Waghen' are also frequent in Bruges at the time; a Victor Waghere, bookbinder, worked for St Donatian's in 1435 and 1450: Dewitte, *Boek*, nos. 119 and 156. See also 'Bernardus' in Appendix A.

67. See *Vlaamse kunst*, no. 61.

68. Judith Cohen, *Masses*, (facsimiles).

69. I am grateful to Profs. Otto Pächt (Vienna), Julian T. Brown (London), Albert Derolez (Ghent) and Gerard Lieftinck (Leiden) for their suggestions which they kindly made to me on the basis of photocopies.

70. The fragments are now kept in the Bibl. Royale, Brussels, MS IV. 829. This was a gradual, probably from a parish church in or near Ghent, but had been used as binding material for volumes concerning parishes near Bruges.

71. Bruges, Grootseminarie, Archief, MSS D 7 and D 8. See Alfons Dewitte, *Muziek rond Memling – Het Orgel*, O.C.M.W. and Festival van Vlaanderen Brugge 1979 (exhibition catalogue), p. 17; Dewitte, *Boek*, p. 90. The liturgical contents of the graduals show that they were copied between 4 December 1467 and *c.*1483; no other graduals were newly copied as a pair for St Donatian's in this period. Both graduals must have contained large sequentiaries which were removed later.

72. *Fn 176* and *Ric 2356*. See Joshua Rifkin, 'Scribal Concordances for Some Renaissance Manuscripts in Florentine Libraries', *JAMS* 26 (1973), p. 318.

73. This can at least be inferred from the contacts of both composers with the singers of S. Giovanni in Florence. See D'Accone, 'Singers', p. 331ff.; and Frank D'Accone, 'Heinrich Isaac in Florence: New and Unpublished Documents', *MQ* 49 (1963), pp. 464–83.

74. P. Guidi and E. Pellegrinetti, *Inventari del vescovato della Cattedrale e di altre chiese di Lucca* (Studi e Testi 34) (Rome: Biblioteca Apostolica Vaticana, 1921), p. 256ff.

75. Luigi Nerici, *Storia della musica in Lucca* (Lucca: Giusti, 1879), p. 42ff.

76. Trenta had already been sent to Vienna in 1459 on an important diplomatic mission. His travel to Bruges and England is documented by his own letters: see J. D. Mansi, ed., *Stephani Baluzii Tutelensis Miscellanea*, 4 vols. (Lucca, 1761–62), vol. 1, p. 490ff. The letter of papal dispensation for Charles the Bold's marriage (17 May 1468) is in Archives Départmentales du Nord, Lille, Sceaux Demay 5776 (*Inventaire Sommaire*, no. B429).

77. Adolf Gottlob, *Aus der Camera Apostolica des 15.Jahrhunderts* (Innsbruck, 1889), p. 297f.

78. Albert Seay, ed., Johannes Hothby, *Tres tractatuli contra Bartholomeum Ramum*, (CSM 10) (American Institute of Musicology, 1964), p. 65. The editor (see introduction p. 1) erroneously relates the *Dialogus* to Ramos, but the *Dialogus* does not criticise, as Seay supposes, Ramos's *Musica practica* of 1482, and appears to be written at a time when Hothby had as yet no knowledge of Ramos's theories. See also Albert Seay, 'The *Dialogus Johannis Ottobi de Arte Musica*', *JAMS* 8 (1955) p. 86ff.; Strohm, 'Politics', p. 312, n. 22.

9. Biblioteca El Escorial, MS c.III.23. The name has been wrongly transcribed as 'thil'r' in Manfred Bukofzer, 'Über Leben und Werke Dunstables', *ActaMus* 8 (1936), p. 104f., where Bernardo Ycart is suggested as the person referred to; another incorrect identification with Henry Knoep is given in Robert Stevenson, *Spanish Music in the Age of Columbus* (The Hague, 1960), p. 54. The treatise is dated Seville, 7 July 1480.

0. Transcribed and discussed in Gottlieb, *Cyclic Masses* (after *Tr 89*, nos. 736–740) as *Missa sine nomine*.

1. Albert Seay, ed., *Johannis Tinctoris Opera Theoretica*, (CSM 22), 2a: *Proportionale musices* (Stuttgart, 1978 American Institute of Musicology), p. 46ff.

2. Reynolds, 'Origins', p. 283.

.3. Marix, *Histoire*, p. 191ff. and *passim*. See also p. 25 above.

84. Günther Weiss ed., *Introitus-Tropen I* (Monumenta Monodica Medii Aevi 3), (Kassel, etc., 1970), no. 351.

85. See p. 81 above. A particularly fine miniature with the 'Tree of Jesse' and musician prophets can be found in René Wangermee, *La musique flamande* (Bruxelles, 1965), p. 7.

   For the motet of Antoine Busnois on *Stirps Jesse*, see Edgar Sparks, *Cantus Firmus in Mass and Motet* (Berkeley, 1963), p. 222ff.

86. See Alejandro E. Planchart, 'Guillaume Dufay's Masses: Notes and Revisions', *MQ* 58 (1972), p. 12ff. The *Caput* mass had received some discussion already in the pioneering article by Manfred Bukofzer, '*Caput*: A Liturgico-Musical Study', in Bukofzer, *Studies*, pp. 217–310. For the transmission of the work in the sources, see Reinhard Strohm, 'Quellenkritische Untersuchungen an der *Missa 'Caput'*, in *Renaissance-Handschriften. Kolloquium Wolfenbüttel 1980*, Tagungsbericht (forthcoming).

87. See Bent, *Dufay*, pp. 408–413.

88. In an unpublished colloquium given at King's College, London (1976).

89. For Le Rouge's 'isomelic' technique, see Eduard Reeser, 'Een 'isomelische mis' uit den tijd van Dufay', *TVNM* 16 (1946), pp. 151–176. The work is published in Rudolf Flotzinger, ed., *Trienter Codices. Siebente Auswahl* (DTÖ 120) (Graz/Vienna, 1970).

90. Sylvia Kenney, ed., Walter Frye, *Collected Works*, (CMM 19) (American Institute of Musicology, 1960).

91. Edited in Bent, *Four Anonymous Masses*.

92. See *New Grove* (David Fallows).

93. An inventory of the manuscript is in Bernhard Meier, 'Die Handschrift Porto 714 als Quelle zur Tonartenlehre des 15. Jahrhunderts', *MD* 7 (1953), pp. 75–97. See also David Fallows, 'Robertus de Anglia and the Oporto Song Collection', in *Source Materials and the Interpretation of Music: a Memorial Volume to Thurston Dart*, ed. I. D. Bent and M. Tilmouth (London, 1983), pp. 99–128.

94. Several polyphonic settings are discussed in Harrison, *Britain*, p. 296 and plate 22; p. 298, n. 6.

95. Published as *Missa sine nomine* in Feininger, *MPLSER*, ser. I, vol. 2, no. 5.

96. The attribution to Dufay has been proposed by Llorens, *Capellae Sixtinae*

Codices, p. 19. Laurentius Feininger (see n. 95 above) suggested Dunstable.

97. See also Bent, *Dufay*, p. 404f.
98. See p. 100 above, and Strohm, 'Nos amis'.
99. Published in Feininger, *MPLSER*, ser. I, vol. 1, fasc. 2 (Rome, 1948).
100. See Gottlieb, *Cyclic Masses*, p. 85ff. and transcription.
101. Allan W. Atlas, 'Conflicting Attributions in Italian Sources of the Franco-Netherlandish Chanson *c*.1465–*c*.1505', in *Music in Medieval and Early Modern Europe: Patronage, Sources and Texts*, ed. Iain Fenlon (Cambridge, 1981), p. 269 and nos. 28 and 43. Atlas suggests that Basin is only the reviser of both pieces. David Fallows, art. 'Basin, Adrien' in *New Grove*, attributes both chansons to Adrien Basin.
102. Perkins, *Mellon Chansonnier*, 1, p. 17ff. For a discussion of the sources of *Nos amis*, see vol. 2, p. 420ff. (no. 56).
103. This section also contains *'Or me veult'*, the presumably English work predating 1440 and connected with Isabella of Portugal or courtly balls in Bruges; see p. 116. For further evidence of musical contacts between Bruges and Naples, see pp. 137 – 8.
104. Heinrich Besseler, ed., *Guglielmi Dufay Opera Omnia*, (CMM 1) (American Institute of Musicology, 1951/1962), 3.
105. Not Carissimi, as often stated: Dr Wolfgang Witzenmann (Rome) kindly informed me that the work which has been attributed to Carissimi is a composition of the sixteenth century.
106. Lewis Lockwood, 'Aspects of the *'L'homme armé'* Tradition', *PRMA* 100 (1973–74), pp. 97–122.
107. Cohen, *Masses*, p. 25 and plate after p. 10. More recently, it has been suggested that all six masses have been composed by Caron: see Don Giller, 'The Naples L'Homme Armé Masses and Caron', *Current Musicology* (1982).
108. See Perkins, *Mellon Chansonnier*, no. 34. In an unpublished conference paper (Oxford, 1976), David Fallows stressed that the melody, with its rhythm, must be considerably older than the Morton setting.
109. This implies that Busnois may have used another intermediate model with more than one text; his mass could well be of the 1460s.
110. A document quoted in Wilkins, *Music*, p. 128, supports this interpretation.
111. For example in Oswald's *Los, Frau und hör des Hornes Schall*: Ivana Pelnar, ed., *Die mehrstimmigen Lieder Oswalds von Wolkenstein*, (Münchner Editionen zur Musikgeschichte 2) (Tutzing: Schneider, 1981), p. 120ff.
112. See Johannes Ockeghem, *Collected Works*, ed. Dragan Plamenac, 2nd rev. edn. (American Musicological Society, 1966), 2, no. 16. As regards the attribution, see especially vol. 2, p. XXXVII.
113. Kenney, 'Origins', p. 87.
114. The *Missa 'Orsus, orsus'* by Johannes Martini, which predates 1480 (occurrence in *ModC*, fol. 1v ff.), is based on an anonymous chanson preserved in the chansonnier Pavia, MS Aldini 362. For the mass by Isaac, see Martin Staehelin, *Die Messen Heinrich Isaacs* (Berne, 1977), 3, pp. 86–94. The anonymous chanson *Chargé de deuil* occurs several times in

Florentine chansonniers which precede Isaac's arrival in Florence in 1484: for example, *Fn 176* and *Ric 2356*.

115. See *New Grove* (Brian Trowell).

116. Planarius *SD*, fol. 123r (17 August 1489).

117. Robert J. Snow, 'The Mass-Motet cycle: A Mid-Fifteenth-Century Experiment', in *Essays in Honor of Dragan Plamenac on His 70th Birthday*, ed. R. J. Snow (Pittsburgh, 1969), pp. 301–320.

118. Published in John Plummer, *Four Motets*, ed. Brian Trowell (Banbury: The Plainsong and Medieval Society, 1968), no. 2.

119. See also Sylvia Kenney, 'In Praise of the Lauda', in *Aspects of Medieval and Renaissance Music. A Birthday Offering to Gustave Reese*, ed. Jan LaRue (New York: Norton, 1966), pp. 489–499; Sylvia Kenney, 'Four Settings of "Ave regina celorum" ', in *Liber Amicorum Charles van den Borren*, ed. A. Vander Linden (Antwerp, 1964), pp. 98–104.

120. On an interesting group of motets based on the 'O-Antiphons', see Richard H. Hoppin, 'A Fifteenth-Century "Christmas Oratorio"', in *Essays on Music in Honor of Archibald Thompson Davison* (Harvard University Press, 1957), pp. 41–49.

121. See Peter Wagner, *Gregorianische Formenlehre* (Einführung in die Gregorianischen Melodien 3) (Leipzig, 1921), p. 151ff.

122. See Edward Lerner, 'The Polyphonic Magnificat in Fifteenth-Century Italy', *MQ* 50 (1964), pp. 44–58; Winfried Kirsch, *Die Quellen der mehrstimmigen Magnificat- und Te Deum-Vertonungen bis zur Mitte des 16. Jahrhunderts* (Tutzing, 1966).

123. For the Busnois Magnificat, see Kirsch (n. 122 above), no. 636. The second work, Kirsch, no. 190, 'may be his also', according to Reese, *Renaissance*, p. 108. Charles Hamm proposed Busnois as the author of the third (Kirsch, no. 368) in his article 'The Manuscript San Pietro B 80', *RBdM* 14 (1960), p. 45.

124. Lockwood, 'Strategies', p. 246ff.

125. Lockwood, 'Strategies', p. 236ff.; D'Accone, 'Singers', p. 334ff.

126. Gilliodts, *Inventaire*, 6, doc. no. 1192.

127. Lewis Lockwood, 'Dufay and Ferrara', in Atlas, *Dufay Conference*, p. 7ff.

128. Perkins, *Mellon Chansonnier* vol. 1, p. 26. According to Ronald Woodley, the musical text of the chansonnier may well have been copied by Tinctoris himself (*The Proportionale Musices of Iohannes Tinctoris: a critical edition, translation and study*, D.Phil. diss., University of Oxford, 1982, vol. 1, p. 116). For some recent observations on the dedicatory nature of the whole manuscript see Jaap van Benthem, 'Concerning Johannes Tinctoris and the preparation of the "Princess" Chansonnier', *TVNM*, 32 (1982), pp. 24–29.

129. Dewitte, *SD*, p. 144, n. 59. Possibly, the painting was connected with the guild of crossbowmen of St George.

130. On the map and the Lomellini painting, see Erwin Panofsky, *Early Netherlandish Painting* (New York, etc.: Icon Editions, 1971), 1, p. 361, n. 2/7.

131. Martha K. Hanen, *The Chansonnier El Escorial, Ms.IV.a.24*, Ph.D diss., University of Chicago, 1973.

132. Dragan Plamenac, 'A Reconstruction of the French Chansonnier in the Biblioteca Colombina, Seville', *MQ* 37 (1951), pp. 501–542, and 38 (1952), pp. 85–117 and 245–277; *idem, Facsimile Reproduction of the Manuscripts Sevilla 5-I-43 and Paris, n. a. fr. 4379 (Part I)*, (Publications of Mediaeval Musical Manuscripts 8) (Brooklyn, 1962).

133. See Perkins, *Mellon Chansonnier*, 1, p. 10ff.

134. Alessandra Macinghi negli Strozzi, *Briefe*, ed. Alfred Doren (Jena, 1927).

135. See D'Accone, 'Singers'; A. Grunzweig, *Correspondance de la filiale de Bruges des Medici* (Bruxelles, 1931); R. de Roover, *The Rise and Decline of the Medici Bank 1397–1494* (Harvard Studies in Business History 21) (Harvard University Press, 1963). The chansonnier Rome, Biblioteca Apostolica Vaticana, Urb. lat. 1411, written in black notation, is very likely to have been a gift of a Flemish musician to Piero de' Medici.

136. See especially Abi Warburg, *Flandrische Kunst und florentinische Frührenaissance* (1902), in *Gesammelte Schriften*, 1, (Leipzig, 1932), pp. 185–206 and 370–380.

137. See Martin Staehelin, *Die Messen Heinrich Isaacs* (Berne, 1977), 2, pp. 50, 54 and 60.

138. Grunzweig, *Correspondance* (see n. 135 above), p. XXV. See also A. Rochon, *La jeunesse de Laurent de Médicis* (Paris, 1963).

139. Reinhard Strohm, 'Giovanni Arnolfini and the Lucca Choirbook', *RIdM* 20 (1985) (forthcoming).

140. See D'Accone, 'Singers', p. 356 (for 1482) and p. 337 (for 1484).

141. Mario Battistini, *La Confrérie de Sainte-Barbe des Flamands à Florence* (Bruxelles: Commission Royale d'Histoire, 1931).

142. Carapezza, *Regina Angelorum*.

143. Little is known about the painter of two of them, the 'Master of the embroidered foliage' (Friedländer), but he certainly worked in Bruges towards 1500. The painter of the panel in the Kress collection, Washington, is the 'Master of the Legend of St Lucy', named after his painting in St James's, Bruges. He worked for churches and confraternities of Bruges, even for merchants from the Baltic; many of his works have once been in Spain. See Nicole Verhaegen, 'Le Maître de la Légende de Sainte Lucie: Précisions sur son oeuvre', *Bulletin de l'Institut Royal du Patrimoine Artistique*, 2, (1959), pp. 73–82; Dirk de Vos, *Stedelijke Musea Brugge: Catalogus Schilderijen 15de en 16de eeuw* (Bruges, 1979), p. 147ff.

144. Sylvia Kenney, 'Four Settings' (see n. 119 above).

145. 'Quellenkritische Untersuchungen . . .' (see n. 86 above).

146. Margaret Bent, ed., *Four Anonymous Masses*, p. 174.

147. See Kenney, 'Origins'.

148. Reynolds, 'Origins'; Charles Hamm, 'The Manuscript San Pietro B 80', *RBdM* 14 (1960), pp. 40–55.

149. On this mass, see Eric F. Fiedler, 'Heinrich Finck, Gaspar van Weerbeke und die Göttin Venus', in *Renaissance-Studien, Helmuth Osthoff zum 80. Geburtstag*, ed. L. Finscher (Tutzing, 1979), pp. 29–55.

150. This anonymous mass has been published as a work of Guillermus Faugues in Feininger, *MPLSER*, ser. I, vol. 3. Tinctoris, in fact,

mentions a *Missa 'Vinus'* by Faugues in his *Proportionale*, p. 46, which exhibits the same mensural peculiarity as the anonymous work in *CS 14*. This attribution has been rejected by George C. Schuetze, *An Introduction to Faugues* (Musicological Studies 2) (Brooklyn, 1960), on purely stylistic grounds. The strange title *'Vinnus vinna'* may refer to a poem by Hugo Primas of Orléans contained in the manuscript 493 of the City Library of Bruges, which seems to have belonged, in the fifteenth century, to a canon Jacques de Vidale of Arras (fol. 242v, later addition): 'Datur in convivio vinus vina vinum, Masculinum deficit atque femininum, Sed in neutro genere vinum fit divinum'. This refers to fasting in Lent, of course, as 'vina' or 'vinna' is the 'fin' of the fish which is served at the dinner-table; 'vinnus' must mean something similar; the poet clearly preferred 'vinum' – wine! Can 'Jacques de Vidale' be the composer Jacques Vide?

151. Edited by Donald W. Shipley in *Das Chorwerk* 123 (Wolfenbüttel, 1977). This remarkable work may have been written for a church in the Low Countries, where the verse 'O crux lignum' of the sequence *Laudes crucis attollamus* was used separately on a specific feast – this was the case in Bruges (see p. 145) but also elsewhere; certainly in Utrecht.

152. See Johannes Ockeghem, *Collected Works* (see n. 112 above), nos. 12, 9, 4 and 7. The connections of Ockeghem with Bruges are still a puzzle. We know only of his celebrated visit in August, 1484 (See Vander Straeten, *Musique*, 1, p. 100f.); far-reaching speculations have been made by René Bernard Lenaerts, 'Bemerkungen über Ockeghem und seinen Kompositionsstil', in *Convivium Musicorum. Festschrift Wolfgang Boetticher* (Berlin: Merseburger, 1974), pp. 163–167. Lenaerts suggests that Ockeghem came into contact with English music in Bruges during his service in the chapel of Duke Charles of Bourbon (1448–1452) or even earlier, and that this accounts for the similarity of his 'florid' style with that of the *Eton Choirbook* (*c*.1490). I think that this similarity is only apparent.

153. Higinio Anglés, *La música en la Corte de los Reyes Católicos*, 2nd edn. (Barcelona, 1960), 1, pp. 106–112.

154. Published in Alexander Agricola, *Opera Omnia*, ed. by Edward Lerner (CMM 22/5) (American Institute of Musicology, 1970), 5, no. 68. In another source (*Bologna Q 17*) the label is *'Cecus'*, and in a third source (Formschneider 1538), *'Cecorum'* (plural!).

155. See Weinmann, *Tinctoris*.

156. See the list of his extant works by Chris Maas, 'Towards a New Obrecht Edition: A Preliminary Worklist', *TVNM* 26 (1976), pp. 84–108.

157. Most of them are published in Johannes Wolf, ed., *Werken van Jacob Obrecht*, 7 (Amsterdam-Leipzig, 1921; repr. Gregg, 1968), and in A. Smijers, ed., *Van Ockeghem tot Sweelinck*, (Amsterdam, 1941) part 3.

158. For their constitution and possible repertory, see Polk, *Wind Bands*.

159. A Netherlands choirbook which contains only *Salve Reginas*, many of them with secular cantus firmi, is the codex Mus. MS 34 of the Bavarian State Library, Munich (*c*.1520).

160. Edited in *Werken van Jacob Obrecht* (see n. 157 above), 6; and in A. Smijers,

ed., Jacobus Obrecht, *Opera omnia*, Edition altera, (Amsterdam, 1958), 2; some motets in codex *Seg* are still unedited.

161. See n. 58 above.

162. Schabacker, *Petrus Christus*, remarks on this painting (cat. no. 9), p. 98: 'The prayer to St. Veronica surmounted by the Holy Face of the Sudarium might indicate one of the wealthy cloth merchants of which Bruges possessed a good number and whose trade fell under Veronica's protection. The more specific possibility that he might be a Lucchese silk merchant is suggested by the fact that the *Volto Santo* was especially venerated in that Italian town and among its merchant colonies abroad.' It may be added that the *Volto Santo* was venerated all over Europe, and that a sitting lion with a shield is shown as a statuette in the margin of the panel – possibly the lion of St Mark's, Venice.

163. Dewitte, *Boek*, p. 94.

164. R.-A. Parmentier, *Beschrijving van de Getijden- en Gebedenboeken van het Kabinet Houtart te Brugge* (Bruges, 1929), p. 69.

165. I am grateful to Profs. Chris Maas and Barton Hudson for their kindness in informing me of variants between the two sources of the work, *CS 35* and the Jena choirbook 32. The Jena version (not used in Wolf's edition), which they regard as the more authentic one, contains an additional duet to the words 'Et incarnatus sepultus est'; therefore, *O clavis David* and the segment of the responsory text coincide with the words from 'Et resurrexit' onwards, whereas in Wolf's edition, they start at 'Et incarnatus est'. In either case, the additional texts coincide with 'Et resurrexit tertia die'. It should be noted that the mass may contain further unrecognised *cantus firmi*, of which neither source gives the text – for example in the head-motive.

166. Gildeboek Wiltwerkers, Stadsarchief Brugge no. 345, Peltiers, liasse 45, fol. 20v.

167. The personal connection of the *Missa 'L'homme armé'* with Busnois was first suggested by Oliver Strunk, 'Origins of the *L'homme armé* Mass', *Bulletin of the AMS* 2 (1936), p. 25f. For *Caput*, see Alejandro E. Planchart, 'Fifteenth-Century Masses: Notes on Performance and Chronology', *Studi Musicali* 10 (1981), pp. 13–29. Planchart's demonstration of the purely 'organistic' role of the cantus firmus seems to fit performance practices in Bruges as described in this book; but he places Obrecht's *Missa 'Caput'* in the 1470s, when the composer had no known connections with Bruges; the participation of the organ, even in such a way, could easily have been widespread in the Netherlands.

168. See *Census Catalogue*, 2, p. 165f. Some masses in this codex may well have reached Ferrara by 1485. Jean Cordier, who invited Obrecht to Ferrara on 2 October 1487, reported to the chapter of St Donatian's that Duke Ercole already knew and loved Obrecht's works; see De Schrevel, p. 160.

169. The copies of Obrecht's masses in Munich, Bayerische Staatsbibl., Mus. ms. 3154, have been dated, on the evidence of watermarks, by Thomas Noblitt, 'Die Datierung der Handschrift Mus. ms. 3154 der Staats-bibliothek München', *Mf* 27 (1974), pp. 36–56. It emerges that *Beata viscera, Carminum II (Scoen lief)* and *Rosa playsant* were copied before *c.*1493,

Je ne demande before *c.*1491. On the style of *Plurimorum carminum I (Adieu mes amours)*, see M. Staehelin, 'Obrechtiana', *TVNM* 25 (1975), p. 25ff. and n. 130.

170. Dewitte, *Boek*, p. 95.

171. Staehelin, 'Obrechtiana' (see n. 168 above) p. 20ff. emphasises the humanist imagery and diction of this text; he overlooks, however, the coincidence of the metre with *O quam glorifica*.

172. See *Census Catalogue*, 2, p. 72ff.; Lenaerts, *Nederlands polifonies lied*, p. 9ff. The chansonnier contains 78 pieces, 25 of which are Flemish songs; these have been edited by Johannes Wolf, *25 driestemmige Oud-Nederlandsche Liederen* (Uitgave der Vereeniging voor Noord-Nederlands Muziek-geschiedenis XXX) (Amsterdam, 1910). According to the *Census Catalogue*, the codex was written *c.*1505–6 for Jérôme Lauweryn of Watervliet (†1509), an official of Philip the Fair; Joshua Rifkin recog-nised a scribal concordance with the Brussels-Tournai partbooks (see following note), which would suggest that the codex originated in Bruges.

173. See *Census Catalogue*, 1, p. 97ff.; Lenaerts, *Nederlands polifonies lied*, p. 12ff. Of this set of partbooks, only the tenor partbook (Tournai, Bibl. de la ville, MS 94) and the discant partbook (Brussels, Bibl. Royale, MSS IV 90) survive. There are only 24 songs, six with Flemish texts. The manu-script is decorated with lovely miniatures in the manner of the 'Books of Hours' produced by Simon Bening and his school (facsimiles in Lenaerts; also in Bernard Huys, *Muzikale Schatten uit de Koninklijke Biblio-theek Albert I* (Brussels, 1957), no. 7). An initial on fol. 21 (Tournai) con-tains the date 1511. The partbooks are bound by Ludovicus Bloc of Bruges and exhibit his typical blind-pressed covers 'Ludovicus Bloc / ob laudem / xpisti librum hunc / recte ligavi'.

174. Cambrai, Bibl. Municipale, MS 125–128: four partbooks with ex-libris of the Bruges merchant and poet Zegher van Male, dated 1542. The contents are masses, motets, chansons and instrumental dances by B. Appenzeller, A. Willaert, Johannes Lupi, Lupus Hellinck, Jan Richafort, Philippe Verdelot, Josquin, Mouton, Gombert, Clemens non Papa and others. The many witty illustrations are of great historical interest. See Alfons Dewitte, 'De Codex Cambrai 124 (125–128) van Zeghere van Male', *Het Brugs Ommeland: Tijdschrift van de Heemkundige Kring Maurits van Coppenolle*, 19 (Sint-Andries/Brugge, 1979), no. 4, pp. 267–280; George K. Diehl, *The Partbooks of a Renaissance Merchant, Cambrai: Bibliothèque Municipale, MSS 125–128*, Ph.D. diss., Univ. of Pennsylvania, 1974 (Univ. Microfilms, Ann Arbor, 75–2718).

175. Dewitte, *SD*, p. 130.

176. Jozef Robijns, 'Eine Musikhandschrift des frühen 16. Jahrhunderts im Zeichen der Verehrung unserer lieben Frau der Sieben Schmerzen', *Kirchenmusikalisches Jahrbuch* 44 (1960), pp. 28–43.

177. The codex has been dated about 1508–1511 by Kellman (see following note), p. 211; it thus postdates the first marriage of Charles de Clerc (b. 28 March 1477), who was the son of Jean de Clerc (†1516), a city councillor of Arras, and the elder brother of Robert, abbot of Ter Duinen

(†1557). The de Clercs of Arras acquired the Flemish township of Bouvekercke, but did not have particularly close ties with Bruges. Many references to the family history are contained in a Book of Hours (Brit. Library, Add. 19416), which belonged to the family from about 1470 until about 1530; on fol. 8v, there is a miniature of Our Lady of the Seven Sorrows. The family does not seem to be connected with Jean de Clerc, son of Lievin, a bookseller of Bruges and probably a patron of Caxton, who was, in turn, related to the families La Bie and Perrot.

178. This group of about 50 splendid choirbooks, copied by Martin Bourgeois, Petrus Alamire and others between *c*.1495 and *c*.1534, has been thoroughly investigated by Herbert Kellman. See, most recently, H. Kellman, 'Josquin and the Courts of Netherlands and France: The Evidence of the Sources', in Lowinsky, *Josquin Des Prez*, pp. 181–216.

———◆•••◆———

Musicians employed in churches of Bruges until *c.*1510

Excluded from the following list are musicians who held prebends *in absentia*, like Vide, Grenon, Binchois, Dufay, Weerbeke, or who were sometimes present but did not fulfill specifically musical functions in the church, like the ducal musicians Jean de Visée, Jean de Watignies or Mathieu de Bracle. A few doubtful cases (Fraxinis, Rembert) are included, however. Composers are marked with an asterisk.

Normally, the dates given are those of the appointment to an office. Where these are not available, the date is that of the first mention of the musician as holding that office, then preceded by 'cit.'. The sources of information are quoted in brackets; for full references, see bibliography. Information contained between two full stops is drawn from the same source; that source is the chapter minutes of St Donatian's and Our Lady's unless otherwise indicated.

Other abbreviations:

Can.	canon
capp.	cappellanus
cler.	clericus (mostly: installatus)
confr.	confrater (i.e. member of a confraternity), confraternity
OL	Our Lady's
SB	St Basil's (administratively part of St Donatian's)
SD	St Donatian's
SG	St Giles's
SJ	St James's
SS	St Saviour's

The alphabetical order follows the pragmatic principle explained in the introduction of this book. Where only father's names are available, they are treated as surnames, but indicated by 'f.' (= filius) if the source gives this information. Musicians for whom no surname could be found are listed separately at the end according to first names.

*   *   *

ABSALONIS, ARNOLDUS. Capp. SD 1440s; rebellious singer 1449 (see p. 26); † before 7.10.1489.

ALCMAER(E), JOHANNES. Copied music for SD 1467 (Dewitte, *Boek*, 90)

ALLERIS, CHRISTIANUS. Cler. singer SD. 8.11.1484.

AMOURET (AMOURY), JACQUES. Singer Savoy court 1454–57 (Bouquet, 283). Cler. SD 13.2.1458. Turned down succentorship SD 5.12.1459. Capp. SD 27.3.1460. Singer Burgundian court 1470–74 (Marix, 124).

ARNOLDI, VICTOR. Capp. SD cit. 1438; rebellious singer 1449 (see p. 26).

ATRIO, JASPAR DE. Cler. Tenorista OL cit. 8.7.1485. Singer still in 1500 (Dewitte, *OL*, 114).

BAELDE, CHRISTIANUS. Virgifer SD cit. 1467; capp. SD cit. 1468. Copied music for SD 1471–1503 (Dewitte, *Boek*, 82, 91ff.).

BALDE, JOHANNES. [OL] Organist SD 23.6.1412–1413. Cler. OL *c.*1420s (Confr. *OL*).

BANC, MATTHIAS DE. Capp. SD cit. 1438. Succentor SD 21.8.1438 for 6–8 weeks.

BAND, JOHANNES. Capp. SD cit. after 1438. Rebellious singer 1449 (see p. 26).

BARBIER,WILLELMUS TASSET dictus. Cler. SD cit. 5.10.1360; succentor SD 13.8.1365–28.4.67; † Dec. 1367.

*BASIN, PIERRE. Cler. SD 23.6.1460; succentor SD 13.8.65–23.6.66; can. 1467– † 19.4.97; succentor 17.1.91–28.3.91. Ducal chaplain and councillor from 1467 (Doorslaer, 29, Marix). Confr. OL van der Sne 1471/2. Composer? (see p. 129).

BEECLINC, BALDUINUS. Cler. singer SD 16.6.1473.

BELLE, CORNELIUS VAN. [OL] Choirboy OL cit. 13.10.1490 (Acta *SD*).

BERGIS, RUBERTINUS DE. [OL] Cler. singer OL cit. 24.5.1490.

BEROUT, JACOBUS. Choirboy SD cit. 19.2.1420.

BLIEKERE, PETRUS DE. [OL] Cler. SD 9.9.1481; capp. SD 5.11.84. Capp. OL 7.9.87. † 6.9.1520.

BLIJMAN, JOHANNES. Cler. tenorista SD 3.11.1468; capp. SD cit. 1489. Turned down succentorship SD 28.3.91. † 1510.

BLEYSERE, ACHILLES DE. Cler. singer SD cit. 9.12.1405, 17.8.1414.

BLOUME, PAULUS. [OL, SS] Organist SD 1439–20.9.47; † 1479 (Dewitte *SD*, 173). Cler. OL (confr. *OL*) *c.*1440. Confr. *SS*.

BOLLAERT, PHILIPPUS. [SS] SD 2.6.1456. Capp. SS 1474 (Cartulary *SS*); organist SS cit. 1506. † before 1510.

*BOUBERT, JOHANNES. Cler. SD 10.5.1452. Succentor SD, with Cornelius Heyns, 23.6.1452–22.6.54, then alone until 29.4.61. His son was choirboy SD before 3.12.61. Composer (see Tinctoris, *Proportionale*, p. 49).

BOUCHOUT, JOHANNES. [OL] 'Almanus'. Cler. contratenor OL 10.10.1480–3.10.81.

*BRAUWERE (BRAXATORIS), NICASIUS DE. [SS] Succentor SS cit. 1484/5 (City accounts). Composer (see p. 86).

BRUNIJNC (DE BRUNE), VICTOR. [OL] Can. SD 1493. Cler. OL 4.7.1496; succentor OL until 2.4.99. Copied music for SD 1501 and 1513 (Dewitte, *Boek*, 82). Probably the singer 'Victore de Bruges' in ducal chapel Milan 1474–75 (Sartori, 64ff.). Hired by Weerbeke in Flanders 1474?

*BUSNOIS, ANTOINE. [SS] Succentor SS, until he died before 6.11.1492 Confr. *SS* (fol. 22r). Composer (see p. 55).

BUUS, JACOBUS [OL, SS] Cler. organist OL 22.3.1499. Succentor SS cit. 1504 (Van de Casteele, 142).

CALEWE, AUGUSTINUS DE. [OL] Cler. singer OL 24.5.1490; capp. OL 8.6.92.

CAMPIOENS (CHAMPION), JOHANNES. Scolasticus SD 1361–83. See p. 19.

CAPELLA, JOHANNES DE. [OL] Capp. organist OL cit. 9.3.1496–cit. 16.5.98.

CAPELLA, PETRUS DE. [OL] Capp. organist OL cit. 18.8.1488–cit. 21.6.90. † 1502? (Dewitte, *OL*,123).

CASEMAN, JACOBUS. Cler.(?) SD; rebellious singer 1449 (see p. 26).

CLENQUEMEURE, PETRUS. Capp. SD cit. 1472/3 (Weale: *Accounts SD*. Can. SD 6.6.85. Still present as singer 1501.

CLERICI, JOHANNES. [OL] Succentor SD 8.11.1497, coming from St Omer; resigned immediately; succentor OL 2.4.1499–29.3.1500 (De Schrevel, 175–178; Dewitte, *OL*, 118).

*CLIBANO, JACOBUS DE. [OL] Cler. SD 15.6.1429; succentor SD 23.12.29–24.6.33; capp. SD cit. 1438. Capp. OL 1436 (Cartulary *OL*). Resigned an office in Bruges 13.6.49 (Acta *SD*). Composer (see p. 117).

*CLIBANO, JERONIMUS DE. [OL] Capp. succentor SD, from s'Hertoghenbosch, 1.12.1492–16.8.97 (de Schrevel, 165ff.). Chaplain of Philip the Fair 5.8.1500 (Doorslaer, 143ff.). Probably cler. OL 26.6.1501–1.11.1501, then travel to Spain (Acta *OL)*. † before 17.5.1503. Composer.

CLITA, CHRISTIANUS DE. Cler. singer SD 13.3.1486.

COENE, SYMON. Cler. singer SD 5.4.1419; capp. SD cit. 1438; † before 1460.

COLINS, MARTINUS. [OL] Capp. tenorista SD from *c*.1467. Can. SD 27.10.84. Organist SD 1485–87 (Dewitte, *SD*, 173). Capp. OL 1485 (Acta *OL*). Copied more than 100 works into the choirbooks of SD (see p. 30). Several times in the 1480s in chapel of Maximilian of Habsburg (Acta *SD*). Probably the 'Martin tenoristre' in chapel of Mary of Burgundy 1482 (Doorslaer, 28). † 23.5.91.

COOPMAN, JACOBUS. [OL] Cler. singer OL 23.2.1486.

COOTS, PETRUS. Succentor and organist SD 12.7.1399–7.4.1400.

CORDIER, JOHANNES. Cler. singer SD 23.7.1460. Can. SD 1482 (Foppens). Succentor SD 9.10.97–10.11.98; † 28.9.1501 (De Schrevel, 167–175). Left SD for the Medici chapel in February, 1467 (see p. 37). Singer in the chapels of Florence, Rome, Milan, Naples, Habsburg.

*COUTREMAN, JACOBUS. [OL] Cler. succentor SD 13.10.1417–19.1.22 and 24.12.27–23.12.29 (De Schrevel, 152ff.; Dewitte, *SD* 139). Organist SD 1427– † 1432 (Dewitte, *SD* 173). Copied music for SD (Dewitte, *Boek*, 85). Cler. OL in the 1420s (Confr. *OL*). Composer (see p. 21).

CRAUWEEL, JOHANNES. Candidate for organist's post SD 2.11.1482.

CREKELE, EGIDIUS. [SS] Cler. SD cit. 27.4.1485; capp. SD. Cler. tenorista SS 21.5.95; can. SS 1502 (Duclos: *Acta SS*).

DAMME, CORNELIUS VAN DER. Choirboy SD until 30.9.1481.

DATH, RICHARDUS. [OL] Cler. singer OL 7.9.1498 (Dewitte, *OL* 125).

DEBBOUT (DUBBOUT, DE WOUT), PETRUS. [OL] Cler. singer OL 25.10.1492.

DEELERS, PIERKIN see GODEMAERS

DEISTER (DEYSEN), VICTOR. Capp. succentor SD 22.4.1387; still in Bruges 1399 (De Schrevel, 150).

DHONDT (DONT), JOHANNES. [SJ]. Curate SJ; copied music for SJ 1463/4 and 1466/7 (Accounts *SJ*).

*DIVITIS (DE RYCKE), ANTONIUS. Cler. succentor SD 13.6.1501–20.3.1504. Composer.

DOORNE (DOORME?), JACOBUS. [OL] Cler. singer OL 3.9.1495. Because of his installation (as succentor?), Aliamus de Groote resigned succentorship OL.

DRIESSCHE, GUILLERMUS VAN DEN. Cler. SD 1421; *coadjutor* of succentor Coutreman 21.7.1421. Bookseller; sold motet-book to SD 1421 (Dewitte, *Boek*, 94).

DULLAERT, PHILIPPUS. [OL] Choirboy SD cit. 3.8.1422; cler. 12.8.33; capp. SD before 1441. Led the singers' rebellion 1449 (see p. 26). Capp. OL cit. 12.8.52 (Cartulary *OL*). † *c*.1463.

*ECGHAERT (EGARDUS?), JOHANNES. Succentor SD 21.8.1370; capp. SB 21.5.71. Probably the composer 'Egardus' (see p. 112).

*FABRI, THOMAS. [OL] Cler. SD 29.3.1412; succentor 23.6.12–1415 (followed by P. Zoeteman 18.12.1415). Cler. OL (Confr. *OL*, no date). Composer (see p. 106 ff.).

FERNANDEZ, JOHANNES. Organist SD 21.1.1482–4.3.82 as deputy for R. de Wreede. Blind musician of international fame (see p. 88).

FINE, ARNOLDUS DE. Capp. singer cit. 1438; rebellious singer 1449 (see p. 26). Copied liturgical books for SD 1452–53 (Dewitte, *Boek*, 89).

FRAXINIS (FRAEYE), JOHANNES DE. Can. SD 1440–69. Singer Savoy court 1456–63 (Bouquet, 283). Perhaps the papal singer Jo. de Fraccinis 1448 and 1451 (Haberl, 225ff.), but present in Bruges 16.5.49.

FRUEYTEN, CLAEYS. [SS] Copied music into discant book of SS 1482/3 and 28.10.83 (Accounts *SS*).

GALLANT, JACOBUS. [OL] Organist OL 1444/5 (Accounts *OL*).

GALLICI. [SS] Cler. singer SS *c*.1500 (Duclos: *Acta SS*).

GENAYS, JOHANNES DE [OL] (i.e. of Geneva?). Cler. succentor OL 27.7.1489–15.3.91.

GLADIO, LEONARDUS f. JUDOCI AERNOUDS DE . Capp. SD 4.4.1384; can. SD cit. 1394. Capp. OL *c*.1410 (Confr. *OL*). Copied music for SD 1400–1416 (Dewitte, *Boek*, 73ff.). † before February, 1420.

GOEDEMAERS, PIERKIN. [SJ] Copied motets for SJ 1463/4 (Accounts *SJ*) – or this was Pierkin Deelers, *custos* of SJ (Dewitte, *SJ* 337).

GOSSAERT, f. FRANCISCI GOSSAERT of Ghent. Choirboy SD 30.9.1481.

GOUY, JACOBUS DE. [OL] Cler. tenorista SD 13.10.1484– † 30.5.85. Cler. OL (Confr. *OL*).

GRAC(H), JOHANNES, of Bourbourg. [SJ] Capp. SD 1490; copied mass by Obrecht for SD 1491 (Dewitte, *Boex*, 94). Succentor SJ 1498–99 (Dewitte, *SJ*, 347).

GRAPPE, CLAEYS. [SJ] Organist confr. Dry Tree from 1497 (Accounts Dry Tree). Organist SD 1502–06 (Dewitte, *SD* 173). Organist SJ 1515– † 1517 (Dewitte, *SJ*, 348).

GRISEL, RYCQUAERT. [SG] Organist SG until 1488 (Dewitte, *SG*, 99).

*GROOTE, ALIAMUS DE. [OL] The spelling 'Aliamus' is consistent in many sources. A. de Groote *sen*.: Capp. OL cit. 1458 (Cartulary *OL*). Succentor OL *c.*1470–75? (see p. 44). Succentor SD 5.7.75–7.2.85 and 7.9.1500– † 1501. Succentor OL 15.3.91–3.9.95. Poet and composer; member of confr. OL van der Sne and Holy Ghost (see p. 70).

GROOTE, ALIAMUS DE *jun*. [OL, SS] Succentor SS cit. 1500–1503 (De Schrevel); succentor OL until 1507; succentor SD cit. 1508–13 (Dewitte, *OL*, 119).

GROOTE, LAURENTIUS DE. Capp. singer SD cit. 1438; rebellious singer 1449 (see p. 26).

HECKE, JAN VAN DEN. [SJ] Organist SJ 1419–21 (Dewitte, *SJ*, 348).

*HEYNS, CORNELIUS. Cler. singer SD 25.10.1447; capp. succentor 23.6.52 – with J. Boubert – until 22.6.54; succentor SD 1462–24.12.65. † 1485 (Weale: *Accounts SD*). Composer (see p. 131). Not identical with Cistercian monk Cornelius Heyns, who copied Seneca MS in 1477 (Leiden UB, BPL 45 A).

HEYNS, JOHANNES. Cler.(?) singer SD: rebellious singer in 1449 (see p. 26).

HILLE, JAN VAN. [SJ] Organist SJ 1487–1506 (Dewitte, *SJ*, 348).

HILLE, JUDOCUS VAN. [OL] Cler. singer OL cit. 1497 (Dewitte, *OL*, 126).

HOLLANDRINUS, JOHANNES. Choirboy SD until 1497 (De Schrevel, 55).

HONIE (HONIN?), JACOBUS. [OL, SJ] Organist OL 22.3.1499–1540 (Dewitte, *OL*, 123). Organist confr. Dry Tree cit. 1507/08 (Accounts Dry Tree). Organist SJ 1511–13 (Dewitte, *SJ*, 348).

HUGHELOOT, MICHAEL. Capp. SD cit. after 1438; rebellious singer 1449 (see p. 26).

HUUSMAN, JACOBUS. [OL] Cler. singer SD cit. 4.12.1441. Cler. OL 1420s, under the name of 'Jacobus Huusman alias metter lute' (Confr. *OL*).

JONGHE see JUVENIS.

*JOYE, GILLES. Cler. singer SD cit. 16.5.1449 (charter OL). Capp. SB 3.11.60. Can. SD 1459 (Foppens). Admitted to prebend 25.7.61 (Acta *SD*). Ducal chaplain from 1467 (Doorslaer, 23, Marix). † 31.12.1483. Composer (see p. 27 ff.).

JUVENIS (DE JONGHE), ADRIANUS. [SG] Organist SG cit. 1482 (Acta *SD*) as candidate for succession of R. de Wreede.

JUVENIS, JOHANNES. Choirboy SD until 30.9.1481; cler. SD cit. 1488.

KNUUT, WALTERUS. Capp. SD cit. 1438; rebellious singer 1449 (see p. 26).

LAMBERTS, JOHANNES. Cler. tenorista SD 21.10.1461.

LE CANU, THOMAS. Cler. singer SD 19.7.1442; capp. SD 1451. Copied passions 1448, mass 1455 for SD (Dewitte, *Boek*, 88ff.).

LE CRISTENIER, STEPHANUS. Cler. tenorista SD 26.1.1462. Copied masses for SD 1463 (Dewitte, *Boek*, 90). Capp. SD still cit. 1490.

LEONIS, CORNELIUS. Cler. singer SD cit. 7.1.1452.

LOO, CORNELIUS VAN. Capp. SS 1480s (Cartulary *SS*). Chaplain of Mary of Burgundy 1482 (Doorslaer, 28).

LOVANIO, LAURENTIUS DE. [OL] Cler. singer OL 8.8.1492.

LUUC, JAN. Cler. SD from *c*.1399; cit. 17.8.1414 (see p. 26).

LUUCX, JACOBUS. Cler. SD cit. 27.6.1454; succentor SD 23.6.66–26.4.68.

MAES, JACOBUS. Cler. singer SD cit. 27.9.1480.

MAES, JOHANNES [SS] Capp. SS cit. 1474, resigned in favour of Ph. Bollaert; † after 1510. Perhaps the Johannes Maas who sang at St Peter's, Rome, in 1467 (Haberl 237).

MANESSIER, EUSTACIUS. Capp. singer SD cit. 22.6.1448 and 3.12.1460.

MARGAS, JOHANNES. Capp. SD 1472/3 (Accounts *SD*). Papal singer 1479 (Haberl, 241); capp. SD 1480 (Haberl, 232).

*MARTINI, GEORGIUS f. JOHANNIS. Can. SD 1431– †14.8.38. Gave a 'liber scientie musicarum' to SD (Dewitte, *Boek*, 87). Capp. singer of Treviso cathedral 1427–31 (d'Alessi). Papal singer 1431–32 (Schuler, *Eugen IV*). Composer (see p. 117).

MAYOUL, NICOLAUS *jun.* Cler. singer SD cit. 23.1.1477 (*prima missa*). Franciscan friar 30.1.82. Chaplain of Maximilian of Habsburg(?), Philip the Fair (Doorslaer, 150f.). Curate SS 6.8.86–87 (Cartulary *SS*).

METTERESSE, EUSTACIUS. Resigned clerkship SD before 30.8.1451. (see also MANESSIER).

MICHAELIS, EGIDIUS f. Capp. singer SD 3.6.1405; capp. SB 12.9.1409. Succentor SD cit. 1410–12 (succeeded by Th. Fabri). Mag. Univ. Louvain 1435 (De Schrevel, 151).

*MIJS, BALDUINUS. Secretary and notary SD *c*.1475. Capp. SD cit. 27.3.80. Composer (Dewitte, *Boek*, 92).

MOENS, BERTINUS. Capp. SB cit. 1438. Curate SS 1439. Capp. SD until †1480. Copied music for SD 1472 (Dewitte, *Boek*, 92).

MOERIJNC, CORNELIUS [OL, SS] Organist OL perhaps 1462/3 ('Heer Cornelis') (Accounts *OL*). Organist OL cit. 1474; Vicarius OL cit. 1485. Copied Obituary OL in 1474 (see p. 44). Confr. *SS*.

MOERSCH(MOERE), PASCHASIUS VAN DER. Cler. singer SD 21.6.1460.

MOERSCH(MOERE), PETRUS VAN DER. Choirboy SD 21.4.1421; capp. SD 13.12.34.

MONACHI, JACOBUS. Choirboy SD cit. 6.8.1425; capp. SD 20.2.36; suggested 'Ludum de sacramento' 27.5.58.

NACHTEGALE, PIETER. [SJ] Succentor SJ 1444–51 (Dewitte, *SJ*, 347).

NEPOTIS, LUDOVICUS. Cler. tenorista SD cit. 1498/9 (Weale: *Accounts SD*) until after 1500.

*OBRECHT, JACOBUS. Succentor SD 13.10.1485–17.1.91 and 13.12.1498–3.9.1500. Capp. SD 2.5.1489. Composer (see p. 144 ff.).

ONDANCH, JOHANNES. Capp. SD cit. 16.8.1370; capp. SB 1390; can. SD cit. 1394– † 1425 (date of will). Ducal organist 1384 (Wright, *Burgundy*, 57). See p. 19.

OSTENDIS, JOHANNES DE. Choirboy SD until 8.8.1491.

PAES, PETRUS. [OL, SS] Organist SD 1432–39 (Dewitte, *SD*, 173). Cler. SD cit. 18.12.41. Capp. OL 3.9.50–1458 (Cartulary *OL*). Confr. *SS*.

PAILLET(TE), PHILIPPE. Choirboy SD until 1491. Cler. SD 1499 (De Schrevel, 99). 1501 chaplain of Philip the Fair, and certainly identical with 'Philipot de Bruges' (Doorslaer, 153).

PARIS, EUSTACIUS DE. Organist SD 2.6.1483–1501.

PASTORIS, CESAR. [OL] Cler. singer OL 23.4.1501.

PASTORIS, JOHANNES. [OL] Succentor OL 7.7.1500. (Brother of Cesar).

PATINIER, PETRUS. [OL] Cler. singer OL cit. 19.6.1486.

PEERBOME, JOHANNES. Capp. SD cit. after 1438; rebellious singer 1449.

PETAULT, ESTIENNE. Can. SD 27.8.1438; † before 24.9.42. Ducal chaplain (Marix).

PETIT, JEAN LE. [OL] Vicarius SD 1507/8; succentor OL 31.1.1508–1514 (Dewitte, *OL*, 121).

PIJPE, JUDOCUS. [OL] Cler. singer OL 5.11.1486.

PIPELARE, JOHANNES, Mag. Cler. tenorista SD cit. 27.3.1493–1498/9 (Acta and Accounts *SD*). Singer at St Peter's, Rome, April 1499–1502 (Haberl, 240).

PLATEA, JOHANNES DE. Cler. singer SD cit. 26.4.1468, when he departed for Liège.

PLOUVIER, JOHANNES. [OL] Cler. singer SD 30.8.1445; Capp. OL *c.*1451, vicarius OL 1454, later can. OL (Confr. *OL*). Perhaps the same as Jean Plouvier, chaplain of Philip the Fair 1492–1505 (Doorslaer, 153).

POLINCHOVE, PERCHEVALDUS DE. Capp. singer SD 30.9.1462; succentor 13.6.–1.10.60 and 26.8.68–5.7.75. Capp. SB 5.7.75. Copied the two extant graduals of St Donatian's in 1468 (see p. 121). † 5.11.1505.

PONT, JOHANNES DE. Capp. SD cit. 1377. (Dewitte, *SD*, 173 identifies him with the organist SD 1387, but this was J. de Prato.)

PRATO (PRATIS), JOHANNES DE. Organist SD 1385–88 (Accounts *SD*); capp. SD 24.1.1390. Probably identical with Johannes de Prato, 'cantor' SD cit. 17.2.1361.

*PRATO (PRATIS), PASCHASIUS DE (Pasquier Desprez). [OL, SS] Capp. OL 1459–60 (Cartulary *OL*). Capp. SS 1465 (Cartulary *SS*). Capp. SD cit. 23.12.1470; can. SD 1479– † 15.11.81. His prebend XVII was reserved to noble graduates (Foppens). Ducal chaplain 1464 (Marix). Confr. OL van der Sne 1471/2 (Accounts). Perhaps the composer cited by Tinctoris (*Proportionale* p. 23) as author of a mass, with the words 'nescio quis Pasquin'.

RAEDT, WALTERUS DE. [SS] Capp. SS *c.*1480; for 30 years capp. of chapel of cordwainers SS; died as can. SS 13.5.1510 (Cartulary SS and Mullie). Perhaps the 'Dominus Walterus' who took over succentorship after death of Busnois 6.11.1492, sharing with 'Denis' (van Spiere?) (Duclos: *Acta SS*).

RAES, JOHANNES. [SJ] Succentor SJ 1499–1504 (Dewitte, *SJ*, 337). Perhaps the same as Jo. de Raedt, a Carmelite priest (charter of the convent 28.9.1457). Perhaps the same as 'Johannes Raat', singer at St Peter's, Rome, 1467–68, and in the papal chapel 1470–84 (Reynolds, 281; Haberl, 230ff.).

RANARII, SIMON. Succentor SD 29.7.1422–22.6.26. Singer of King Sigismund (Schuler, *Konstanz*, 158).

RAPPONDE, JOHANNES. Choirboy SD 6.3.1426. Perhaps a relative of the merchants from Lucca, Dino Rapondi (see p. 15) and Filippo Rapondi.

RAVESCOTE, JACOBUS VAN. Succentor SD interim 25.5.1425 (with J. Storkin).

REKENARE, PASCHASIUS DE. Choirboy SD 3.8.1422.

REMBERT, NICOLAUS. Can. SD 1489–98, probably *in absentia*. From 1475 singer at St Peter's, Rome (Haberl, 237). At SD successor of Rosa.

REYNEVILLE, JOHANNES. Choirboy SD until 14.8.1482. Cler. singer OL 8.11.90.

ROBERTI, JOHANNES. Succentor SD 23.6.1435–23.6.52. Copied music for SD 1452 (Dewitte, *Boek*, 89). † July 1467.

ROGERII, JOHANNES f. Organist SD 1306/7(!) (Dewitte, *SD*, 134).

ROGIAULT, GUILLERMUS DE. [OL] Capp. OL 8.5.1457 (Cartulary *OL*). Cler. SD 24.4.59; succentor SD 29.4.61–24.12.61, although not a musical specialist.

ROSA, GUILLERMUS. Can. SD 1476– † 28.7.89. Resident and cit. in musical functions. Papal singer 1469–75 (Haberl, 230, 233); tenorista St Peter's 1472 (Haberl, 237). At SD succeeded by N. Rembert.

RYKELIN, JOHANNES Cler. singer SD cit. 4.5.1481. Capp. SD 1485; succentor 7.2.(?)85–13.10.85 and 2.10.87–15.8.88 as deputy of Obrecht.

RYN, JOHANNES VAN. Cler. tenorista SD 2.5.1468, from Antwerp. Capp. OL Antwerp 1477 (Doorslaer, 156).

SAARLOT, KAROLUS. Cler. SD cit. 31.1.1381, for leave of absence to go to Rome. Organist SD 1384–87 (Accounts *SD*).

SAINT-VAAST, LÉON DE. Can. SD 18.6.1492; resident at least in 1498. *Sommelier* of Philip the Fair 1497, *chantre* 1502 (Doorslaer, 157).

SANDEWIN, ROBERTUS. [OL, SS] Nominated for clerkship SD 30.12.1409 on behalf of Pope Alexander V. Cler. SD 14.1.1411; can. SD 1414– † 13.3.1453. Can. OL *c.*1420 (Confr. *OL*). Capp. SS 1424; papal singer at Council of Constance 1418 (Schuler, *Martin V*, 41) and probably earlier. See also p. 20 f..

SARIGOT DE SCRIVA, NICOLAUS. Cler. singer SD 5.10.1485; pilgrimage to Rome 23.7.89. Perhaps the 'Nicolaus Sardigo' who sang at St Peter's, Rome, 1492 (Haberl, 239). Will proved at SD 1502/3 (Weale: *Accounts SD*).

SLUUS, JOHANNES VAN DER. Choirboy SD *c.*1486.

SMOUT(KIN), JOHANNES. *Custos* St John's, Bruges, 31.1.1452; cler. SD 7.1.58; capp. SD 1470. Copied music for SD in 1467 (Ockeghem's *Missa 'L'homme armé'*), 1468 and 1470 (Dewitte, *Boek*, 90ff.).

SPASBOEN, FRANCISCUS. Choirboy SD 21.4.1421 and cit. 3.8.22.

SPIERE, DENIJS VAN. [SJ, SS] Cler. tenorista SJ 1463–65 (Accounts *SJ*). Copied music for SJ 1488 (Dewitte, *SJ*, 337). Perhaps the 'Denis' who was interim succentor(?) at SS 1492/3 with 'Walterus' (de Raedt?). (Duclos: *Acta SS*).

SPIERINCK, THEODORUS. Organist – not of Bruges? – who tested organ of SD 12.5.1449 (Dewitte, *SD*, 143).

SPOET, BALDUINUS. [OL, SS] Cler. singer SD cit. 15.12.1440; cap. SD cit. 1448; rebellious singer 1449 (see p. 26). Capp. OL (Confr. *OL*, no date). Capp. SS– † 1476 (Cartulary *SS*).

STALINHOOFT, ELIGIUS. Cler. SD cit. 9.3.1389; succentor SD 14.4.1400–
1410, succeeded by Michaelis.

STEPHANI, JOHANNES. [OL] Cler. singer OL 10.9.1480.

STORKIN, JOHANNES. Cler. singer SD 10.9.1412; succentor SD interim
25.5.1425, together with J. v. Ravescote; capp. SD cit. 1438; † before
19.3.1473.

TASSET see BARBIER.

TAYAERT, JACOBUS. Cler. singer SD 25.5.1445; friend of G. Joye. Copied
'liber pandecte' (medical glossary) MS 473 of city library, Bruges, in 1473.

TYCK (TIJCKE), JACOBUS. [SJ, SS] Succentor SJ August–December 1463.
Confr. SS. Perhaps a relative of the English composer Henricus Thick (see
p. 123).

VALE, BERNARDINUS. [OL] Cler. singer OL cit. 8.7.1485. Perhaps the
'Bernardinus de Flandria' who sang at St Peter's, Rome, 1486 (Haberl,
238). OL cit. 1486, 1487, 1490, 1498.

VICO, JACQUETUS DE. Cler. SD and candidate for organist's post of R. de
Wreede 6.3.1482; 10.6.82 interim organist.

VICO, JOHANNES DE. Cler. singer 'habens vocem altam' SD 10.10.1480.
Perhaps the illuminator Johannes de Vico SD 1479–81 (see p. 30).

VILT, JAN. [SJ] Copied music for SJ 1489, 1498, 1516? (organ book)
(Dewitte, OL, 113). Member booksellers' guild 1488. Probably not identical
with Johannes Vils (Wils), capp. singer OL 1483 and capp. SD cit. 1488,
† 1495.

*VINDERHOUT (VINDEGOED), PETRUS. Capp. SD 1381– cit. 1394;
† before 7.1.1411. Can. St Pharailde's, Ghent, 4.4.1384. Copied – and
composed? – four 'O Christi pietas' for SD 1381/2 (Accounts SD). See p. 16.

VINELOO, PETRUS VAN, from Sluis. [SS] Succentor SS 12.1.1495 (Duclos:
Acta SS). Nominated succentor SD 17.5.1501; held the post 1505 – † 1507
(De Schrevel).

VOOSDONC (VOYSDONC), JOHANNES. [OL] Choirboy SD until
17.8.1489. Cler. singer OL 1497–98.

VOS, BERNARDUS f. ARNOLDI DE. [OL] Choirboy OL cit. 27.7.1489.

VOS, JOHANNES DE. [OL] Cler. tenorista SD 1481–1511. Copied music for
SD 1482 (Dewitte, Boek, 93). In Antwerp c.1482–85. Succentor SD 28.3.91–
1.12.92. Organist SD 1487 (Dewitte, SD, 173). Succentor OL 1506?
(Dewitte, SJ, 349).

WAELLIN, JOHANNES. Choirboy SD 21.4.1421; cit. 3.8.22.

WEYTS, NICASIUS. [OL, SS] Capp. SS cit. 1488 (Planarius SS). Capp. OL
1450 (Cartulary OL). Mag. scholarum OL (see Meerssman) and SS 1482
(Cartulary SS). Probably the 'Magister Nicasius Weyts Carmelita', author
of counterpoint treatise, in cod. Faenza 117 (see p. 66). † before 18.7.1492
(Duclos: Acta SS).

WILHOUDT, JOHANNES. [SG] Vicecurate SG 1480s (Cartulary SG); not
identical with 'Jan de Cantere', succentor SG (Dewitte, SG, 98).

WILLEMS, PIETER. [SJ] Succentor SJ 1500–1502 (Dewitte, SJ, 337).

*WREEDE, JOHANNES DE. [OL] Nominated cler. SD 30.8.1451, but
rejected because son of Rolandus de Wreede. Cler. OL; capp. OL 23.9.57

(Cartulary *OL*). Left *c*.1460. Composer, working in Spain 1476. See Vander Straeten, *Musique*, 8, p. 455ff.

*WREEDE, ROLANDUS DE. Cler. SD 19.9.1440; organist SD 20.9.47– † 3.2.85; leave of absence for *studium universale* 13.7.67. Composer? (see p. 30f.).

WULFAERT, JAN. [SJ] Cler. organist SD 29.6.1411–23.6.12. Organist SJ 1422–48 (Dewitte, *SJ*, 348).

ZAGHERE. [SS] Cler. singer SS *c*. 1500 (Duclos: *Acta SS*).

ZELANDRIE, ALEXIUS. Organist SD 1354–67 (Dewitte, *SD*, 173).

ZOETEMAN, PETRUS. Cler. SD 3.11.1410; succentor cit. 18.12.1415, 19.1.22–17.6.22 and 24.6.33–23.6.35.

ZOMERE, PETRUS DE. [OL] Cler. singer ('bascontre') OL 26.6.1501– cit. 1523.

ZOMERGHEM, JOHANNES DE. [OL] Cler. singer OL cit. 10.9.1498.

ZOUBURG, PETRUS, alias DE HUSENE. Cler. singer SD 20.4.1485– after 1500.

ZWINEMERSCH, JOHANNES. Cler. SD; capp. SD cit. 29.6.1411; organist SD 1413–1427 (Dewitte, *SD*, 173).

*   *   *

ALBERTUS. Cler. tenorista SD 3.11.68, from Antwerp or Germany.

ANDRAES. [OL] Organist OL cit. 1444–50 (Accounts *OL*).

BERNARDUS. [OL] Copied music, perhaps plainsong only, for SD 1443/4 (Dewitte, *Boek*, 87). Copied for OL 1444/5 (Accounts *OL*). Perhaps Bernard de Waghe(n), magistrate of Sijssele 1430s (charters *OL*).

BERTIN. [SS] Singer SS *c*. 1500 (Duclos: *Acta SS*).

CLEMENS. Cler. singer SD cit. 17.8.1414.

COPPIN. [SJ] Organist SJ 1422 (Dewitte, *SJ*, 348). Not identical with the following?

COPPIN. [OL] Organist OL 1462/3 (Accounts *OL*). Perhaps Coppin Bucquel de Bruges, ducal chaplain 1465–74 (Marix).

DAMMAERT DE FORCTEN. Choirboy SD 21.4.1421. Son or pupil of Johannes Ondanch. Or, son of citizen Dammaert de Straeten (De Schrevel, 54ff.).

GHISELBRECHT. [SG] Tenorista SG 1487 (Cartulary *SG*).

GILLIS. [SJ] Organist SJ cit. 1461 (Dewitte, *SJ*, 348).

GOUTIER. [SS] Singer SS *c*.1500 (Duclos: *Acta SS*).

JAN DE CANTERE. [SG] Succentor(?) SG cit. 1486/7 (Cartulary *SG*). Dewitte (*SG*, 98) seems to identify him with Jan Wilhoudt, vicecurate SG.

JOHANNES. [SS] Singer SS *c*.1500 (Duclos: *Acta SS*).

KAROLUS. Succentor SD interim 17.6.1422–29.7.22. Perhaps Karolus de Campis, can. SD *c*.1438–54, prebend IX.

OLIVERUS. Cler. singer SD 14.12.1405; cit. 17.7.1414. Perhaps Oliverus de Beka, capp. SD cit. 1419.

PHILIPPUS (VAN WETTERE?). [SS] Singer SS *c*.1500 (Duclos: *Acta SS*).

PHILIPS. [SG] Organist SG 1488 (Dewitte, *SG* 99).

RIQUAERT. [SJ] Succentor SJ 1421 (Dewitte, *SJ* 347).

ROBIJN. [SS] Singer SS *c.*1500 (Duclos: *Acta SS*).

SALVATOR. [SS] Singer SS *c.*1500 (Duclos: *Acta SS*).

SIMON. [SS] Singer SS *c.*1500 (Duclos: *Acta SS*).

STASSINETUS (DE COPPELAERE?). Cler. singer SD 2.12.1482.

VALENTIN DE CANTERE. [SJ] Succentor SJ 1463 (Until August) and 1464 (Accounts *SJ*).

VINCENTIUS. Organist SD 1406 (Dewitte, *SD*, 173).

WALTERUS. [SS] Succentor SS after Busnois 1492/3 (Duclos: *Acta SS*). See RAEDT.

WINNOCUS. Cler. tenorista SD cit. 1470/1 (Weale: *Accounts SD*). Perhaps the 'Vinocus tenorista' who sang at St Peter's, Rome, 1476–78 (Haberl, 237).

———◆———

Catalogue of Lucca, Archivio di Stato, Biblioteca Manoscritti 238 (*Las 238*)

The catalogue follows the order in which the fragments are presently kept. This results from a reconstruction, undertaken by the author in 1976 and 1978. Although subsequent research has suggested that some items may originally have been placed elsewhere in the codex (nos. 5a and 5b, 7a and perhaps 13 and 14), the reconstructed order of the gatherings, folios and compositions has not been altered here; only no. 25 has been allocated to the second Magnificat (*olim* no. 26), because it became apparent that no. 25 of the reconstruction was not a separate work, but part of no. 24. The bifolium 41/44 is preserved in Pisa, Archivio Arcivescovile, Biblioteca Maffi.

The catalogue lists in separate columns the gathering (Roman numerals), the number of the work (Arabic numerals), the folio numbers and the description of the work. Below the folio numbers, capital letters indicate the scribal hands, which correspond to the chronological layers of the compilation:

A^1 = Waghes, first stage of copying (*c*.1467–1469?)
A^2 = Waghe(s), second stage of copying (*c*.1469–1470?)
B = Italian scribe, 1470s
C = Italian scribe, *c*.1485
D = Italian scribe, *c*.1500

The gatherings have been numbered in order to show which works once belonged to the same gathering and which did not. 'II/III' etc. means that a composition bridges two adjacent gatherings. In the motet section (nos. 15–23), it cannot be established how many original gatherings there were; all these folios have been assembled together as one gathering 'XVI', although more than one gathering was involved.

The individual gatherings contain the following bifolios:

I	1/10, 2/9, 3/8, 4/7, 5/6	X	31/34, 32/33
II	11/18, 12/17, 13/16, 14/15	XI	35/36
III	19/20	XII	37/40, 38/39
IV	21/22	XIII	41/44, 42/43
V	23/24	XIV	45/46
VI	24*bis*/24*ter*	XV	46*bis*/48*bis*, 47/48
VII	25/26	XVI	49/54, 50/53, 51/52
VIII	27/30, 28/29	XVII	55/58, 56/57
IX	30*bis* (single folio)		

In the description of the works, the following conventions have been observed:

The first line gives the author, if named in the codex, but 'Anon.' if no author is named; neither indication occurs where the beginning of the work, and therefore an attribution, is missing. The name of the composer follows in square brackets, if it is available in another source. The title of the work is completed, if necessary, with the help of internal evidence or from other sources, in either case in square brackets.

The second line lists the voices and their clefs – in square brackets if reconstructed – in the order from top left to bottom left and then from top right to bottom right of an opening. Left-hand (l.h.) and right-hand (r.h) voices are divided by a diagonal dash.

The third line (and the following lines where applicable) lists the surviving sections and voices of the work, followed by an estimate of how many pages are missing.

In the lists of concordances, the lack of an attribution is not normally mentioned. For sources given in Italics, see **List of Sources**. The concordant sources are listed in approximately chronological order.

Abbreviations: Conc. = Concordance; Ct = Contratenor, S = Superius; T = Tenor.

*

Gathering · Work		Folio	Description
I		1r originally blank	
I	1	1v–10v A¹	Henricus Tik: *Missa [de B.M.V.]* [S]c¹♭/ Ct c³♭, T c³♭. Complete except for Ct of Agnus I–III (1p.). Conc. (all anonymous): *Tr 90* fol. 348v–349r (no. 1060) (Sanctus only); *Tr 89* fol. 366v–374r (nos. 736–740); *Strah* fol. 84v–85r (Sanctus only).
II	2	11v–17r A¹	P[etrus] de Domarto: *Missa Spiritus almus* [S]c², T 1 c⁴ / Ct c⁴, T 2 F³. Kyrie; Gloria I; l.h. voices Gloria II ('Qui tollis' – end); r.h. voices Sanctus; Benedictus; Agnus (8 pp. missing). Conc.: *Tr 88* fol. 401v–410r (nos. 497–501); *ModC* fol. 117v–129r; *CS 14* fol. 38v–47r.
II/III	3	17v–20v A¹	Anon.: *Missa Caput* (with prosula *Deus creator*) [S]c¹, T c³ / Ct 1 c³, Ct 2 c⁴. Kyrie; l.h. voices Gloria I; r.h. voices Agnus I–II; l.h. voices Agnus III (13 pp. missing). Conc. (erroneously 'Duffay' in *Tr 88*): Coventry MS A 3 fol. 1–v (part of Agnus); *Tr 93* fol. 126v–128r (Gloria), 236v–238r (Credo), 297v–299 (Sanctus);

			Tr 90 fol. 96v–98r (Gloria), 168v–170r (Credo), 228v–230r (Sanctus);
			Tr 88 fol. 31v–35r (Kyrie, Agnus);
			Tr 89 fol. 246v–256r (all movements);
			London, British Lib., Add. 54324, fol. 6–6v (part of Kyrie).
IV		21r blank	
IV	4	21v	Walterus Ffrie: *Missa [So ys emprentid]*
		A¹	[S]c²♭ / [Ct, T ?]
			L.h. voice of Kyrie (*c*.19 pp. missing).
			No conc.
IV/V	5	22r–24v	*Missa* (with prosula *Omnipotens pater*)
		A¹	[S]c²♭ / T c³♭, Ct c⁴♭.
			R.h. voices Kyrie II; l.h. (= all) voices Kyrie III; R.h. voices Credo II ('et incarnatus' – end); l.h. voice Sanctus; r.h. voices Agnus I–II; l.h. voice Agnus III (14 pp. missing).
			No conc.
VI	5a	24*bis* r–v	*Missa Quem malignus spiritus* (with prosula *Rex genitor*)
		A¹	[S]c² / Ct c⁴, T c⁴.
			R.h. voices Gloria I; l.h. voice Gloria II ('Qui tollis' – end) (*c*.18 pp. missing).
			Conc.:
			Cambridge, Univ. Lib. MS Ji.V.18 fol. 219v–228r;
			Tr 93 fol. 130v–133r (Gloria), 240v–242v (Credo), 303v–308r (Sanctus, Agnus);
			Tr 90 fol. 100v–103r (Gloria), 172v–175r (Credo), 234v–239r (Sanctus, Agnus).
VI	5b	24*ter* r–v	*Missa O rosa bella* (I)
		A¹	[S]c¹♭ / Ct c⁴♭, T c⁴♭.
			R.h. voices Gloria I; l.h. voice Gloria II ('Quoniam' – end) (*c*.18 pp. missing).
			Conc.:
			Tr 88 fol. 363v–372r.
VII	6	25r–26v	*Missa Te gloriosus* (with prosula *Conditor Kyrie*)
		A¹	[S]g², T c³, Medius c⁴ / [Ct]c³, T 2 c⁴.
			R.h. voices Kyrie III; Gloria I; l.h. voices Gloria II ('Domine fili' – end) (*c*.20 pp. missing).
			No conc.
VIII	7	27r–30v	*Missa [Sancta Maria virgo]*
		A¹	[S]c¹, T c⁴, Ct F³ / [S 2?]c³, Ct 2 c⁴.
			R.h. voices Gloria II ('Qui tollis' – end); Credo I; l.h. voices Credo II ('consubstantialem' – 'sepultus est'); r.h. voices Sanctus I; Pleni +

Osanna I; l.h. voice Benedictus (Osanna II
ut supra) (*c*.16 pp. missing).
No conc.

IX   7a   30*bis* r–v   *Missa* [*de Sancto Andrea?*]
                    (single fol.)
                    A¹   [S]c¹, Ct bassus c⁴♭ / [Ct altus]c³♭, T c³♭.
                    R.h. voices Credo II ('Crucifixus' – end); l.h.
                        voices Sanctus (ending before 'Sabaoth')
                        (*c*.20 pp. missing).
                    Conc.:
                    CS 14 fol. 65v–75r.

X/XI   8   31r–35r   *Missa Alma redemptoris mater* (with prosula *Deus
                                        creator*)
                    A¹   [S]c¹, T bassus c⁵ / Ct c³♮, T c³♭.
                    R.h. voices Credo I; Credo II ('Et incarnatus' –
                        'erit finis'); Credo III; Sanctus, Osanna I;
                        l.h. voices Benedictus, Osanna II; r.h. voices
                        Agnus III (*c*.13 pp. missing).
                    London, British Lib. Add. 54324 fol. 1r has
                        part of Kyrie: no conc. for movements in
                        Las 238.

XI   9   35v–36v   Anon. [Heinrich Isaac:] *Missa* [*Chargé de deuil*]
                    C   [S]c¹, T c³ / [Ct altus]c³, Ct bassus c³.
                    L.h. voices Kyrie I; r.h. voices Credo II; l.h.
                        voices Credo III (– end) (*c*.23 pp. missing).
                    Conc.: see Staehelin, *Isaac* (Ch. VI, n. 114
                        here), 3, p. 30ff.

XII/XIII 10   37r–42v   *Missa Hec dies*
                    A²   [S]c¹, T c⁴ / [Ct altus]c³, Ct bassus c⁴.
                    R.h. voices Kyrie III; Gloria I; l.h. voices
                        Gloria II ('Qui tollis' – end); r.h. voices
                        Credo IV ('Confiteor' – end); Sanctus,
                        Osanna I, Benedictus, Osanna II; Agnus I;
                        l.h. voices Agnus II (*c*.14 pp. missing).
                    No conc.

XIII   11   43r–44v   *Missa* [*Nos amis*]
                    A²   [S]c¹, T c⁴ / [Ct altus]c⁴, Ct bassus F³.
                    R.h. voices Gloria II ('Qui tollis' – end); Credo
                        I; l.h. voices Credo II ('Et incarnatus' – end);
                        (*c*.16 pp. missing).
                    No conc.

XIV   12   45r–46v   [Guillaume Dufay:] *Missa 'L'homme armé'*
                    A²   [S]c¹, T c³♭ / Ct c³♭, T 2 c⁴♭.
                    R.h. voices Osanna I, Benedictus, Osanna II;
                        Agnus I–II; l.h. voices Agnus III (*c*.16 pp.
                        missing).
                    Conc.:
                    CS 14 fol. 101v–105r (Kyrie, Gloria);
                    CS 49 fol. 36v–55r;

			Edinburgh, Nat. Lib. of Scotland, Adv. MS 5.I.15 fol. 24v–40r.
XV	13	46*bis* r–v, 47r–v B	[Cornelius Heyns:] *Missa* [*'Pour quelque paine'*] [S]c¹, T c⁴ / [Ct altus]c³, Baritonans c⁴. R.h. voices Credo I; l.h. voices Credo II ('Crucifixus' – end); r.h. voices Sanctus; l.h. voices Osanna I, Benedictus, Osanna II (*c.*16 pp. missing). Conc.: *Br 5557* fol. 99v–109r (attr. 'Ockeghem'?); *CS 51* fol. 18v–27r (attr. Cornelius Heyns).
		48r blank	
XV	14	48v–48*bis* v C	[Johannes Martini:] *Missa Orsus, orsus* [S]c¹, T c³ / [Ct altus]c³, [Ct bassus]c⁵. L.h. voices Kyrie; r.h. voices Gloria I; l.h. voices Gloria II ('Qui tollis' – end) (*c.*15 pp. missing). Conc.: *ModC* fol. 1v–11r; *CS 51* fol. 145v–155r; Verona, Bibl. Capitolare MS 755 fol. 85v–95r; Verona, Bibl. Capitolare MS 761 fol. 89v–100r.
XVI	15	49r A²	Motet *A cordibus fidelium* [S g², T c³?]/ [S 2?]c¹, Ct c³. R.h. voices part I (3 pp. missing). No conc.
XVI	16	49v A²	[John] Stone: Motet *Deo gratias agamus* [S]c¹♭, Ct c³♭ / [T c³♭, Ct 2 c⁴♭?] L.h. voices part I (3 pp. missing). No conc.
XVI	17	50r–v A²	Motet *Ave mater gloriosa / Virga iesse generosa* [S]c¹, T c³♭ / Ct concordans cum alio Ct c³♭, Ct concordans cum omnibus c⁴♭. R.h. voices of part I; l.h. voices of part II (2 pp. missing). No conc.
XVI	18	51r A²	Motet *O rex gentium* [S c³♭?, Ct bassus F⁴♭?]/ T c⁵♭, Ct c⁵♭ R.h. voices of complete work (1 p. missing). No conc.
XVI	19	51v A²	Anon.: Motet [*A*]*gimus tibi gratias* [S]c¹ / [Ct c³?, T c³?] L.h. voice of complete work (1 p. missing). No conc.
XVI	20	52r A²	Motet *Ave gloriosa mater salvatoris* [S c¹♭?, T c³♭?] / [Ct 1]c³♭, Ct 2 c⁴♭. R.h. voices of part II (3 pp. missing). No conc.

XVI	21	52v–53r A²	Anon. [John Plummer:] Motet *Tota pulchra es* (I) [S]c¹ / [Ct c³b, T c⁴b]. L.h. voice of part I; r.h. voices of part II (2 pp. missing). Conc. (attributed): *ModB* fol. 104v–105r.

XVI	22	
		
		A²
			Anon. [John Plummer?] Motet *O pulcherrima
			    mulierum*
			[S]c² / [Ct c²?, T c⁵?]
			L.h. voice of complete work (1 p. missing).
			Conc. (all anonymous):
			Tr 93 fol. 368v–369r;
			Tr 88 fol. 69v–70r (with added Ct 2);
			Munich, Bayer. Staatsbibliothek, Mus. MS
			    3232 ('Schedelsches Liederbuch') fol. 79v–80r
			    (with added Ct 2);
			Berlin, Staatl. Kupferstichkabinett, MS 78.C.28
			    fol. 49v–50v (lacking the last of four pp.);
			Ric 2356 fol. 33v–34r (= 39v–40r);
			Sev (work mentioned in the index, but lost);
			Paris, Bibl. Nat., f. fr. 15123 ('Pixérécourt
			    chansonnier') fol. 1v–3r.

XVI	23	54r–v A²	Motet *Vidi speciosam* [S]c², T c⁴ / Ct[altus]c⁴, Ct [bassus]F³. R.h. voices of part I; l.h. voices of part II (2 pp. missing). Conc.: *CS 15* fol. 199v–201r.

XVII	24	55r–56v
		A²
			Magnificat secundi toni
			[S]c²b–c³b, Ct 1 F³b–F⁴b / T F³b, Ct 2 F³b–F⁴b
			R.h. voices verses 1–3 (but Ct 1 instead of T);
			    l.h. voices vv. 4–6; r.h. voices vv. 7–9; l.h.
			    voices vv. 10–12 (4 pp. missing).
			No conc.

XVII	25 (olim 26)	57r–v D 58r–v blank.	*Magnificat* (no tone) [S]c¹b, T c⁴b / Ct[altus]c⁴b, Bassus F⁴bb. R.h. voices vv. 2, 4, 8, 10; l.h. voices vv. 6, 12 (2 pp. missing).

The unica of *Las 238*

Ex. 1. Motet *Comes Flandrie/Rector creatorum/In cimbalis*

Text underlay often unclear; *Sm222* has more text (see p. 167 n. 5). Triplum b.21 perhaps 'refectione'; b.42 'isto'; b.50 'astrola debet'; b.55 'state'. Tenor b.62–64 'tutis divi gremius' (?), adopted reading from *Sm222*.

Ex. 2. Thomas Fabri: Rondeau *D(ie) mey so lieflic wol ghebloit*

Top voice b.6–7 reading uncertain. Triplum b.16 third note a; b.21 third note c'. Tenor b.23 second note B.

Ex. 3. Thomas Fabri: Ballade ('*refrein*') *Ach Vlaendere vrie*

2. Ach, Vlaendern wat macht bedreden
   dattu zo sere ziis ghehaet,
   en du ne daets noyt goede lieden,
   die te di quamen, eenich quaet,
   maer hoghen staet hebsi hoet gaet,
   comsi van verren of van by. Ach, Vlaendre etc.

3. Ach, Vlaendere nu zi voort mere
   eendraechtich binden lande diin,
   en diene [?] dine gherechten heere,
   vor waer hi es een prinche fiin,
   zo soltu ziin zonder ghepiin
   in allen tiden zonder sy. Ach, Vlaendre etc.

4. Ach, Vlaendern der vruechden aert,
   bewaren moeti goed alteen,
   en dinen grawen so wide vermaert
   behoede got voor thelsche ween,
   dat man ne ghoen noch grave [?] gheen
   met rechten roupe mere 'o wy! Ach, Vlaendre' etc.
   nw well got

Several uncertain readings of rhythm, as dots and stems have partly disappeared, for example in Superius b.5–8, 17, 39, Contra b.9. Superius b.15 'willen' (a Germanism), adopted reading Flemish 'wylen' i.e. 'of old'.

Ex. 4. Thomas Fabri: Canon *Sinceram salutem care*

2. O ros Bachi me rorare, veni tibi supplicare -- nostis me -- quod vis migrare fugam illam prope mare.

3. Melodiam te man[d]are, hanc quisque investigare potest perscrutando, quare facta probant satis clare.

4. Vos intendo visitare, tecum Bachum lacerare, Brugis meque recreare et ut - re - mi - fa - sol - la - re.

5. Tu cum fare nil temptare atque [?] carmina grammare, docet alpha gubernare, te dignare quod salvare.

6. Sinceram salutem care mande vobis, o Buclare etc. hin ist hin.

First voice b.2 reading uncertain. Second voice: clef one third too high throughout.

Ex. 5. Jacobus de Clibano: *Agnus dei*

[Agnus 3 da capo al 𝄐]

The mensuration sign '∅' for b.1–14 and 21–25 would usually indicate duple diminution, i.e. the beat (semibreve) is twice as fast as in the other sections. To express this,
note-values have been halved in b.15–20 and 26–37, quartered in b.1–14 and 21–25.
However, a slightly faster tempo for b.15–20 and 26–37 may be in order. Superius
b.28–37 mensuration sign '3' (proportio sesquialtera).

Ex. 6. Motet *O sanctissime presul/O Christi pietas*

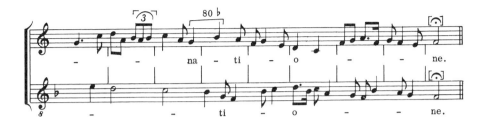

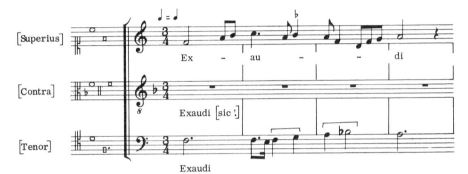

Transcribed from the facsimile edition of *Tr 92*, Bibliopola, Rome 1969–70. Contra b.17 blackened breve; b.41 first note semibreve; b.107 second note e.

Ex. 7. Mass *Alma redemptoris mater, Sanctus*

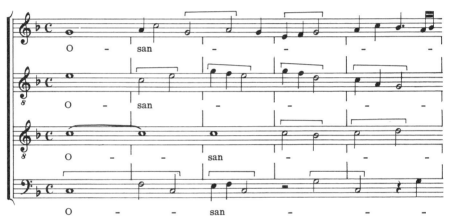

Superius b.3 first note missing. Tenor b.49–66 only 4 bars rest plus double-bar. Bassus b.50–66 only 6 bars rest plus single bar. Mensuration sign at b.82 is 'Ȼ'. As exact doubling of tempo is unlikely, the reduction of the note-values has been maintained, but a faster tempo is recommended from b.82.

Ex. 8. Mass *Hec dies, Sanctus – Benedictus*

Proportional signs: Superius b.14–16 '⊘'; b.35–43 '꜌'; Altus b.14–16 '꜌'; b.35–43 '3'.
All these signs have the same effect and are not strictly correct or even necessary.
Superius b.50–51 '3' (sesquialtera). Superius b.107 d'-c'. Tenor b.119–122 rests missing.
Tenor and Bassus notated in double augmentation throughout b.1–58.

Ex. 9a. Adrien Basin: Rondeau *Nos amys*

vous   a prins sa pla – ce,   vo –

-tre fran-chois   en vain u – – sés.

2. Vous n'estes point des plus rusés
   pour prendre tel beste a la chace.
   Nos amys ... l'amoureuse grace.

3. Envers aultres vous excusés,
   j'ay plus leal qui me pourchace;
   pour ce queres qui pour vous face,
   c'est a ung mot : plus n'y penses.

4. Nos amys ... en vain usés.

Transcribed from facsimile edition: Perkins, *Mellon Chansonnier.* Here and in ex. 9b, the minim of the original is the beat, and note-values have therefore only been halved.

Ex. 9b. Mass *Nos amis, Patrem* and *Cum sancto spiritu*

Et ascendit: duet superius – contra
Confiteor: duet contra altus – contra bassus

Altus b.35 rest missing; b.42 first note missing. Tenor b.41 text label 'Et in unum', no further text. Superius b.120 last two notes original semiminims; b.143–145 notes partly illegible, partly substituted by a later hand.

Reconstruction of *Cum sancto spiritu*

Ex. 10. (Adrien?) Basin: *Madame faites-moy savoir*

Transcribed from: D. Plamenac ed., *Facsimile Reproduction of the MSS Sevilla 5-I-43 and Paris, N.a.fr.4379 (part I)* (Brooklyn, 1962).

Ex. 11. (Adrien?) Basin: *Vien avante morte dolente*

Note-values halved, as the original minim is the beat (as in ex. 9a/b).

Ex. 12. (John Plummer?): Motet *O pulcherrima mulierum*

Transcribed from the facsimile edition of *Tr 93*, Bibliopola, Rome 1969–70. Superius b.12 last note missing; b.53–54 two equal original minims across barline. Tenor b.36 semibreve-minim-minim-semibreve. Contra b.14 after second note: dotted minim a – semiminim g – semibreve e; b.25–29 reading corrupt, adopted reading from *Tr 88* fol. 70r.

BIBLIOGRAPHY

Music manuscripts

Ao	Aosta, Biblioteca del Seminario Maggiore, MS without shelfmark.
BL	Bologna, Civico Museo Bibliografico Musicale, MS Q 15.
Br 5557	Brussels, Bibliothèque Royale Albert Ier, MS 5557.
Br 9085	Brussels, Bibliothèque Royale Albert Ier, MS 9085.
Cas 2856	Rome, Biblioteca Casanatense, MS 2856.
CS 14 [etc.]	Vatican City, Biblioteca Apostolica Vaticana, Cappella Sistina MSS 14, 15, 26, 35, 49, 51, 160.
Em	Munich, Bayerische Staatsbibliothek, Clm 14274.
Esc A	El Escorial, Monastero de San Lorenzo, Biblioteca y Archivio, MS V.III.24.
Esc B	El Escorial, Monastero de San Lorenzo, Biblioteca y Archivio, MS IV.a.24.
Fn 112bis	Florence, Biblioteca Nazionale, MS Magliabechi XIX, 112*bis*.
Fn 176	Florence, Biblioteca Nazionale, MS Magliabechi XIX, 176.
FZ 117	Faenza, Biblioteca Comunale, MS 117.
HEI	Heiligenkreuz, Bibliothek des Zisterzienserstifts, frag. without shelfmark.
Las 238	Lucca, Archivio di Stato, Biblioteca Manoscritti 238.
Lbm 54324	London, British Library, Reference Division, Add. MS 54324.
Lu 2720	Leiden, Universiteitsbibliotheek, MS BPL 2720.
MachA	Paris, Bibliothèque Nationale, MS fr. 1584.
Mel	New Haven, Yale University, Beinecke Library, MS 91 ('Mellon chansonnier').
ModA	Modena, Biblioteca Estense, MS α.M.5.24 (*olim* lat. 568).
ModB	Modena, Biblioteca Estense, MS α.X.1.11 (*olim* lat. 471).
ModC	Modena, Biblioteca Estense, MS α.M.1.13 (*olim* lat. 456).
ModD	Modena, Biblioteca Estense, MS α.M.1.2 (*olim* lat. 457).
Nn VI E 40	Naples, Biblioteca Nazionale, MS VI E 40.
Nst 9/9a	Nuremberg, Stadtbibliothek, MS frg. lat. 9 and 9a (*olim* Cent. V, 61 and Cent. III, 25).
Ox 213	Oxford, Bodleian Library, MS Canonici misc. 213.
PC II and III	Paris, Bibliothèque Nationale, MS n. a. fr. 4379, parts II and III.
Pn 4917	Paris, Bibliothèque Nationale, MS n. a. fr. 4917.
Pn 6771	Paris, Bibliothèque Nationale, MS n. a. fr. 6771 ('Reina codex').
Pr	Prague, Státní knihovna ČSSR – Universitetní knihovna, MS XI.E.9.

Ric 2356	Florence, Biblioteca Riccardiana, MS 2356.
Seg	Segovia, Archivio de la Catedral, MS without shelfmark.
Sev	Seville, Biblioteca Colombina, MS 5-I-43, and Paris, Bibliothèque Nationale, MS n. a. fr. 4379, part I.
Sm 222	Strasbourg, Bibliothèque Municipale, MS 222.C.22 (destroyed).
SP	Vatican City, Biblioteca Apostolica Vaticana, MS San Pietro B 80.
Stra	Prague, Památník Národniho Písemnictví, MS D.G.47.
Tr 87 [etc.]	Trento, Castello del Buon Consiglio, MS 87, 88, 89, 90, 91, 92.
Tr 93	Trento, Archivio della Cattedrale, MS '93' (new shelfmark; now also deposited in the Castello del Buon Consiglio).
Uu 37	Utrecht, Universiteitsbibliotheek, MS 6 E 37.

Archival sources

Accounts *OL*	Kerkrekeningen Onze-Lieve-Vrouw (1445–74, with interruptions), Rijksarchief Brugge, Nieuw Kerkarchief no. 1403.
Accounts *SD*	Rekeningen Kerkfabriek Sint-Donaas, Bisschoppelijk Archief Brugge, Reeks G. nos. 1–7 (1375–1499).
Accounts *SJ*	Kerkrekeningen Sint-Jacob, Rijksarchief Brugge, reg. 42 (1419–29); 4 (1443–67); 35 (1487–94).
Accounts *SS*	Kerkrekeningen Sint-Salvators, Bisschoppelijk Archief Brugge, Reeks S. nos. 616–617 (*olim* 701–702).
Acta *OL*	Acta capitularia Onze-Lieve-Vrouw (from 1480), Rijksarchief Brugge, Onze-Lieve-Vrouw, prov. no. 332.
Acta *SD*	Acta capitularia Sint-Donaas, Bisschoppelijk Archief Brugge, Reeks A. nos. 47–57 (1345–1506).
Cartulary *CC*	Cartularium Liber Oblongus, Archief van het Klooster van de Ongeschoeide Karmelieten, Brugge.
Cartulary *OL*	'Hec est tabula beneficiorum . . .', Rijksarchief Brugge, Onze-Lieve-Vrouw R. 39, (prov. no. 398).
Cartulary *SS*	Oorkondenboek Communiteit (1442–96), Bisschoppelijk Archief Brugge, Reeks S. no. 289 (*olim* 243).
Cathalogus prepositorum omnium ecclesie beate marie Brugensis, MS 4289 (18128), Bibliothèque Royale, Brussels.	
City Accounts	Stadsrekeningen Brugge (1280–1794), Stadsarchief Brugge no. 216.
Confraternity *OL*	'Confraternitas Beate Marie Brugensis me possidet . . .' (fol. 3:) 'Anno Domini (1298)', MS without shelfmark, Provinciaalbibliotheek van West-Vlaanderen, Brugge.
Confraternity *SS*	'Institutio confraternitatis presentis Anno (1397) . . .' Rijksarchief Brugge, Découvertes no. 101.
Planarius *OL*	Reg. 179, Archive of the O.C.M.W., Bruges.
Planarius *SD*	Liber Planarius Sancti Donatiani Brugensis, Bisschoppelijk Archief Brugge, Reeks A. no. 141.

Duclos: *Acta SS* Manuscript notes of Adolphe Duclos, copied from the lost volume of chapter minutes of St Saviour's, 1490–1516, MS folder, Bisschoppelijk Archief Brugge.

Weale: *Accounts SD* Nota's William H. J. Weale, Stadsbibliotheek Brugge, MS 599 (transcribed from account books of St Donatian's and some other churches).

Literature and editions of music

Apel, W., ed., *French Secular Compositions of the Fourteenth Century* (CMM 53) (3 vols., American Institute of Musicology, 1970–72)

ASEB Annales de la Société d'Émulation de Bruges (Handelingen van het Genootschap van Geschiedenis) (Bruges, 1839ff.)

Atlas, A. W., ed., *Dufay Quincentenary Conference* (Brooklyn, 1976)

Bent, M. and I., 'Dufay, Dunstable, Plummer: A New Source', *JAMS* 22 (1969), pp. 394–424

Bent, M., ed., *Four Anonymous Masses* (*Missa Fuit homo, Quem malignus spiritus, Salve sancta parens, Veterem hominem*) (Early English Church Music 22: Fifteenth-Century Liturgical Music II) (London, 1979)

Bouquet, M. T., 'La cappella musicale dei Duchi di Savoia dal 1450 al 1500', *RIdM* 3 (1968), pp. 233–85

Bowles, E. A., *Musikleben im 15. Jahrhundert* (Musikgeschichte in Bildern vol. III/8 (Leipzig, 1977)

Bukofzer, M., *Studies in Medieval and Renaissance Music* (New York, 1950; repr. 1978)

Carapezza, P. E., 'Regina Angelorum in musica picta: Walter Frye e il "Maître au feuillage brodé" ', *RIdM* 10 (1975), pp. 134–54

Cartellieri, O., *The Court of Burgundy* (London, 1929)

Census Catalogue of Manuscript Sources of Polyphonic Music 1400–1550, compiled by the Illinois Musicological Archives for Renaissance Manuscript Studies, 1 and 2 (American Institute of Musicology, Stuttgart, 1979 and 1982)

Cohen, J., *The Six Anonymous L'homme armé Masses in Naples, Biblioteca Nazionale MS VI E 40* (MSD 21) (American Institute of Musicology, 1968)

D'Accone, F., 'The Singers of San Giovanni in Florence during the Fifteenth Century', *JAMS*, 14 (1961), pp. 305–58

D'Alessi, G., *Il tipografo fiammingo Gherardo de Lisa* (Treviso, 1925)

Derolez, A., *Corpus Catalogorum Belgii: De Middeleeuwse bibliotheekscatalogi der Zuidelijke Nederlanden I. Provincie West-Vlaanderen* (Brussels, 1966)

De Schrevel, A. C., *Histoire du Séminaire de Bruges* (2 vols., Bruges, 1895) Vol. 1: *ASEB* 37 (ser. 4, tom. 10, 1887); vol. 2: *ASEB* 33 (ser. 4, tom. 6, 1883)

De Smedt, O., *De Engelse Natie te Antwerpen in de 16de eeuw (1496–1582)* (2 vols., Antwerpen, 1950)

Dewitte, A., 'Boek-en bibliotheekwezen in de Brugse Sint-Donaaskerk XIII^c– XVe eeuw', in *Sint-Donaas en de voormalige Brugse Katedraal*, (Bruges, 1978) pp. 61–95

——, 'De Geestelijkheid van de Brugse Lievevrouwkerk in de 16de eeuw', *ASEB* 107 (1970), pp. 100–35 (Dewitte *OL*)

——, 'Scholen en onderwijs te Brugge gedurende de Middeleeuwen', *ASEB* 109 (1972), pp. 145–217

——, 'Gegevens betreffende het muziekleven in de voormalige Sint-Donaaskerk te Brugge', *ASEB* 111 (1974), pp. 129–74 (Dewitte *SD*)

——, 'Zangmeesters, "Schoolmeesters" en Organisten aan de Sint-Gilleskerk te Brugge, ca.1471–ca.1570', *Biekorf* 77 (1976), pp. 89–99 (Dewitte *SG*)

——, 'Zangmeesters, organisten en schoolmeesters aan de Sint-Jacobparochie te Brugge 1419–1591', *Biekorf* 72 (1971), pp. 332–49 (Dewitte *SJ*)

Doorslaer, G. v., 'La chapelle musicale de Philippe le Beau', *Revue Belge d'archéologie et d'histoire d'art* 4 (1934), pp. 21–57 and 139–65

Duclos, A., *Bruges: Histoire et souvenirs* (Bruges, 1910; repr. 1976)

EMH Early Music History: Studies in Medieval and Early Modern Music ed. I. Fenlon (Cambridge, 1981–)

[Foppens, J.], *Compendium Chronologicum Episcoporum Brugensium, necnon prepositorum, Decanorum, et Canonicorum ecclesie Cathedralis S. Donatiani Brugensis* (Bruges, 1731)

Gilliodts-Van Severen, L., *Cartulaire de l'ancien estaple de Bruges* (Société d'Émulation: Chroniques) (4 vols., Bruges, 1904–6)

——, *Inventaire des archives de la ville de Bruges. Section Première: Inventaire des chartes* (Table analytique and Glossaire Flamand by Edwin Galliard) (9 vols., Bruges, 1871–85)

——, *Le ménéstrels de Bruges* (Essais d'archéologie Brugeoise 2) (Bruges, 1912)

Gottlieb, L. E., *The Cyclic Masses of Trent Codex 89* (Ph.D diss., University of California, Los Angeles, 1958) (microfilm: CU 3237)

Günther, U., 'Zur Biographie einiger Komponisten der Ars subtilior', *AMW* 21 (1964), pp. 172–99

——, ed., *The Motets of the Manuscripts Chantilly, Musée Condé, 564* (olim *1047*) *and Modena, Biblioteca Estense, a.M.5,24* (olim *lat. 568*) (CMM 39) (American Institute of Musicology, 1965)

Haberl, F. X., *Die römische 'Schola cantorum' und die päpstlichen Kapellsänger bis zur Mitte des 16. Jahrhunderts* (Bausteine zur Musikgeschichte 3) (Leipzig, 1888) = *VfMW* 3 (1887) pp. 189–296

Harrison, F. Ll., *Music in Medieval Britain*, 2nd edn. (London, 1963)

——, ed., *Motets of French Provenance* (Polyphonic Music of the Fourteenth Century 5) (Monaco, 1968)

Heeroma, K. and Lindenburg, C. W. H., eds., *Liederen en Gedichten uit het Gruuthuse Handschrift* (Leiden, 1966)

Kenney, S., 'Origins and Chronology of the Brussels Manuscript 5557 in the Bibliothèque Royale de Belgique', *RBdM* 6 (1952), pp. 75–100

Laborde, Comte L. E. de, *Les Ducs de Bourgogne* (3 vols., Paris, 1349–52)

Leech-Wilkinson, D., 'Un libro di appunti di un suonatore di tromba del quindicesimo secolo', *RIdM* 16 (1981), pp. 16–39

Lenaerts, R. B., *Het Nederlands polifonies lied in de zestiende eeuw* (Mechelen-Amsterdam, 1933)

Letts, M., *Bruges and its Past*, 2nd rev. edn. (Bruges-London, 1926)

Llorens, J. M., *Capellae Sixtinae Codices musicis notis instructi sive manu scripti sive praelo expressi* (Studi e testi 202) (Vatican City, 1960)

Lockwood, L., 'Strategies of Music Patronage in the Fifteenth Century: The

Cappella of Ercole I d'Este', in *Music in Medieval and Early Modern Europe: Patronage, Sources and Texts*, ed. I. Fenlon (Cambridge, 1981), pp. 227–48

Lowinsky, E. E. and Blackburn, B., eds., *Josquin Des Prez: Proceedings of the International Josquin Festival-Conference . . . New York City 1971* (London, 1976)

Marix, J., *Histoire de la Musique et des Musiciens de la Cour de Bourgogne sous le règne de Philippe le Bon (1420–1467)* (Collection d'Études Musicologiques 28) (Strasbourg, 1939)

Marix, J., *Les Musiciens de la Cour de Bourgogne au XVᵉ siècle* (Paris, 1937)

Meersseman, G. G., OP, 'L'Epistolaire de Jean van den Veren et le début de l'humanisme en Flandre', *Humanistica Lovanensia* 19 (Louvain, 1970), pp. 119–200

Mirot, L. and Lazzareschi, E., 'Un mercante di Lucca in Fiandra: Giovanni Arnolfini', *Bollettino Storico Lucchese* 12 (1940), pp. 81–105

Moreau, E. de, SJ, *Histoire de l'église en Belgique*, vol. 4: *L'Eglise aux Pays-Bas sous les ducs de Bourgogne et Charles-Quint 1378–1559* (Brussels, 1949)

MPLSER Monumenta Polyphoniae Liturgicae Sacrae Ecclesiae Romanae, ed. L. Feininger (Rome, 1947–)

New Grove Dictionary of Music and Musicians, The, ed. S. Sadie (20 vols., London, 1980)

Perkins, L. L. and Garey, H., eds., *The Mellon Chansonnier* (2 vols., New York–London, 1979)

Pirro, A., *Histoire de la Musique de la fin du XIVᵉ siècle à la fin du XVIᵉ* (Paris, 1940)

Polk, K., *Flemish Wind Bands in the Late Middle Ages: A Study in Improvisatory Instrumental Practices* (Ph.D diss., University of California, Berkeley, 1968) (University Microfilms, Ann Arbor, UM 69-3674)

Reaney, G., ed., *Early Fifteenth-Century Music* (CMM 11) (6 vols., American Institute of Musicology, 1955–)

——, 'New Sources of Ars Nova Music', *MD* 19 (1965), pp. 53–67

Reese, G., *Music in the Renaissance*, rev. edn. (London, 1959)

Reynolds, C., 'The Origins of San Pietro B 80 and the Development of a Roman Sacred Repertory', *EMH* 1 (1981), pp. 257–304

RISM B IV² *Manuscripts of Polyphonic Music (c.1320–1440)*, ed. G. Reaney (Répertoire International des Sources Musicales B IV²) (Munich-Duisburg, 1969)

RISM B IV³,⁴ *Handschriften mit mehrstimmiger Musik des 14., 15. und 16. Jahrhunderts*, ed. K. v. Fischer and M. Lütolf (Répertoire International des Sources Musicales B IV³ and B IV⁴) (Munich-Duisburg, 1972)

Sartori, C., 'Josquin des Pres cantore del Duomo di Milano', *Annales Musicologiques* 4 (1956), pp. 55–83

Schabacker, P. H., *Petrus Christus* (Utrecht, 1974)

Schuler, M., 'Zur Geschichte der Kapelle Papst Eugens IV', *Acta Mus* 40 (1968), pp. 220–7

——, 'Die Musik in Konstanz während des Konzils 1414 bis 1418', *Acta Mus* 38 (1966), pp. 150–68

——, 'Zur Geschichte der Kapelle Papst Martins V', *AMW* 25 (1968), pp. 30–45

Smijers, A., *De Illustre Lieve Vrouwe Broederschap te 's-Hertogenbosch* (Amsterdam,

1932) = *TVNM* 12 (1928), pp. 40–62 and 115–67; 13 (1929–32), pp. 46–100 and 181ff.

Strohm, R., 'Die Missa super "Nos amis" von Johannes Tinctoris', *Mf* 32 (1979), pp. 34–51

——, 'European Politics and the Distribution of Music in the Early Fifteenth Century', *EMH* 1 (1981), pp. 305–23

Thielemans, M. R., *Bourgogne et Angleterre: Relations politiques et économiques entre les Pays-Bas Bourguignons et l'Angleterre 1435–1467* (Brussels, 1966)

Tinctoris, J., *Proportionale Musices*, ed. A. Seay, in *Johannis Tinctoris Opera Theoretica* (CSM 22), 2a (American Institute of Musicology, 1978)

Van de Casteele, D. and Van der Straeten, E., 'Maîtres de chant et organistes de Saint-Donatien et de Saint-Sauveur à Bruges', *ASEB* 23 (1870), pp. 105–74

Van de Casteele, D., 'Préludes historiques sur la ghilde des ménéstrels à Bruges', *ASEB* 20 (1868), pp. 53–144

Van der Straeten, E., *Les ménéstrels aux Pays-Bas* (Brussels, 1878)

——, *La musique aux Pays-Bas avant le XIXᵉ siècle*, (8 vols., Brussels, 1867–88; repr. New York, 1969, with a new Introduction by E. E. Lowinsky)

Vandewalle, A., *Beknopte Inventaris van het Stadsarchief van Brugge. Deel I: Oud Archief* (Bruges, 1979)

Van Houtte, J. A., *Bruges: Essai d'histoire urbaine* (Brussels, 1967)

Vlaamse kunst op perkament. Handschriften en miniaturen te Brugge van de 12de tot de 16de eeuw, exhibition catalogue, Gruuthusemuseum Brugge (Bruges, 1981)

Wangermée, R., *La musique Flamande* (Brussels, 1965)

Weale, W. H. J., 'Obituaire du Couvent des Carmes à Bruges', *ASEB* 50 (1900), pp. 153–288

Weinmann, K., *Johannes Tinctoris (1445–1511) und sein unbekannter Traktat 'De inventione et usu musicae'* (1909, repr. Tutzing, 1961)

Wilkins, N., *Music in the Age of Chaucer* (Chaucer Studies 1) (Cambridge, 1979)

Wolf, J., ed., *Werken van Jacob Obrecht* (7 vols., Amsterdam–Leipzig, 1908–21; repr. 1968)

Wright, C., *Music at the Court of Burgundy 1364–1419: A Documentary History* (Musicological Studies 28) (Institute of Medieval Music, 1979)

——, 'Dufay at Cambrai: Discoveries and Revisions', *JAMS* 28 (1975), pp. 163–229

INDEX

(Appendix A not included)